Argentina's Lost Patrol

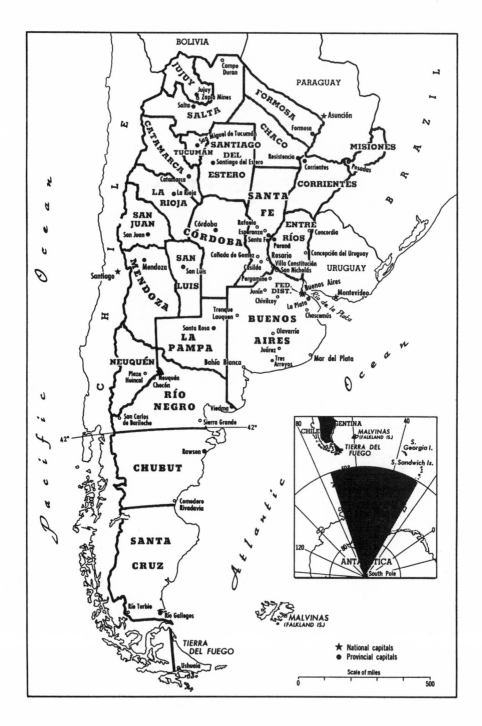

From *Argentina, A City and a Nation,* by James R. Scobie. Copyright © 1964, 1971 by Oxford University Press, Inc. Reprinted by permission.

Argentina's Lost Patrol

Armed Struggle 1969-1979

María José Moyano

Yale University Press
New Haven and London

Designed by James J. Johnson.
Set in Times Roman type by Tseng
Information Systems, Inc.

Printed in the United States of America by
BookCrafters, Inc., Chelsea, Michigan.

Library of Congress
Cataloging-in-Publication Data
Moyano, María José.
Argentina's lost patrol : armed struggle,
1969–1979 / María José Moyano.
p. cm.
Includes bibliographical references and index.
ISBN 0–300–06122–6 (alk. paper)
1. Argentina—Politics and government—
1955–1983. 2. Government, Resistance
to—Argentina—History. 3. Guerrillas—
Argentina—History. 4. Violence—
Argentina—History. I. Title.
F2849.2.M68 1995
320.982—dc20   94-35509
                                    CIP

A catalogue record for this book is available
from the British Library.

The paper in this book meets the guidelines for
permanence and durability of the Committee
on Production Guidelines for Book Longevity
of the Council on Library Resources.

10 9 8 7 6 5 4 3 2 1

To My Mother

Contents

List of Figures, ix

List of Tables, x

Acknowledgments, xi

List of Abbreviations, xii

1
The Lost Patrol, 1

2
Politics in Argentina after 1955 and the
Development of the Guerrilla Movement, 11

Part I   Patterns of Violence

3
Armed Struggle, 50

4
Collective Violent Protest, 63

5
Right-Wing Violence, 75

6
Patterns of Violence Compared, 88

Part II   The Guerrilla Movement

7

Guerrilla Lives, 101

8

Ideological and Organizational Somersaults, 131

9

The Lost Patrol Revisited, 156

Notes, 167

Bibliography, 207

Index, 223

Figures

2.1   Splits and Mergers in Peronist Armed Organizations   23
2.2   Splits and Mergers in Marxist Armed Organizations   24
6.1   Incidents of Armed Struggle and Collective Violent Protest,
      1969–79   90
6.2   Incidents of Agitational and Enforcement Violence, 1969–79   94
8.1   Initial Guerrilla Structure   139
8.2   Guerrilla Structure Circa 1972   140
8.3   Structure of the PRT-ERP   141
8.4   Structure of the ERP, 1974   147
8.5   Structure of the Politico-Military Organization Montoneros, 1974   149
8.6   Structure of Montoneros After 1976   153

Tables

2.1	Election Results, March 1973	32
2.2	Election Results, September 1973	37
3.1	Location of Guerrilla Attacks, 1969–79	52
3.2	Groups Responsible for Guerrilla Attacks (Excluding Bombings), 1969–79	53
3.3	Participants in Guerrilla Attacks (Excluding Bombings), 1969–79	54
3.4	Guerrilla Operations, 1969–79	56
3.5	Motives Behind Kidnappings, 1969–79	58
3.6	Kidnappings with Highest Ransoms, 1969–79	59
4.1	Collective Violent Protest, January 1, 1969–May 24, 1973	66
4.2	Collective Violent Protest, May 25, 1973–March 23, 1976	70
4.3	Collective Violent Protest, March 24, 1976–December 31, 1979	73
5.1	Right-Wing Violence, January 1, 1969–May 24, 1973	78
5.2	Right-Wing Violence, May 25, 1973–March 23, 1976	81
5.3	Right-Wing Violence, March 24, 1976–December 31, 1979	85
7.1	Guerrilla Casualties, 1969–79	106
7.2	Biographical Data on Guerrilla Combatants, 1969–79	110
7.3	Guerrilla Founders Interviewed	115

Acknowledgments

This book would not have been completed without the help of a number of individuals. Foremost among these is Juan José Linz. As a scholar and mentor he has set standards that few can hope to emulate. I am also grateful to Rocío and Juan Linz for their friendship, their affection, and their hospitality.

Vaughn Altemus, John Arquilla, Eileen Burgin, Marcelo Cavarozzi, Margaret Keck, George Moyser, Barnett Rubin, James Scott, and Paul Stockton provided intellectual advice at different stages. I will be forever indebted to James McGuire, Peter Stavrakis, James Wirtz, and the anonymous reader at Yale University Press for the care with which they read, edited, and (in the case of the first three) discussed portions of this work with me.

Several Argentine scholars and intellectuals gave me invaluable assistance in carrying out my research: Carlos "Chacho" Alvarez, Carlos Escudé, Rubén Heguilein, Norberto Ivancich, and Alfredo Vásquez. Patricia Baxendale and Carola Garrido helped with the task of collecting data on violence for the years 1974–75 and 1977–79, and Brent Pollock helped with bibliographical citations. I must also thank the men and women who granted me interviews. Whether former combatants, members of the security forces, or political figures, they will probably feel equally disappointed if they ever read this book.

Close friends furnished their emotional support: April Alliston, Horacio Cocchi, Silvia Colazingari, Jacinto Fombona, James McGuire, Miriam Smith, Regina and Peter Stavrakis, and Albert Vourvoulias. Norma Turconi deserves special mention. Over the years, she has been a faithful friend and an unwavering source of strength, and she has patiently sat through endless discussions about the tragic events portrayed in this study.

I owe my deepest gratitude to the most influential person in my life, my mother.

Abbreviations

AAA	Alianza Anticomunista Argentina
	Argentine Anti-Communist Alliance
AE	Agrupación Evita de la Rama Femenina
	Evita Group of the Feminine Branch
APF	Alianza Popular Federalista
	Federalist Popular Alliance
APR	Alianza Popular Revolucionaria
	Revolutionary Popular Alliance
CGT	Confederación General del Trabajo
	General Confederation of Labor
CPL	Comandos Populares de Liberación
	Liberation Popular Commandos
EM	Ejército Montonero
	Montonero Army
ERP	Ejército Revolucionario del Pueblo
	People's Revolutionary Army
ERP FR	Ejército Revolucionario del Pueblo Fracción Roja
	People's Revolutionary Army Red Fraction
ERP 22	Ejército Revolucionario del Pueblo 22 de Agosto
	People's Revolutionary Army 22 August
ESMA	Escuela de Mecánica de la Armada
	Navy Mechanics School
ETA	Euskadi Ta Askatasuna
	Basque Homeland and Freedom
FAL	Fuerzas Armadas de Liberación
	Liberation Armed Forces
FAP	Fuerzas Armadas Peronistas
	Peronist Armed Forces
FAP CN	Fuerzas Armadas Peronistas Comando Nacional
	Peronist Armed Forces National Command

FAP 17	Fuerzas Armadas Peronistas 17 de Octubre Peronist Armed Forces 17 October
FAR	Fuerzas Armadas Revolucionarias Revolutionary Armed Forces
FAS	Frente Anti-Imperialista y por el Socialismo Anti-Imperialist Pro-Socialist Front
FLQ	Front de Libération du Québec Front for the Liberation of Quebec
FRECILINA	Frente Cívico de Liberación Nacional Civic Front for National Liberation
FREJULI	Frente Justicialista de Liberación Justicialist Liberation Front
FRIP	Frente Revolucionario Indoamericano Popular Popular Indoamerican Revolutionary Front
GAN	Gran Acuerdo Nacional Great National Agreement
GT	Grupo de Tareas Task Force
IRA	Irish Republican Army
JP	Juventud Peronista Peronist Youth
JTP	Juventud Trabajadora Peronista Peronist Working Youth
JUP	Juventud Universitaria Peronista Peronist University Youth
MPM	Movimiento Peronista Montonero Montonero Peronist Movement
MSB	Movimiento Sindical de Base Rank and File Union Movement
MVP	Movimiento de Villeros Peronistas Movement of Peronist Slum Dwellers
PCR	Partido Comunista Revolucionario Revolutionary Communist Party
PM	Partido Montonero Montonero Party
PRT	Partido Revolucionario de los Trabajadores Workers' Revolutionary Party
UCR	Unión Cívica Radical Radical Civic Union
UES	Unión de Estudiantes Secundarios Union of Secondary School Students

1

The Lost Patrol

Naturally if we believe that the crisis of capitalism is definitive, we can only advocate a more or less immediate transition to socialism . . . and declare peronism belongs in a museum. We would all like this to happen, but in practice our theory has galloped kilometers ahead of reality. When that occurs, the vanguard runs the risk of becoming a lost patrol.

RODOLFO WALSH, *Los Papeles de Walsh* (1976)

Rodolfo Walsh was the dean of investigative journalism in Argentina. Two of his books have become classics of Argentine literature as well as politics: *Operación Masacre,* in which he describes the summary execution of 27 men (9 of them civilians) following an abortive pro-Peronist rebellion in 1956; and *Quién Mató a Rosendo?* in which he explores the power struggle within the Metalworkers' Union that led to the murder of an activist in 1968.[1] The success of these two books obscured Walsh's other talents, notably as a writer of short stories.

Following the victory of Fidel Castro's forces, Walsh was among the intellectuals who flocked to Cuba and helped launch that country's press agency, Prensa Latina. Beyond his literary and journalistic achievements, in Havana his fame derived from the fact that, with the aid of a second-hand volume on cryptography, he deciphered a telex describing American plans for an invasion of the island. Back in Argentina, sometime in the late 1960s, Rodolfo Walsh became "Esteban," the nom de guerre he adopted when he joined a guerrilla group and rose within the group's power structure to become head of its intelligence department. In that capacity that he wrote a series of reports in 1976–77 collectively known today as the Walsh Papers,[2] in which Esteban argued that the strategy followed by the group was erroneous, in that spectacular military actions did not result in popular support for the guerrillas. Esteban also argued that such operations were almost suicidal in the context of the campaign of illegal repression launched by the military government, known as the "dirty war," which took the form of disappearances—abductions of citizens who were held in clandestine detention centers and eventually killed. Esteban received no response from his superiors. In 1977, as he put it, he "became Rodolfo Walsh once more." On

1

March 24, the first anniversary of the military coup, Walsh wrote an "Open letter from a writer to the Military Junta," denouncing the disappearances, which he mailed to various newspapers and magazines.[3] None of them published it. The following day Rodolfo Walsh was caught and killed by paramilitaries from the Navy Mechanics School. His only daughter, Victoria, also a guerrilla officer, had been killed in action six months earlier.

The story of Rodolfo Walsh is the story of many others in Argentina; the story of a violent life leading to a violent death, and of a militant commitment that overshadowed everything else. It becomes difficult to understand how someone capable of the piercing insights on Argentine politics in *Quién Mató a Rosendo?* should have ended up as a gear in an organization that seemed so out of touch with reality. But Walsh was also atypical. He was significantly older than most guerrillas and, as the Walsh Papers prove, toward the end he recovered his critical faculties and opposed his group's strategy. Most combatants did not and continued to formulate policies and execute military operations devoid of apparent political rationality. This study attempts to explain how and why Argentine guerrillas became the lost patrol.

Broad generalizations about the guerrilla groups that operated in Argentina between 1969 and 1979 are virtually impossible, for a variety of reasons. Initially, there were six major organizations, as well as a myriad of *groupuscules*. Through a series of splits and mergers, by the second half of the decade only two of these organizations were still in existence. Guerrilla membership also varied dramatically. In 1969, there were approximately 200 active combatants. Five years later, these had turned into an army of 5,000, and by the end of the decade, membership had dwindled to 1,000. Argentine guerrillas first went into action against a military government but continued operating following the country's return to constitutional rule in 1973, and were in fact partly responsible for the subsequent breakdown of democracy in 1976, and the establishment of a highly repressive military regime that would become their nemesis. The patterns of violence also changed significantly during the decade. Initially, there was an emphasis on "violence against property, not persons," as the guerrillas concentrated on small-scale attacks against the security forces and Robin Hood type actions like the theft and distribution of food in slum dwellings. During a second stage, kidnappings for ransom were favored. This in turn gave way to widespread assassinations and the staging of spectacular operations involving more than 100 combatants and sophisticated technology. Not surprisingly, changes in both the nature of the regime in which the guerrillas functioned and their operational repertoire brought about concomitant changes in popular support.

What can be stated with confidence is that guerrilla groups are central to an understanding of Argentine politics in the past twenty years. The initial societal reaction following the first guerrilla arrests was one of shock or, as a leading daily put it, "stupor in all circles given the social origin of those who appear to be linked to these events."[4] Those arrested were the children of the middle and upper middle classes rebelling against the values and beliefs of their own social milieu. The initial shock turned into support as the socioeconomic policies of the military regime produced a widespread radicalization of society. Sustained guerrilla activity was to a significant extent responsible for the military's decision to call elections in 1973 and, more important, to allow Juan Perón to return to Argentina after an eighteen-year exile. Following the restoration of Peronism to power, guerrillas were amnestied and offered government posts. Armed organizations intensified their operations after 1973, however, in the process losing the widespread popular support they had enjoyed. They also provoked illegal repression in the form of death squads, first under Peronist rule and then during the dirty war. Guerrilla groups not only provoked extra-legal action; they also helped legitimize it.[5] Many political developments in Argentina over the past twenty years appear as reactions to the activities of guerrilla groups, organizations that have not been comprehensively examined.[6]

The Problem of Definitions

The field's specialists have not formulated a comprehensive and widely accepted definition of terrorism, but their efforts have produced a consensus of sorts. Terrorism is often described as the use or threat of use of violence to achieve political objectives, when such violence is intended to control a population through fear or coerce a government into granting certain concessions.[7]

Several objections to this definition can be raised. First, terrorism has been a feature of a variety of social conflicts—labor struggles, peasant wars, pre- and post-civil war situations. Second, the notion of control through fear must be questioned. The introduction of this element may be the result of an attempt to include state terror in the definition of terrorism. Fear is pivotal to rule by terror: it is through random violence that the state controls entire populations.[8] Whether the British people are terrorized by the Irish Republican Army is highly debatable. As long as the violence is circumscribed to Ulster, British citizens may berate the IRA and complain about defense expenditures in Northern Ireland, but they will not live in fear.[9] Finally, the definition contains an implicit value connotation. Nothing exemplifies this better than the literature's attempt to distinguish between terrorism (as defined above) and guerrilla warfare. The latter is normally characterized as the use of hit-and-run tactics by irregular forces against a stronger military force.[10] Whereas guerrilla warfare is defined by the means it employs, terrorism is defined by the ends it pursues. This has led one author to remark that when we talk about "terrorists," we "imply that the regime itself is *legitimate*. If we call them 'freedom fighters' we imply that the regime is *illegitimate*. If we call them 'guerrillas' we may not be quite sure what we ought to think about the regime."[11]

Attempts to distinguish between terrorism and guerrilla warfare focus on two issues: the discriminate nature of the violence and whether the victims are combatants or noncombatants. In the first case, it is argued that because guerrillas are concerned with winning the hearts and minds of the population, they will use violence sparingly, thus minimizing the danger of accidental deaths, whereas terrorism frequently strikes at the innocent.[12] In the second case, it is pointed out that while guerrillas adhere to the conventions of war and restrict their attacks to military installations and members of the armed and security forces, terrorists target the civilian population.[13] To distinguish between terrorism and guerrilla warfare on the basis of the discriminate nature of the violence implies that there is a threshold of acceptability beyond which death is no longer justifiable. How many accidental deaths should we record before we decide to call a group of insurgents "terrorists"? Differentiation based on the status of the victims also runs into problems. In certain domestic violent conflicts the line separating combatants and noncombatants is more imaginary than real. In addition, in the course of international wars, states have frequently ignored the distinction between combatants and noncombatants.

The distinction between terrorism and guerrilla warfare is important, and we need to be able to differentiate conceptually and analytically between Mao's Red Army and the German Baader-Meinhof Gang. But twentieth-century political history provides a plethora of cases in which that distinction is blurred. In Vietnam, guerrillas resorted to terrorism; and the Algerian National Liberation Front practiced terrorism before launching a guerrilla campaign. The Argentine groups discussed in this study employed both simultaneously—an attack against a military factory in order to steal explosives could be followed by the murder of an industrialist.

The problem is more than semantic, for the definition of terrorism provided earlier normally entails a number of assumptions about the organizations that practice it. Terrorist groups are supposed to be constituted by a small group of men and women suffering from some mental pathology who engage in short campaigns of senseless violence, completely divorced from established social organizations, and without popular support.[14] Reality is more complex. Although the Baader-Meinhof Gang never counted on more than 50 members, the Italian Red Brigades, the Basque Euskadi Ta Askatasuna (ETA), and the IRA are (or have been) considerably larger. Though it is possible for armed organizations to attract a number of pathological individuals, it is highly unlikely that these will number in the hundreds. Groups like the Front for the Liberation of Quebec have had a short life span, yet ETA dates back to 1952 and the IRA to 1916 (or 1858, if one considers the Irish Republican Brotherhood as its forerunner). Finally, though it is easy to write off violence by the French Direct Action or the Baader-Meinhof Gang, few dispute the fact that the actions of ETA or the

IRA have received the support of a not insignificant segment of their respective populations.[15]

Armed organizations in Argentina started off with a handful of members but developed into veritable armies of thousands. Their violence was initially extremely selective and, as later chapters will show, justified in the eyes of wide sectors of society. In the latter half of the decade, armed organizations combined indiscriminate killings of civilians with frontal attacks against military installations analogous to what the literature expects of irregular forces transforming themselves into popular armies. Consequently, both "terrorism" and "guerrilla warfare" mischaracterize the activities of armed organizations in Argentina between 1969 and 1979. For this reason I have chosen the more neutral term "armed struggle" to denote the actions of clandestine groups that systematically resort to military means in order to achieve political ends.[16] This is not a rigorous definition. It is not intended as such. In fact, the field is not likely to produce widely accepted definitions of terms like "terrorism" and "guerrilla warfare" in the foreseeable future. Nor is this vital, since the most interesting issues in the study of political violence do not evolve around semantics. In choosing the term "armed struggle" my only purpose is to avoid characterizations that are imprecise and, in one case, pejorative. It could also be said that in this way I avoid any a priori assumptions about the nature of popular support for armed actions or the targets of such violence. The participants are called "combatants" or "guerrillas," even though they were only occasionally deserving of the latter, because it would be awkward to refer to "individuals engaged in armed struggle" or to "members of armed organizations" throughout this work.

The Militarization of Armed Struggle

It is not easy to explain some of the strategic choices made by Argentine guerrillas. How does one interpret the decision to wage armed struggle against a constitutional government they had been instrumental in electing? Combatants not only wasted the unique opportunities granted them by the amnesty; they also provided the military with an excuse for the ferocious repression unleashed after 1976. And how does one account for the seemingly suicidal decision to continue fighting once the dirty war was launched?

The central thesis of this book is that after 1973 armed struggle became militarized. The term *militarism* has been employed in a variety of contexts. Between the two world wars, and given the German experience, the term denoted a predominance of military considerations in the life of a nation. In Marxist usage, it is almost a synonym for imperialism. It is now used to describe such diverse phenomena as excessive defense expenditures or the primacy of military figures in the politics of Third World states. Whatever the usage, the term always signals deviant behavior. Alfred Vagts makes this clear when he introduces the distinction between military organization and militarism: "The military way is marked by a primary concentration of men and materials on winning specific objectives of power with the utmost efficiency. . . . Militarism . . . presents a vast array of customs, interests, prestige, actions, and thought associated with armies and wars and yet transcending true military purposes. Indeed, militarism is so constituted that it may hamper and defeat the purposes of the military way." [17]

Therefore, it is not redundant to speak of militarism within guerrilla groups. Combatants tend to view armed struggle as a means to advance political objectives through military action, and define their organizations as politico-military structures.[18] For example, reflecting on how accidental deaths during an operation could influence the public's view of his organization, a former Argentine guerrilla told me: "I believed it could have a very negative impact, so I always insisted we had to provide a political content to our military operations." And yet, within guerrilla groups, military considerations tend to predominate over political ones time after time. Three interrelated factors—resocialization, occupational hazards, and bureaucratic imperatives—account for this development.

1. Re-socialization

Individuals are recruited at a relatively early age and in the company of friends. A life of clandestinity turns the guerrilla group into a substitute family, where strong affective ties link guerrillas with their fellow fighters, alive or dead. Emotional bonds with living guerrillas are easily explained. They constitute the combatant's reference group. But dead comrades also carry enormous weight for two reasons. Survivors feel a certain amount of guilt at having survived, and they glorify the dead and take them as examples to be followed.[19] The transformation of the guerrilla group into a surrogate family leads to an obliteration of the individual conscience. Through emotional and/or peer pressure combatants obey policies decided within the upper echelons of the organization, and do not voice their opposition even though they may consider those policies erroneous.

2. Occupational Hazards

An underground life also forces combatants to deal with a certain amount of physical discomfort, since safehouses are not precisely luxury hotels.[20] Combatants must also accept setbacks (death of comrades, arrests, failed operations, separation from their loved ones) and pervasive feelings of being under threat. A simplified world view is part of this effort, and combatants adopt a "friend-foe" conception of political conflict. In the case of Argentine guerrillas, who were fascinated by Clausewitz, the view that war is the continuation of politics by other means was gradually replaced by the idea that politics is war. West

clearly

German combatants wrote off their parents' generation by stating that they were "the generation of Auschwitz." In the case of ETA, Pedro Ibarra Guell points out that the will to fight can only be maintained "as long as I convince myself that outside those engaged in my same struggle there are only groups not worthy of respect." [21]

3. Bureaucratic Imperatives

Guerrilla groups are likely to confront the same problems as more conventional organizations. A sudden increase in membership leads to increased organizational complexity and to the establishment of more rigid authority relations. Careerism appears, as promotion within the organization is premised on the combatant's behavior. Organizational survival therefore appears as a primary goal. [22]

These three interrelated factors are also mutually reinforcing. When individuals define their identity only in connection with a given reference group, the pressure to conform is enormous. In addition, a friend-foe view of politics makes it difficult to conceive of an identity outside one's group. [23] That armed organizations become bureaucratized and hierarchical, providing combatants with a position of power as well as with an identity, also helps explain the reluctance to question orders. For power struggles within guerrilla groups are as ferocious as those within political parties.

It is because of these developments that I speak of militarism within armed organizations. The resort to armed struggle is not in itself militaristic. In certain situations armed struggle might appear as the only viable alternative and might in fact accomplish certain political objectives. Argentine guerrillas could claim credit for bringing Perón back to power, just as ETA could consider itself partly responsible for Madrid's decision to grant autonomy to the Basque provinces. Militarism develops when these groups lose sight of the political objectives that inspired the struggle, when they adopt hierarchical structures that require discipline and uniformity of members and sympathizers alike, and when they close themselves to outside influences but claim to be interpreting the popular will.

Indicators of the development of militarism can be found at the levels of operations, organization, ideology, and individual motivation. At the level of operations, guerrilla units tend to become larger and attempt to take on the armed forces through attacks at military establishments. Also, the initial emphasis on violence against property, not persons that is typical of groups mindful of popular support is abandoned. Assassination become the standard punishment meted out by the guerrillas. The political content assigned to operations is gradually lost, as operations are increasingly designed only to show military might. At the organizational level, guerrillas begin to mimic the armed forces as they introduce ranks and uniforms and abandon the commando or cell structure in favor of platoons, brigades, and companies. Ideological formulations show a hardening of attitudes as wider sectors of the population are included in the category of "enemies" and the guerrillas adopt a heroic view of the struggle that glorifies death in combat. At the level of individual motivation, combatants cease to question and argue. They simply obey.

It should be stressed that this analysis of militarism within armed organizations applies to nonrevolutionary situations. In a revolutionary situation it may be legitimate and in fact advisable to take on the armed forces, to attack military installations (even if it means suffering heavy casualties), or to eliminate dissent within the revolutionary ranks, or at any rate postpone it until victory appears at hand. The problem is that most revolutionary situations are not recognized as such until after the fact, until revolution has occurred. Lenin himself was rather vague on this issue, and in describing a revolutionary situation he argued that three factors had to be verified: a worsening of economic conditions, an increase in mass action, and a ruling class no longer able to impose its domination any longer.[24]

Until 1973 Argentina appeared to be facing a revolutionary situation, but this was no longer the case in 1974. However, the militarization of armed struggle took place over an extended period of time. Therefore, if Argentine guerrillas could be excused for an initial misreading of the situation, they could not be excused for persevering in their error. This inability to correct mistakes is in fact additional evidence of the presence of militarism.

Plan of the Book

The next chapter presents a historical overview of Argentine political history following Perón's downfall in 1955 as well as a brief discussion of the genesis and subsequent development of the different guerrilla groups. This study is then divided into two parts. Part I discusses patterns of violence in Argentina between 1969 and 1979. Chapters 3–5 examine armed struggle, collective violent protest, and right-wing paramilitary violence, respectively. Collective violent protest is discussed with a view to establishing whether it bears any relationship to guerrilla violence or, as the guerrillas would say, whether armed struggle "responds to the pressure of the masses" and is in turn a "motor of the masses." Right-wing violence is included for two reasons. First, illegal repression is inseparable from an explanation of guerrilla motivation because it tends to reinforce group cohesion. Second, paramilitary activity must be considered if one is to test what ETA calls the "action-repression-action" spiral and what Argentine combatants called the "theory of 'the worse, the better' "—that armed operations by guerrilla groups provoke an official response which in turn increases popular support for armed struggle. In chapter 6 I analyze the feedback effect of each of these three types of violence on the other two and explore the possibility that collective violent protest or right-wing violence influenced the militarization of armed struggle.

Part II describes the three factors that account for the development of militarism. Chapter 7 provides a description of the social basis of the Argentine guerrilla groups and an analysis of two aspects of the combatants' motivations: the decision to join and the will to continue the fight. Relying on interviews with former combatants in which they examined their lives before, during, and after their guerrilla experience, I attempt to account for both aspects of motivation. These life histories show that shared experiences, first in legal political organizations and then in the underground, provided participants with strong affective ties with their comrades that made "not letting the others down" the primary consideration. Chapter 8 describes changes over time in the guerrillas' ideological formulations and organizational structure, with particular emphasis on how the combatants viewed the process leading to the seizure of power. The characterization of the conflict as war made dissent unthinkable. Deviation from orthodoxy became treason, an epithet reserved for the enemy. The chapter describes a combination of carrots and sticks: if ideological deviations amounted to betrayal, conformity was rewarded with promotion through an increasingly complex and hierarchical structure.

Finally, the concluding chapter 9 will develop the ideas introduced above in light of the evidence presented in the body of the study.

A Note on Sources

This book relies heavily on primary sources. Argentine and foreign daily newspapers and weekly magazines were used extensively, and Argentine newspapers supplied the statistics on different types of violence and on combatants presented in chapters 3–7.[25] I also consulted a panoply of radical weeklies of the period, some of which were the official organs of individual armed organizations, and an array of position papers and other documents issued by the various guerrilla groups. All these sources can be found in the notes and bibliography, with two exceptions. Two documents by guerrilla combatants were given to me with the stipulation that they could be used but not cited since this would identify the authors and the person that made those documents available to me.

Interviews with 43 former combatants, discussed in depth in chapter 7, were granted on condition that the interviewed individual not be named. Accordingly, I provide only the date and place where the interview took place and the guerrilla group my interviewee belonged to. Any former combatants identified by name are dead, have "disappeared," or, as is the case with top leaders, have become media personalities and could come to no harm as a result of my writing. I also conducted a number of interviews with cabinet ministers and political appointees to administrative posts, members of the judiciary, and military commanders. Some of these interviewees also requested anonymity. Those who did not are identified in the different chapters.

2

Politics in Argentina after 1955 and the Development of the Guerrilla Movement

A former Argentine guerrilla once told me the following story. In 1970, while a student at the Catholic University in Buenos Aires, he was surprised outside the Sociology Department while using an aerosol can to put the finishing touches on a graffito of a *P* over a *V*. Within and outside guerrilla circles, this stood for *Perón Vuelve* (Perón is coming back). The individual who caught the guerrilla was none other than Monsignor Octavio Derisi, the university's president. Monsignor Derisi looked at him, said "I always knew that reality would one day catch up with us," and moved on.

The "reality" Monsignor Derisi referred to was the ouster of Juan Perón in 1955 and his enforced eighteen-year exile. It is against this background that the emergence of armed struggle must be understood. What followed the 1955 coup was a situation of political deadlock. The military and its civilian allies were set on preventing a return of Peronism to power by any means, including repression; while Peronists, primarily within the union movement, protested their political exclusion through strikes and industrial sabotage. If, for some, Peronist rule was unthinkable, Peronists made sure that rule without them became impossible. Youth groups from all along the political spectrum derived one lesson from this period—that the only way to effect political change was through violence. The remainder of civil society pinned its hopes on the 1966 government of General Juan Carlos Onganía, expected to end political deadlock by ensuring a period of social peace that would in turn bring economic development. But disillusionment with Onganía and his policies came swiftly. The 1966–73 military government, popularly known as the *Onganiato*, replaced the Peronism–anti-Peronism antinomy that had existed since 1955 with a confrontation between the military and the rest of society. It also radicalized the middle class and created a climate in which a return of Peronism to power became the only viable alternative.

This chapter describes political developments in Argentina since 1955 and reviews the genesis of the guerrilla movement during the Onganiato and the development and decline of guerrilla groups during the 1973–76 Peronist administrations and the 1976–83 military dictatorship. The political context in which guerrilla groups increased their membership exponentially, became complex organizations, and developed a view of conflict that equated politics with war sets the scene for a discussion of the militarization of armed struggle in subsequent chapters.

Post-Peronist Argentina

There are three key dates in twentieth-century Argentine political history. The first is February 12, 1912, when universal male suffrage was introduced. This allowed for the incorporation of the middle class into politics, led to the victory of the middle-class Radical Party (Unión Cívica Radical or UCR) in the presidential elections of 1916, and ended the sixty-year period of conservative rule. The second key date is February 24, 1946, when the then Colonel Juan Perón was elected president. The Peronist era (1946–55) marked the integration of the working class into the national political arena.[1] It also redefined political identities because the traditional leftist parties, the Socialists and Communists, permanently lost their working-class constituency. After 1946 the working class would by and large identify with Perón's party, successively named Labor Party, Single Party of the National Revolution, Peronist Party, and, after the 1950s, Justicialist Party. The third key date is September 16, 1955, when General Eduardo Lonardi staged the coup that toppled Juan Perón. This event might not have appeared significant at the time. After all, it was the third coup in Argentina in 25 years, and, like its predecessors, it resulted in a brief military interlude followed by a call for elections and the establishment of a civilian administration. Yet for the next 30 years Argentina was plunged into one of the most conflictive periods the country had undergone since independence.[2] The heart of the matter was the debate over the role of Peronism within the polity.

Once Perón was deposed, his followers upheld the achievements of the 1946–55 period:

> pension schemes and protection against layoffs, a working day of statutorily defined length, paid vacations and a new rigorously enforced Sunday rest law, improved working conditions for factory workers, accident compensation, regulated apprenticeships, controls on female and child labor, compulsory and binding conciliation and arbitration procedures, subsidized

housing and legal services, vacation resorts, full legal status for trade unions, employment agencies, and annual bonuses (*aguinaldos*).[3]

To this one could add that the poor and downtrodden whom Perón called "shirtless masses" (*masas descamisadas*) received free food and clothing, subsidized medicines, and other charitable gifts through the Eva Perón Foundation (headed by the president's wife); that Perón gave women the vote; that workers gained seats in the Congress and cabinet posts; and, most important, that Perón offered the working class a new commodity, a sense of dignity. Anti-Peronists, on the other hand, concentrated on the evils of Peronist rule: an economic policy that sacrificed productivity to redistribution and led to fiscal irresponsibility, high inflation, and economic stagnation. Anti-Peronists also stressed the regime's authoritarian tendencies. Perón purged the Supreme Court and the universities, indirectly censored the press by rationing newsprint (and eventually licensed raids on the opposition dailies), reformed the constitution which barred him from reelection, and incited mobs to raid the aristocratic Jockey Club and the UCR headquarters, and, in 1954, to burn churches. Perón's maxims and speeches became the Justicialist doctrine taught in schools and at the service academies. Finally, anti-Peronists stressed corruption in the administration, in particular the Eva Perón Foundation, and the cult of personality that developed around the president and his wife. Perón was known as "the Leader" and "the First Worker of the Republic," and Evita, whose autobiography became compulsory reading in grade schools, was the "Spiritual Chief of the Nation." Their names were given to

railway stations, streets, hospitals, schools, cities and even provinces. Their large portraits hung on every wall, hall, public office, classroom, etc. If we add to this permanent propaganda effort the special celebrations and meetings—which the [official] press used in order to comment for days on the ruling couple's every gesture, every facial expression, every word—we will understand that, after 1950, Perón did not omit any measure to turn his name into the everlasting symbol of the Argentine Nation in all its manifestations.[4]

Following the 1955 coup, anti-Peronists interpreted the Peronist era as a case of "rape of the masses,"[5] and generally believed that once Perón was forced into exile, his followers would forget him. This was the philosophy behind General Lonardi's post-coup slogan, "neither victors nor vanquished" (*ni vencedores ni vencidos*), and of those who initially rallied behind Lonardi: the bourgeoisie, the church, the armed forces, sectors of the middle class, and significant numbers from all opposition parties. When it became apparent that Perón would not be forgotten, the political elite split into two camps. One wing of the UCR was willing to allow Peronists to participate in elections and therefore in the political process. The military, the right, and the majority of Radicals, who were unwilling to do either, won. General Pedro Eugenio Aramburu deposed Lonardi in November 1955, became president, and attacked the Peronist movement. A presidential decree banned the Peronist party and prevented anyone who had held office at the national, provincial, or municipal level between 1946 and 1955 from running for office. Perón, who went into exile first in Paraguay, then in Venezuela and the Dominican Republic, and after 1960 in Madrid, was cashiered and charged in absentia with corruption, smuggling, and treason. The General Confederation of Labor (Confederación General del Trabajo or CGT) was placed under military control and military supervisors were appointed to oversee the various unions. The government also granted legal recognition to more than one union per economic sector in an effort to break the Peronist identity of the union movement. Another decree excluded from future labor activism about 50,000 union activists who had held leadership posts between 1949 and 1955. Evita had died in 1952 and her embalmed body had been deposited at the CGT headquarters. In 1956 Aramburu had the body smuggled out of the country and buried under a false name in an Italian cemetery. The government also banned the use of Peronist slogans and insignias and the display of portraits of Perón and Evita. Perón's name could not appear in print and the press had to resort to euphemisms like "the fugitive tyrant." In 1956 a group of civilians and officers led by General Juan José Valle responded to these developments by staging a pro-Peronist rebellion in Corrientes province. The rebellion failed and 27 men were summarily shot. It was the first time since the civil wars in the mid-nineteenth century that rebellion was punished by death.

After 1955, with Peronism (supported by roughly one third of the electorate) outlawed, Argentina became a semi-democracy.[6] The military and its civilian allies found Peronist participation unacceptable, even though in 1962 and 1965 and at the provincial level Peronists were allowed to run for office as long as they did so under a different party label and did not advocate a return of Perón or 1946–55 policies. Peronists were thus forced to play outside the established rules of the political game. But rule without Peronism proved impossible, since the unions would launch successive "Struggle Plans," which included occupations of factories, violent strikes, and industrial sabotage designed to harass the government until it lifted the ban on their party.

This period, popularly known as the Peronist Resistance or simply "the Resistance" is "a dominant reference point in Peronist political culture."[7] The Resistance's bark was stronger than its bite in that activity never went beyond localized protest and sabotage, but it produced two lasting effects. First, a left wing emerged within Peronism, formed by the so-called combative unions (combativos), and a myriad of student groupings. The combativos were a small minority within the labor movement and the student groups failed to establish a strong and unified organization. Daniel James accurately characterizes the emergence of this left wing as a reflex action because it was mainly a reaction against the union bosses' willingness to ally themselves with whoever was in power in exchange for the right to maintain total control over their unions. In the 1950s the Peronist left "developed very little alternative ideology, very little separate existence. Politically, it remained firmly rooted within the Perón–anti-Perón dichotomy that was the chief defining characteristic of Argentine politics in this period. This meant that the distinguishing characteristic of the Left, the *duros*, could only be defined objectively as loyalty to Perón and his orders."[8] In the late 1960s the Peronist left developed a program of radical reform and received the massive support of youth sectors. The emergence of the Peronist left gradually produced the second legacy of the Resistance: the traditional left changed its attitude toward Peronism. Since the 1940s, Socialists and Communists had viewed Peronism as a fascist movement, drawing parallels between Perón and Mussolini, and had supported the 1955 coup. As Peronism developed a left wing supporting an anticapitalist and anti-imperialist message and stressing direct action, sectors of the traditional leftist parties came to view Peronism as a revolutionary force. The radicalization of the Peronist left and the "peronization" of sectors of the traditional left would be vital to the development of armed struggle in the late sixties.)

Governments after 1955 oscillated between failed attempts to co-opt and destroy the Peronist movement. No party could offer itself as a viable alternative to Peronism because no party could claim to represent any significant portion of the population. Socialists, Communists, and other parties on the left had by the late fifties become negligible, torn by ideological debates and the emergence of the ultraleft) The conservatives never recovered from the introduction of universal male suffrage, and the Radicals split into several factions which gave birth to new parties. Not restricted to the Radical party, these splits developed into the ridiculous figure of 225 parties for the 1965 congressional elections, and frequently originated not on ideological but on personal grounds.[9] Contrary to what happened in Venezuela or Colombia after 1958, where the political arena was narrowed so as to minimize conflict, Argentina witnessed a host of new forms of political action. When more than one third of the electorate is excluded from the decision-making process, the temptation to resort to extra-institutional, even extra-legal forms of pressure becomes too strong to resist. Governments from 1955 to 1966 were besieged from their inauguration by short-term demands from different sectors of society. The CGT staged Struggle Plans, students occupied universities, the Church threatened excommunication, and the military organized the next coup, in anticipation of which all the parties, including the president's, began plotting. Policy making was thus reduced to satisfying whichever sector happened to be most vociferous at any given time.[10]

Between 1955 and 1966 Argentina was governed by five presidents, two generals, and three civilians, none of whom finished his term: civilians were deposed and soldiers were forced to retreat to the barracks and call new elections. Economic stagnation and political immobilism in "a society which increasingly perceived itself as unable to generate consensual solutions autonomously"[11] gradually eroded the legitimacy not only of governments but also of the system. The previous constitutional transfer of power in Argentina in the twentieth century, before Carlos Menem succeeded Raúl Alfonsín in July 1989, had taken place in 1928. In 1938 Roberto M. Ortiz succeeded Agustín P. Justo, but elections were fraudulent and recognized as such at the time. Perón had amended the constitution so that it would allow him to be re-elected in 1952. In the absence of a democratic tradition, the system was not valued per se but as long as it produced the desired results. As the failure of democracy became apparent, the appeal of authoritarian solutions increased. For a population that consistently voiced the need for new faces in politics, a "strong hand," even a "new Franco,"[12] General Juan Carlos Onganía was, in 1966, the panacea.

1966–73: The Argentine Revolution

The 1966 coup, the fifth in Argentina since 1930, differed substantially from its predecessors. Traditionally, the military had intervened in politics following what Alfred Stepan calls the "moderator pattern" in civil-military relations. Assiduously courted by civilian elites, the military staged coups in what were considered crisis situations, like the electoral victory of a leftist candidate or the implementation of a policy too radical for the military's taste. But the consensus among civilian and military elites was that the military would hand over power to a civilian administration after a short interval. This moderator pattern was broken in 1966 when Juan Carlos Onganía seized power with no intention of relinquishing it. Onganía and the armed forces talked about a ten-to-fifteen-year period of military rule in which the country would have to go through three phases of change: economic, social, and political. Economic rationalization would be followed by the development of "healthy" social corporations and only later by political institutionalization.[13] The fact that the coup bore the rather pompous name of Argentine Revolution pointed to the serious transformations the military were contemplating. The Onganiato was characterized at the time as a "provisional technical dictatorship,"[14] its aim being to modernize the economy and put an end to a decade of inefficiency, corruption, disorder, and instability.

A survey taken a week after the June 1966 coup revealed its considerable support: 66 percent of the population declared itself happy with the change in government, 27 percent was neither happy nor unhappy, and only 6 percent opposed the military takeover. In another survey, 77 percent of respondents answered the "revolution" of June 28, 1966, was "necessary." Scarcely two years later, 70 percent of those surveyed considered General Onganía equal to or worse than his civilian predecessor Arturo Illia, who had been in power from 1963 to 1966.[15] What was initially disaffection from the Onganiato through shattered hopes eventually became a marked radicalization of Argentine society; a rejection of everything the military regime stood for, stemming not from what the "revolutionaries" of 1966 promised to do but from the way they went about doing it. Broad sectors of Argentine society deposited in Onganía their last hopes of escaping the 1955–66 deadlock. However, as the next section will show, the military government's response to specific politico-economic challenges created a spiral of violence, eroded that initial societal support, and favorably predisposed the population to another authoritarian experiment of an opposite ideological nature—armed struggle.

Radicalization in the Sixties

Analysts of the 1966–1973 period have suggested that the reasons for the radicalization that followed the 1966 coup were mainly economic, and that the pauperization of the middle class as a consequence of the regime's economic policy led to its joining the Peronist ranks just as the working class was about to shed its Peronist ideology and become an authentic class movement.[16] This is not entirely accurate.

Onganía's Economy Minister, Adalbert Krieger Vasena, launched his economic plan in early 1967. The Krieger Vasena plan was based on a strong devaluation (40 percent) and a two-year wage freeze. In the best developmentalist tradition, devaluation was supposed to encourage foreign investment. To keep internal prices down, there would be a tax on agrarian exports, and these funds would go toward eliminating the deficit and allowing the government to engage in a massive public works program. The wage freeze was supposed to keep costs down. The ultimate goal was to curb inflation, cut down industrial costs and modernize the industrial sector, and create the international confidence that would open new lines of credit for Argentina. Until mid-1969 the plan was extremely successful. Inflation went down dramatically, there was a growth in investments, and the transformation did not entail extremely high social costs.[17] However, it is also true that different societal sectors were dissatisfied with the plan: the working class was bearing the brunt of economic transformation, economic rationalization hit small and middle enterprises severely, and the agrarian sector was displeased with its enforced participation in the economic effort.[18] Scholars who emphasize the economic causes of radicalization in the sixties point to the 1969 student-worker riots in Córdoba as proof,[19] but the riots cannot be ascribed to Krieger Vasena's policy because the economic crisis occurred after those events and was, in some sense, a consequence of them. The radicalization of Argentine society must not be viewed merely as a reaction against economic cycles. New antagonisms and new problems had emerged which went beyond the idea of economic injustice. The radicalization was due, to the extent that they can be separated, not so much to economic but to political causes.

The 1966 Argentine version of the bureaucratic-authoritarian state was characterized by a relatively low level of threat prior to its inauguration, and consequently by a low level of state repression.[20] Indeed, the Onganía regime was viewed as a *dictablanda,* a benign dictatorship. However, the regime's bigotry and paternalistic style quickly dispelled that impression. Onganía began by dissolving political parties, banning all types of political activity and launching a crusade against communism represented by the National Security Doctrine, which he had helped develop in the early sixties. This was in keeping with Onganía's ideas about the three phases (economic, social, and political) his regime should go through, but it had the negative effect of stimulating the development of myths and search for panaceas which have long characterized Argentine society.[21]

Onganía's decision to rule out by decree the very existence of politics was due not so much to the autocratic will of his regime but to the vision he held of his own role within Argentina. For Onganía genuinely believed he had the sacred duty to reshape and remoralize his country. This morality crusade took several forms. Books were burned, the Maipo and Nacional cabarets (equivalents of the Lido in Paris) were closed down because they were considered indecent, censorship commissions were set up to eliminate corruption on television and in the cinema. The Argentine population might have remained indifferent, just as it had when political activity was banned, were it not for the fact that the government's crusade (which even involved entrusting the country to the Virgin Mary's protection) appeared grotesquely medieval to a nation obsessed with replicating the latest European fads and cultural patterns.

This "onslaught on culture," as it came to be known, was accompanied by the closing down of a number of publications on grounds ranging from publishing communist propaganda to publishing cartoons of the president.[22] But the event which epitomizes the cultural policy of the Argentine Revolution was the "intervention" in all national universities, which became known as the Night of the Long Batons. The University Reform of 1918 had established the principle of "university autonomy" by which universities were governed by a "tripartite council" of professors, students, and alumni; and university grounds were off limits to police and military forces. Intervention meant the removal of the governing authorities, elected by this tripartite council, and their replacement by government-appointed officials—the end of university "autonomy."

Some time before the coup, during a public ceremony in front of the Department of Exact Sciences of the University of Buenos Aires, students had climbed to the top floor and poured coins and insults on the military contingent present. Thus, the only sector within Argentine society that actively opposed the coup was making its repudiation public. On July 29, 1966, when the news about the intervention became known, these same students decided to occupy the building as a sign of protest. The military, which had not forgotten the previous insult, broke into the building and with an unusual display of brutality forced students and professors out. More than 200 people were detained and more than 30 were hospitalized. The same procedure was repeated at the Department of Architecture for no apparent reason (the students were in class) and at other universities throughout the country. The Night of the Long Batons acquired international overtones because among those beaten at the Department of Exact Sciences was Professor Warren Ambrose from the Massachusetts Institute of Technology, who described the incident:

> The police entered firing tear gas and ordered everyone to face the wall with our hands up. . . . As we stood blinded by the tear gas against the walls of the classrooms, the police then began hitting us. Then one by one we were taken out and forced to run between rows of police spaced about 10 feet apart. That is when I got seven or eight wallops and a broken finger. No one resisted. We were all terrified, what with the curses and gas. Prof. Carlos Varsavsky, director of the new radio observatory in La Plata, received a fractured skull then. The eminent geologist Félix González Bonorino, who is about 70, had his head bloodied. Those of us on our feet after running the gantlet were herded into trucks and taken to a police station. . . . I was released at 3 A.M. but few of the others taken with me were freed at that time. At no time was any explanation given us for the police beatings, which is incomprehensible to me.[23]

The State Department lodged a protest and forced the Argentine Foreign Ministry to issue an apology.

The president of the University of Buenos Aires, eight of his ten deans, and one hundred and eighty-four professors from the Department of Exact Sciences resigned immediately. Within several days the presidents of five of the eight national universities also resigned. It was the first stage in a continuous exile of academics. An attempt was made to portray the Night of the Long Batons as a leftist maneuver designed to discredit the government. The left, according to this version, had deliberately exposed its forces so that it would have some martyrs to display. However, this thesis could in no way explain, after the initial blunder, the government's persistent harassing of the universities. That the Night of the Long Batons was a mistake, and that it brought serious consequences, is even acknowledged by two of the most prominent government officials of the time.[24] Always mindful of what the rest of the world thinks of them, Argentines were profoundly embarrassed by this display of barbarism. Argentines were also extremely proud of their university system, considered the best in Latin America at the time, and the exile of academics brought about a sharp decline in the quality of university education and research, for which they blamed the Onganiato. University students would not forget the incident and would become the regime's main source of opposition.

Three other events contributed to the radicalization of public opinion: the violent riot in Córdoba city in May 1969, known as the *Cordobazo* (the blow from Córdoba); a similar incident in March 1971, popularly called the *Viborazo* (the viper's blow); and the Trelew massacre in 1972.

Events leading to the Cordobazo can be traced back to a government decision to raise the price of meal tickets at the University of the Northeast.[25] This led to demonstrations in Corrientes where a student was shot dead on May 15, 1969. His death sparked more demonstrations, and on May 17 a student was killed in Rosario. There were further marches and demonstrations and, on May 20, a student was blinded by a grenade in Córdoba. On May 21 another student was shot in the back during a demonstration in Rosario, and students in Salta attacked the local country club. By this time students were marching throughout the country and the May 25 Independence Day parades and festivities had to be canceled. In Córdoba province, student protest coincided with labor unrest due to summary dismissals at the Santa Isabel (IKA-Renault) car factory. During a general strike called for May 29, students and workers took to the streets, occupied the city, erected barricades, and destroyed and burned shops, cars, and buses. Their progress through the city was unhampered by the police or the military until that evening, and fighting continued the following day. After the two-day riots, 14 people were dead and large portions of the city were smoking ruins. The population, and above all the government, were shocked by this sudden breach of the *pax onganiana*. The official interpretation was that the Cordobazo was a carefully planned attack on the government, intended to anticipate further "subversive" operations. In fact, the Cordobazo was a spontaneous act by students and workers, two sectors of society which had different grievances but no channels through which these could be expressed. As a result of these events, these two groups, which had up to that moment functioned quite independently from each other, began to see the advantages of engaging in joint action.[26]

The Cordobazo showed that the social peace and social order on which Onganía's sole claim to power rested had evaporated. There could be no further discussion of a ten-year dictatorship to change the face of Argentina. Open recognition by the government that the Cordobazo expressed legitimate grievances, accompanied by effective measures for their redress, would not have altered the outcome but could have made the transition to democracy a less violent, antimilitary procedure. But the government set up a military government in Córdoba, court-martialed the insurgents, and closed down Córdoba university.

Onganía was deposed in June 1970 in a "coup within the coup." Neither his successor, General Roberto M. Levingston, nor the regime's gray eminence, General Alejandro A. Lanusse, could erase from public memory the events of the Cordobazo and its aftermath. Levingston attempted to continue ruling the country with a heavy hand. In February 1971, workers at the Fiat car factory in Córdoba occupied the plant to protest layoffs. Levingston asked the province's governor, Bernardo Bas, to end the factory occupation by any means, including force. Bas, who after the Cordobazo and the subsequent military occupation of the province had brought about some stability and enjoyed considerable popularity, refused. Levingston deposed him and appointed Camilo Uriburu, whose inaugural speech called all forces opposing the regime "subversive" and compared armed struggle to "a viper with a hundred heads." This phrase gave its name to the Viborazo, a second Cordobazo which was more of an insurrectional class movement than the first.[27] Two days of violence (March 12–14, 1971) brought two deaths, about thirty injuries, and nearly three hundred detainees. On March 23 Uriburu was replaced by Rear Admiral Helbio Guozden, the ninth governor appointed to unruly Córdoba in less than five years. The following day Levingston was forced to step down and Lanusse became president. This second "coup within the coup" provided further evidence of the failure of the Argentine Revolution as the usual military retreat and talk of elections took place. Lanusse announced on April 1 that the government would elaborate a new law of political parties, legalizing them and allowing them to reorganize. But no election date was mentioned.

The Guerrilla Movement up to 1972

Even though the Onganía dictatorship provided the context in which armed struggle became a salient activity, Argentina experienced three failed attempts at rural guerrilla warfare between 1959 and 1968. Throughout the decade, emulating the Cuban example, insurgents across Latin America would attempt to establish *focos*, rural guerrilla nuclei expected to create the conditions for revolution in developing countries where such "objective" conditions did not exist.[28]

In September 1959, a group of about 20 people known as the *Uturuncos* ("tigermen" in Quechua, an indian language) established two guerrilla camps in the hills of Tucumán province. Once these groups went into action, commanded by Enrique Manuel Mena and Félix Seravalle, other fighting fronts were expected to open in the provinces of Salta, Jujuy, and Santiago del Estero, accompanied by urban insurrections and a military revolt led by general Miguel Iñíguez. The objective was to depose president Arturo Frondizi (1958–62) and force the return of Perón to power. Iñíguez backed down and the urban insurrection never materialized. After a single operation, the seizure of Frías police station on Christmas Day 1959, the group was rounded up by the police.[29]

In 1963, a second attempt was led by Jorge Ricardo Masseti, a journalist for Radio El Mundo in Buenos Aires who had interviewed Fidel Castro at Sierra Maestra and subsequently been recruited to organize the Cuban press agency

Prensa Latina. In June 1963 Masseti and three Sierra Maestra veterans entered Argentina via Bolivia and started recruiting members for the People's Guerrilla Army (Ejército Guerrillero del Pueblo or EGP). For the next ten months the group ambled between Salta and Jujuy provinces. In April 1964 the group literally stumbled upon a gendarmery patrol and killed one gendarme. It was the only military action by the EGP, which only came to the attention of the public and the authorities because it sent president Arturo Illia a letter calling on him to resign.[30] Even though the group totaled probably fewer than 30 members, Masseti had taken the time to draft a complex disciplinary code, under whose provisions two would-be deserters were shot. Three others died of hunger, sixteen were caught by the gendarmery in April 1964, and Masseti vanished into thin air.

The last rural guerrilla episode was organized by members of the Peronist Youth (Juventud Peronista or JP) who, after Perón's failed attempt to return to Argentina in 1964, concluded an insurrection was the only way out. These JP militants planned to set up a foco in Tucumán which would be followed by an urban guerrilla campaign. The group carried out a few bank robberies, the proceeds of which were used to buy supplies, all prior to the establishment of a guerrilla camp at Taco Ralo. Led by Néstor Verdinelli, Carlos Caride, and Envar El Kadri, the thirteen men and one woman who formed the 17 October Montonero Detachment of the Peronist Armed Forces (Destacamento Montonero 17 de Octubre de las Fuerzas Armadas Peronistas or FAP) came from different provinces. They wanted to create the impression that this was a nationwide campaign, and the geographical provenance of the guerrillas would be made known after the first major operation.[31] But as soon as the group arrived in Tucumán the police stumbled onto it while looking for smugglers. The captured guerrillas persuaded the authorities that this was simply another mad attempt at *foquismo,* so the urban contingent remained undetected. Miguel Zabala Rodríguez, the attorney defending the Taco Ralo fourteen, acted as courier between the two groups.[32]

The year 1969, which represented a switch from rural to urban armed struggle, inaugurated a decade of uninterrupted, escalating guerrilla activity. Six major groups, portrayed in figures 2.1 and 2.2, went into action during the year: the reconstituted FAP; the Shirtless Commando (Comando Descamisados); the Montoneros; the Revolutionary Armed Forces (Fuerzas Armadas Revolucionarias or FAR); the People's Revolutionary Army (Ejército Revolucionario del Pueblo or ERP); and the Liberation Armed Forces (Fuerzas Armadas de Liberación or FAL). While the last two were Marxist, the rest identified themselves with Peronism. During that first year, the groups carried out their attacks anonymously, and would each choose a major operation in 1970 to make their existence known to the public.

The reconstituted FAP went public with the occupation of a slum dwelling,

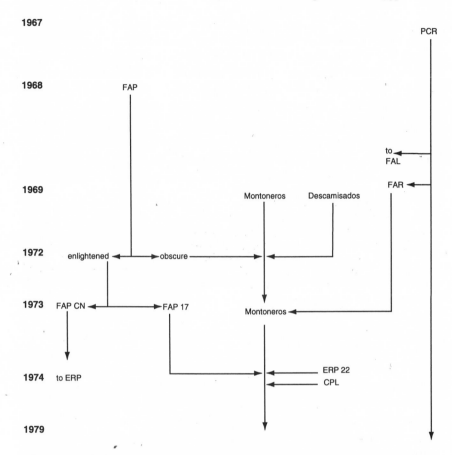

Figure 2.1. Splits and Mergers in Peronist Armed Organizations

Villa Piolín, on January 6, 1970. Policemen guarding the place were stripped of their weapons, and FAP distributed toys among Villa Piolín's children. During these early years, FAP was viewed as the "most Peronist" of armed organizations because of its ties to combative unions and to veterans of the Resistance. FAP was also the strongest of Peronist armed organizations because it spent the better part of 1969–70 devoted to "equipment" operations—theft of arms and money. This allowed FAP to offer protection to Tupamaro combatants escaping repression in Uruguay, and to loan money and materiel to other Peronist armed organizations. But by 1972 the group was torn by an internal debate between the "enlightened" and the "obscure." The former argued that this was a time to regroup and develop adequate ideological formulations. The latter held that FAP's strength had always resided in its atheoretical behavior. The quarrel resolved itself when the "obscure" left FAP and joined the Montoneros.[33]

Though it is generally believed that 12 individuals founded the Montoneros,

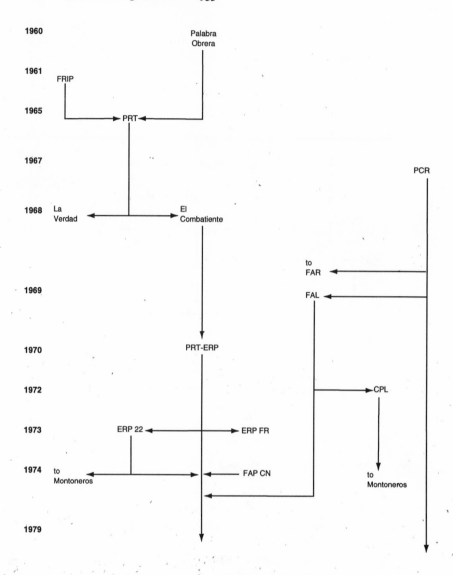

Figure 2.2. Splits and Mergers in Marxist Armed Organizations

the origins of the organization are more complex. Four groups coalesced before its launching: a Santa Fe contingent made up of Catholic Action activists;
a group from Córdoba mostly made up of university students; individuals from
Buenos Aires province with prior activism in certain combative unions; and
the Buenos Aires city group, several of whose members were graduates of the
National Buenos Aires School (Colegio Nacional Buenos Aires), a prestigious
state-owned high school. The Montoneros went public with two spectacular

operations. On May 29, 1970, Army Day as well as the first anniversary of the Cordobazo, Montoneros kidnapped former president General Pedro Eugenio Aramburu. The retired general was taken to an estate belonging to the family of one Montonero founder and was put on revolutionary trial. Aramburu was found guilty of executing General Valle and the other 1956 rebels, of stealing Evita's body from the CGT, and of repressing the Peronist movement after 1955. A communiqué sent to the press on June 1, 1970, read: "TO THE PEOPLE OF OUR NATION: The leadership of MONTONEROS announces that Pedro Eugenio Aramburu was executed today at 07:00 hs. God our Lord have mercy on his soul. PERON OR DEATH! LONG LIVE THE MOTHERLAND! MONTONEROS." [34] The kidnapping and murder of Aramburu turned Montoneros into a household name among Peronists. It also cost Onganía the presidency. On July 1, 1970, the Montoneros staged their second spectacular feat, the seizure of the town of La Calera in Córdoba. In 40 minutes, the group occupied and robbed the bank, robbed arms from the police station, occupied the town hall and the post office, played the Peronist March, and distributed leaflets. Two combatants were arrested during the getaway, however, and information they furnished to the police decimated the organization through deaths and detentions. The Montoneros were forced to seek protection from FAP, and turned to political work while regrouping. In a two-year maneuver, the organization seized control of the JP groups at the universities. This was a stroke of genius which would turn the Montoneros into the only spokespeople for the radicalized sectors of Peronism, an umbrella of organizations which came to be known as the Revolutionary Tendency, or simply as the Tendency. [35]

The original Descamisados were mostly members of the youth wing of the Christian Democratic Party and were heavily imbued with the ideas of radical Catholicism. The "peronization" of the group derived from a re-evaluation of the social policies of the 1946–55 Peronist era. The Descamisado founders shared two radicalizing experiences. First, some of the founders participated in the University Working Camps. Organized by two progressive priests, these camps provided middle-class students with first-hand experience of how workers in the most depressed areas of northern Argentina lived. Second, Descamisado founders were active in the post-1966 student resistance to Onganía. Following the Cordobazo, and led by Horacio Mendizábal, Norberto Habegger, and Oscar de Gregorio, the group underwent military training and staged its first operations, primarily Robin Hood type distribution of food in slums and small-scale theft of arms, money, medical supplies, and wigs. The Descamisados chose to make their existence public by occupying a movie theater at La Tablada in the province of Buenos Aires. They showed an eight-minute short in which Perón praised armed struggle, then they distributed leaflets and left. [36] Until they merged with Montoneros in late 1972, the Descamisados remained a relatively small group which managed to combine political work in working-class neighborhoods with military actions very effectively. Their military actions were planned to the last detail—throughout the Argentine Revolution the group boasted only one death and one detention.[37]

The founders of FAR and FAL were originally Communist party dissidents who in 1967 had split to form the Revolutionary Communist party (Partido Comunista Revolucionario, PCR). By their own admission, both organizations had originally considered launching a rural guerrilla campaign in support of Ernesto (Che) Guevara's Bolivian adventure and had subsequently reappraised their strategy in light of Che's failure.[38] But FAR had also proceeded to revise its views on Peronism and had become "peronized."[39] Barely two weeks after the Cordobazo, FAR firebombed 15 Minimax supermarkets to protest a visit to Argentina by the Minimax owner, Nelson Rockefeller. But FAR chose to go public with the seizure of the town of Garín in Buenos Aires province on July 30, 1970. The operation, inspired by a similar feat by the Tupamaros a year earlier, was a model of military precision and economy of effort which characterized FAR's early years. In 11 minutes the group robbed the local bank, stole all armaments from the police station, cut the town's radio and telephone communications, occupied the train station and a bar, distributed leaflets, and withdrew. Unfortunately, the Garín operation resulted in the death of one police officer and of FAR's Raquel Gelín, the first Argentine woman ever to die in combat. FAL first became known to the public when it kidnapped the Paraguayan consul Waldemar Sánchez on March 24, 1970. The group expected to exchange Sánchez for two imprisoned militants. One militant had died, presumably under torture, and the government refused to trade the other. FAL released Sánchez unharmed. More successful was the attack on a guardhouse outside the Military Academy at Campo de Mayo on April 5, 1970, when FAL took off with the guards' weapons. Unlike the other groups, FAL was plagued from its inception by internal squabbles which would lead to its apparent extinction by 1972, after a substantial sector calling itself Liberation Popular Commandos (Comandos Populares de Liberación or CPL) splintered off and announced it would support a future Peronist administration.[40]

The ERP was the only organization established as the armed wing of a political party. In 1965, a group active among sugar cane workers in the northwest, the Popular Indoamerican Revolutionary Front (Frente Revolucionario Indoamericano Popular or FRIP) merged with a Buenos Aires group called Worker's Word (Palabra Obrera) to form the Workers' Revolutionary Party (Partido Revolucionario de los Trabajadores or PRT). The PRT was an uneasy alliance from the start, blending the FRIP's nationalist and anti-imperialist exaltation of the indian heritage in Latin America with Palabra Obrera's trotskyism. During the Fourth Party Congress in 1968 the PRT split into two factions. El Combatiente, led by Mario Santucho, advocated armed struggle; La Verdad, led by Nahuel Moreno, rejected it. La Verdad, comprising one third of the original PRT membership, was expelled from the party.[41] At the Fifth Party Congress in 1970 the PRT decided to launch the ERP as the party's armed wing. Party and army were supposed to be separate entities. Originally, the PRT adopted Marxism-Leninism whereas the ERP defined itself as merely anti-imperialist. But in practice these distinctions became blurred, all the more so since the leadership of the ERP tended to occupy positions in the PRT's Central Committee. In fact, during the year prior to the launching of the ERP, members of the PRT had begun staging "equipment" operations in Rosario. But the official launching of the ERP came in September 1970 with an attack and theft of arms at a Rosario police station. Distributions of foodstuffs in slums, occupations of schools and factories, and other operations of "armed propaganda" followed in quick succession. In May 1971 the ERP carried out the first political kidnapping for ransom in Argentine history. The victim was Stanley Sylvester, manager of the Swift meat-packing plant and honorary consul in Rosario. A $50,000 ransom was used to purchase food and clothing for the poor, and Sylvester was released unharmed.[42]

The political impact of armed struggle could not be emphasized enough. To begin with, guerrilla groups demonstrated an operational ability to strike, and strike repeatedly—there were 114 armed operations in 1969, 434 in 1970, and 654 in 1971. One should also mention the initial societal surprise at the social origin of guerrillas, when the identities of combatants were revealed through arrests and deaths. As two progressive priests acquainted with some of the guerrilla founders put it, the guerrillas "are not drawn from the masses. . . . They were born and they grew up listening [to their elders] vomit abuse against peronism. What drives them to react violently against the social milieu in which they grew up? . . . the conviction that only violence will sweep away social injustice. . . . That is why they believe fervently in socialism. . . . That is why they look favorably upon peronism."[43] And "the *great families* [are] scared because their own children s—— on the society they have built."[44] But the Onganiato's policies had produced a societal radicalization not restricted to the students and workers who participated in events like the Cordobazo and the Viborazo. By 1971, according to survey data, 45.5 percent of respondents in Greater Buenos Aires and 49.5 percent in the rest of the country considered armed struggle "justified," and those expressing support for the guerrillas were primarily drawn from the middle and upper classes.[45] Conservative journalist Raúl Abdala would complain that

every attack, every kidnapping—with or without a subsequent murder—are seen by many as a statement, better still, as a morally valid action, and even as the only alternative left to bring about "structural change". . . . [normally] peaceful people . . . applaud as an act of social justice the obtention of a multimillionaire ransom and the murder of a kidnap victim, or in any event attempt unsuccessfully to hide their sympathy towards these excesses, justifying them with arguments whose coherence nobody tries to sustain to any degree . . . [the guerrillas] count on a panoply of approvals, complacencies and connivances, from the justification that proceeds from the party committees and forums, to the benediction offered by our "modern" men of the cloth.[46]

Once armed struggle emerged on the political scene, one of the regime's main concerns became that of isolating the guerrillas from their societal support. To this effect, in September 1971 Lanusse announced that the electoral campaign would begin in October 1972, and general elections would take place in March 1973. At the same time that he satisfied popular demands for re-democratization, Lanusse implemented new measures against armed organizations. The death penalty had already been introduced following the kidnapping of Aramburu, even though it would never be applied. In May 1971 Lanusse modified the Criminal Code, introducing harsher penalties for various crimes, and launched a special tribunal to deal exclusively with crimes committed by members of guerrilla groups, the Federal Penal Chamber of the Nation (Cámara Federal en lo Penal de la Nación). The rationale behind the creation of this tribunal was that the same individual could be indicted for crimes committed in different provinces, and the existence of one tribunal with national jurisdiction would facilitate the administration of justice. This tribunal consisted of nine justices divided into three courts with three justices each. Each court tried cases, and there was no appeal except on grounds of arbitrariness, when the case could go to the Supreme Court. Another innovation involved the establishment of "maximum security" prisons. The Argentine Criminal Code has never included the category of political prisoner, but beginning in 1971, guerrilla prisoners were isolated from common criminals and subject to more rigorous prison conditions, first at Devoto prison in Greater Buenos Aires and later also at Rawson prison in Chubut.[47] Lanusse's policies achieved some tangible results—substantial numbers of guerrilla cadres were either imprisoned or killed in combat, and the total number of armed operations in 1972 (352) was the lowest since 1969.

The Trelew Massacre

Lanusse is one of the most astute politicians the Argentine army has ever produced. He nevertheless committed a serious blunder which, together with the Night of the Long Batons, the Cordobazo, and the Viborazo, would give the impression of a ruthless regime intent on perpetuating itself—the Trelew massacre.

On August 15, 1972, ERP, FAR, and Montonero inmates attempted to escape from the Rawson Maximum Security prison. It was an elaborate plan. Combatants seized the prison while a support group outside provided transportation from the prison to nearby Trelew airport. Another support group boarded the Trelew-Buenos Aires flight to hijack the plane. The escapees were to board the plane at Trelew and fly to Chile, since Salvador Allende was unlikely to turn them over to the Argentine military.

However, the plan did not unfold as anticipated. The buses expected to transport 100 escapees to Trelew airport never materialized. The top 25 guerrilla cadres traveled to the airport by cab. The plane had been hijacked and forced to wait on the runway for the delayed escapees, but the pilot had alerted the control tower, which in turn called for reinforcements from a naval base nearby. When the first six escapees arrived at the airport they boarded the plane. The Navy was on its way, so the plane took off as the remaining 19 combatants arrived at the airport. The guerrillas seized the airport but eventually surrendered and were taken into custody and transported to the Almirante Zar naval base near Trelew. The operation did not turn out to be the spectacular blow the guerrillas had planned, but it was something of a media success. Among the six who arrived in Chile were Mario Santucho, top leader of the ERP, Roberto Quieto, top leader of FAR, and Fernando Vaca Narvaja, a founding member of Montoneros and one of the participants in Aramburu's kidnapping and murder. Also, at the press conference at which those left behind at Trelew announced their surrender, the hostages praised the guerrillas' behavior. Hostages and combatants even joked about the country's economy—the guerrillas insisted on paying for the snacks they consumed during the siege and were appalled at the rising price of chocolate.

On August 22, at the Almirante Zar base, sixteen guerrillas were killed and the remaining three were critically wounded. Within forty-eight hours, the government produced three contradictory versions of the events, and the federal judge in charge of the case apparently failed to order autopsies. The final official version, which Rear Admiral Hermes Quijada (Chairman of the Joint Chiefs of Staff) provided in a televised address to the nation, was that Montonero Mariano Pujadas had attempted to seize a guard's gun, and that all 19 were attempting to escape. Inexplicably, the three survivors, who were taken to hospital in Buenos Aires, were allowed to tell a different story: they had all been woken up at 3:30 A.M., made to line up down the corridor between the cells, and machine-gunned. The survivors believed that the Navy made the decision to kill all 19 quite independently and that the president, Lanusse, had no other option but to bow to the fait accompli.[48] Subtleties aside, the incident was a premeditated murder designed to work as exemplary punishment, and as such it was widely viewed at the time.

The CGT went on strike, and marches, demonstrations, and bombings spread throughout the country. The guerrillas took their revenge: in December 1972 FAR killed Rear Admiral Emilio Berisso, chief of naval intelligence, and in April 1973 the ERP killed Quijada and the Montoneros killed Colonel Héctor Iribarren, head of the Third Army Corps' intelligence service. Berisso, Quijada, and

Iribarren were not missed. Chants frequently heard at election rallies in 1972–73 were: "Soon you will see/soon you will see/when we avenge/the Trelew dead"; "so that justice was served/and because the people wanted it/the commandos of the FAR/killed Berisso"; and "Iribarren-Quijada/the liberated motherland." [49]

The March 1973 Elections

If antimilitary feelings had been developing since the Night of the Long Batons, the Lanusse-Perón confrontation in the months prior to the March 1973 elections, and speculation as to whether one or both generals would run, made matters worse. The Perón candidacy became a possibility because, following the legalization of political parties, Lanusse had announced elections would be absolutely free. Evita's body was returned to her husband at his Madrid residence in September 1971, and in April 1972 the last legal charges pending against Perón—treason and smuggling—were dropped. Throughout the period there were persistent rumors that Lanusse would grant Perón a passport to enable him to return to Argentina. A Lanusse candidacy appeared equally probable, however, and speeches and declarations by Lanusse and some of his ministers fueled speculation.

As soon as he became president, Lanusse entered into secret negotiations with Perón. Lanusse offered to allow Peronism to contest presidential elections and expected Perón to disavow armed struggle. It seems that Lanusse also hoped to persuade Perón to stay in Madrid, and that he was seriously considering running for president.[50] When Lanusse floated in early 1972 the idea of a Great National Agreement (Gran Acuerdo Nacional or GAN), intended to overcome the Peronist–anti-Peronist antinomy that had prevailed since 1955, Perón took this as a clear indication that Lanusse intended to be the GAN's presidential candidate. Negotiations broke down, and Perón embarrassed Lanusse by making public his taped conversation with one of Lanusse's envoys. Perón also launched in July 1972 the Civic Front for National Liberation (Frente Cívico de Liberación Nacional or FRECILINA), which would eventually become the Justicialist Liberation Front (Frente Justicialista de Liberación or FREJULI). This still stressed the idea of national unity, but whereas Lanusse's GAN had meant "united against subversion," FRECILINA meant "united against the military."

Lanusse retaliated by announcing that anyone wanting to run for president would have to be living in Argentina by August 25, 1972, and anyone occupying a government post would have to resign by that date. Since Perón could not bow to this and return to Argentina in haste, this was a direct provocation unmitigated by the fact that Lanusse finally excluded himself from the race. A few days later, during a speech at the Military Academy, Lanusse asserted that Perón "lacked the guts" to return.[51] Perón rose to the challenge and arrived in Argentina in November for a one-month stay. Before returning to Spain, he chose

Héctor Cámpora as the FREJULI presidential candidate. A dental surgeon considered a weakling within Peronist circles, Cámpora was highly objectionable to anti-Peronists because of his close links with his party's radicalized left. Cámpora was pushed down Lanusse's throat: he had been away from the country on August 25, and according to the Residency Clause could not run for office. But Lanusse knew that if he objected to Cámpora Perón would choose someone even more distasteful.[52]

As the election approached, rumors began to spread that Lanusse might ban the FREJULI from running or call off the elections altogether. He displayed a further lack of political skill by forbidding Perón from returning to the country until after the elections. Together with the Residency Clause, this strengthened the impression Perón had, once more, been proscribed. The campaign came to a close on March 8, and the following evening Lanusse went on national television and asked the country not to choose "anarchy, messianism, the vilification of institutions, the curtailment of liberties, the implantation of terrorism, and the tyranny or subordination to the will of one man," an unsubtle reference to Perón.[53] The Argentine people, who by that time were tired of having the armed forces dictate to them, went to the polls and made their choice.

The March election presented the Argentine people with nine different tickets. The two major contenders were the UCR and the FREJULI. The major rightist force was the Federalist Popular Alliance (Alianza Popular Federalista or APF), whereas the most important voice for the left was the Revolutionary Popular Alliance (Alianza Popular Revolucionaria, APR). The APF, the APR, and the FREJULI were all coalitions, even though in the case of the FREJULI the potential contribution of the smaller parties was quite negligible. The FREJULI vote was primarily a Peronist vote. The election was unique in many ways. For the first time in ten years the country was going to the polls, and all national, provincial, and municipal authorities would be chosen simultaneously. It was also the first presidential election since 1955 that the Peronist party was allowed to contest. The Lanusse government had introduced several amendments to the constitution: the president and vice-president would be chosen by direct election and not through an electoral college; their terms of office, and those of governors, national and provincial legislators, and municipal officials, were shortened from six to four years; and the provinces and the federal capital would return not the usual two but three senators.[54] The government also decided to adopt the French system of *ballotage:* if no party achieved the 50 percent plus one vote needed for a first ballot victory, a second election would take place between the major contenders, in the hope that the second turn would bring about a victory by a coalition of FREJULI opponents. Table 2.1 shows the election results. The FREJULI ticket had failed to obtain the necessary 50 percent of the vote, but Lanusse realized the futility of calling for a second turn and proclaimed Cámpora the victor. The ballot count revealed the Justicialists had won 20 of the 22

Table 2.1. Election Results, March 1973

Ticket	Party	Votes	Percentage
H. Cámpora/ V. Solano Lima	Justicialist Liberation Front (FREJULI)	5,907,464	49.56
R. Balbín/ E. Gamond	Radical Civic Union (UCR)	2,537,605	21.29
F. Manrique/ R. M. Raymonda	Federalist Popular Alliance (APF)	1,775,867	14.90
O. Alende/ H. Sueldo	Revolutionary Popular Alliance (APR)	885,201	7.43
E. Martínez/ L. Bravo	Republican Federal Alliance (AFR)	347,215	2.91
J. Chamizo/ R. Ondarts	New Force	234,188	1.97
A. Ghioldi/ R. Balestra	Social Democratic Party (PSD)	109,068	0.91
J. C. Coral/ N. Schiapone	Workers' Socialist Party (PST)	73,796	0.62
J. A. Ramos/ J. Silvetti	Popular Left Front (FIP)	48,571	0.41
Total		11,918,975	100

Registered Voters: 14,337,427
Source: La Opinión, March 31, 1973, p. 8.

provincial governorships, 45 of the 65 Senate seats, and 146 of the 243 seats in the Chamber of Deputies.

The results cannot be compared to previous elections because the Peronist party had been proscribed since 1955 and was therefore unable to run for office. Attempts have been made to estimate pro-Peronist strength during the wilderness years on the basis of the number of blank ballots cast,[55] but this is not a reliable indicator since it ignores the existence of provincial neo-Peronist parties, and we cannot be sure all Peronists voted as they were told by their leader, that is to say blank or, in 1958, for Arturo Frondizi.

Support for Peronism in the 1946–55 period came from popular and middle sectors in rural areas, and from the urban working class. Throughout the period, the working class continued to be Peronism's main source of strength, while the middle class remained in opposition.[56] By 1973, although the working class continued to be the backbone of the movement, a substantial proportion of non-workers were now voting Peronist. Just to illustrate the point, the composition of the Peronist vote in Córdoba required a 52 percent vote by nonworkers to be able to reach the total Peronist vote; in Buenos Aires, 46 percent of nonworkers voted Peronist; and 35 percent did so in Tucumán and Rosario.[57] Such middle-class and even upper-class support for Peronism was unheard of in Argentine history.

The FREJULI victory was partly the result of Perón's strategy. Throughout the Onganiato and until the elections, Perón justified the resort to violence by what were euphemistically called "special formations," on the grounds that violence would disappear once its causes were eliminated and the Peronists were once more in power. He openly encouraged the guerrillas and allowed his radicalized young followers to believe a return of Peronism to power would mean the establishment of *socialismo nacional*, an adaptation of the principles of international socialism to Argentine conditions. In a letter to FAP in February 1970, Perón wrote: "the moment is one for struggle, not one for political dialectic, because the dictatorship that scourges the Motherland will not cease its violence unless it is confronted by a greater violence. The People have a right to fight for their future, which today is jeopardized by the irresponsibility of these traitors who have capitulated to yankee imperialism. . . . As long as there are men who, like you, have resolved to fight, the Nation has nothing to fear." [58]

And in June 1971, Perón filmed an interview released in Argentina as "Political and Doctrinaire Updating for the Seizure of Power." In this film, which was directed to the military as well as to the radicalized youth sectors, Perón said:

> There are three courses of action: one is revolutionary war, the other is an insurrection which is spreading through the Army with the generals and all that, and the other is the peaceful line of institutional normalization . . . revolutionary war is a long and bloody war. . . . And maybe that is one road, if there is no other road . . . military insurrection . . . what the military want after an insurrection is another dictatorship. . . . Maybe the best road would be institutional normalization. . . . If there are no elections there will be another resolution [to the situation], the struggle will have to be intensified so that we arrive at those elections. . . . For us Justicialist Government is that which serves the people . . . our revolutionary process articulates individual and collective [needs], it is one form of socialism. Therefore a fair socialism, like the one Justicialism wants, and that is why it is called Justicialism, is that in which a community develops in agreement with [the community's] intrinsic conditions.[59]

But the FREJULI victory was also the logical outcome of events after 1966.[60] The Argentine Revolution began with high hopes and enjoyed the initial support of virtually every sector of Argentine society, but it gradually alienated the entire population. The 1973 vote was therefore to a large extent an antimilitary vote, a reaction led by certain sectors of the middle classes among which Peronism became fashionable and by the students who considered themselves heirs to the Resistance.

1973–76: The Peronist Interregnum

By 1973, Peronism was split into a right wing and a left wing, both vying for supremacy within the movement.[61] With the inauguration of Cámpora on May 25 the left appeared to be firmly in the saddle. The Revolutionary Tendency had managed to get eight of its spokesmen elected to Congress under the FREJULI ticket.[62] It could also count on the support of two members of the cabinet, Esteban Righi (Interior Minister) and Juan Carlos Puig (Foreign Minister); and of the governors of Buenos Aires, Córdoba, Mendoza, Salta, and Santa Cruz. The presidency of the University of Buenos Aires had gone to Rodolfo Puiggrós, a Communist intellectual, and persons with impeccable left-wing credentials were chosen to head several university departments.[63] The Cámpora administration, however, was more valuable to the Tendency for what it promised than for what it initially delivered. The Peronist left had been an invaluable mobilizing force during the election campaign and its influence could certainly be felt in the final party platform.[64] This, and Cámpora's initial measures, seemed to point to the most radicalized administration the country had ever had.

In the international sphere, there was a break with Argentine foreign policy since the fifties, which had stressed alignment behind the United States. The Cámpora government established diplomatic relations with Cuba, North Vietnam, and North Korea, signed trade agreements with Communist countries, and called for a new Pan-American union which excluded the United States. In the domestic sphere, Onganía's antiterrorist legislation was abolished, the Federal Police's Department for Anti-Democratic Information dissolved and its files burnt. Most important, on inauguration day Cámpora granted a presidential pardon for political prisoners that Congress immediately ratified with an amnesty law. By the following day 371 prisoners, most of them guerrilla cadres, had been freed.[65] The wisdom of this measure could be debated even in those euphoric days. The ERP had already published a long declaration entitled "To the People: Why and against what the ERP will continue fighting," which stated that the organization would refrain from attacking the Cámpora administration but reserved the right to continue harassing the security forces. Also, as an augur of things to come, when the FREJULI bloc in the Chamber of Deputies met to discuss the projected amnesty law two days before the inaugural, the deputies began their session by standing in silence for one minute in homage to union leader Dirk Kloosterman, whom the FAP had just killed.[66]

The government was apparently aware of the fact that an amnesty, which incidentally turned armed organizations into legal political groups, might strengthen the guerrillas' hand. But the country had suffered a period of political and normative irregularity that rendered convictions for political offenses highly questionable. The government intended to establish new rules for the political game, in the hope that channels for more conventional forms of political participation would gradually diminish the appeal of armed struggle.[67] Beyond this, the question of amnesty is indicative both of the fragility of the Cámpora government and the relative strength of the guerrillas and their sympathizers. Political prisoners could be freed through a presidential pardon or through an amnesty. The party platform mentioned an amnesty, a congressional prerogative which would have conveyed an aura of consensus among the political parties. But an amnesty law required the intervention of the courts and the judicial application of the law to each individual case. This was unacceptable to the radicalized sectors who, under the slogan "the popular government cannot coexist for one minute with political prisoners" mobilized a crowd estimated at 40,000 to the gates of Devoto prison on the eve of the inaugural, demanding an immediate release. Cámpora was forced to grant a presidential pardon, which unlike the amnesty was implemented immediately. Congress passed the amnesty law the following day, but the impression that remained was that the prisoners had been released through popular pressure.

One month into the "Cámpora Spring," the Revolutionary Tendency suffered its first setback. June 20 was the date of Perón's final return to Argentina. A crowd estimated at three million people[68] had gathered to meet him at Ezeiza airport, and a platform had been built near the airstrip so that Perón could address his followers immediately after landing. For reasons that have never been officially explained, security was entrusted not to the police but to retired Lieutenant Colonel Jorge Osinde, then Undersecretary for Sports and Tourism at the Ministry of Social Welfare. Osinde's forces, recruited from various organizations of the Peronist right, occupied the platform and were posted at different airport buildings nearby.

The Revolutionary Tendency shares some of the blame for the subsequent tragedy. Members of FAR, Montoneros, and their front organizations marched to Ezeiza with the intention of occupying the area immediately adjacent to the platform. Though they were armed with a few handguns, and a machine gun they never used, this time they were using the one weapon they had found so effective during the electoral campaign—mass mobilization. They assumed that their massive presence, their banners, and their slogans would prove to Perón that they were a force to be reckoned with. As members of the Tendency approached the platform from behind, they were told through the public address system that if they "were really soldiers of Perón" they should stop in their tracks. But the Tendency moved on, and Osinde's men on the platform fired their machine guns. The Tendency fired back, and chaos ensued as the huge mass of people attempted to find cover in the nearby woods. Fighting continued for two hours. The battle at the airport, which became known as the Ezeiza massacre, resulted in at least 16 dead and 433 wounded, although official figures were never released and the thorough investigation that the government promised never materialized.[69] There were also reports, never corroborated or disproved, of lynchings and tortures by Osinde's men, which is probably why, in spite of the Tendency's behavior, every book or article mentioning the events at Ezeiza considers the Peronist right responsible for the tragedy.

Perón landed not at Ezeiza but at the Morón Air Force base nearby. His speech the day after these events, however, left no doubt as to his allegiances: "We have to return to the legal and constitutional order as the only guarantee of freedom and justice. . . . Those who naively think they can take control of our Movement or seize the power that the people have re-conquered are mistaken. . . . I advise the stealthy and hidden or disguised enemies to cease in their effort because when the people exhaust their patience they clamor for punishment."[70]

The Ezeiza massacre was the first in a series of political defeats sustained by the Peronist left. If the 1966–73 period had resulted in a confrontation between the military and the rest of society, the Peronist interregnum was marked by the struggle between two visions: the "Peronist Motherland," espoused by the majority of the union movement and of the Peronist political class, and the "Socialist Motherland," held by all youth and guerrilla groups.[71] In the months that followed the Ezeiza massacre, it would become clear to most within and outside the Peronist movement that Perón leaned on the Peronist right to destroy the left.

The September 1973 Elections

On July 13 Cámpora and vice president Vicente Solano Lima resigned under the pretext that once Perón was back nobody else could be president. This was, in fact, "a coup engineered by the [Peronist] right."[72] Raúl Lastiri, president of the Chamber of Deputies, became interim president, and new elections were scheduled for September 23. The Tendency promoted Cámpora for the vice-presidency, but Perón surprised everybody by deciding to run with his wife, María Estela (Isabel) Martínez. Table 2.2 shows the election results.

Until the March 1973 elections Perón justified armed struggle on the grounds that Argentina was ruled by a military dictatorship, and argued that violence would disappear after the Peronist electoral victory. By September it became clear that Perón had been proved wrong. Armed struggle did not end with the Cámpora inaugural. It increased steadily and dramatically during the three years following the return to constitutional rule: in 1973 guerrilla groups staged 205 operations prior to the Cámpora inaugural and 208 operations afterward; and in 1974 and 1975 they staged 807 and 723 operations, respectively. By September 1973 Perón confronted forces he had conjured up, over which he no longer ex-

Table 2.2. Election Results, September 1973

Ticket	Party	Votes	Percentage
J. D. Perón/ I. Perón	FREJULI	7,371,249	61.89
R. Balbín/ F. de la Rúa	UCR	2,905,236	24.39
F. Manrique/ R. M. Raymonda	APF	1,445,981	12.14
J. C. Coral/ F. J. Páez	PST	188,227	1.58
Total		11,910,693	100

Registered Voters: 14,334,253
Source: La Opinión, September 25, 1973, p. 1.

ercised control. Many of those who had voted for the FREJULI in March were becoming alarmed. Perón executed a volte face, decided the era of radical politics had come to an end, and emphasized class conciliation and the elimination of violence as prerequisites for national reconstruction. This time Perón appeared as a staunch defender of the system. He was being elected to do away with the previous progressive experiment and with a clear mandate to wipe out subversion."[73]

Perón's strategy, which he called "integrated democracy," was straightforward (and, in fact, similar to Lanusse's): he would attempt to build bridges with every sector of Argentine society which renounced violence, while he simultaneously waged an all-out war against the guerrillas and the radicalized sectors within the labor movement. Union militancy would be fought with the Social Pact, an agreement between business and labor involving a wage increase and a price-wage freeze. The pact relied on labor's willingness to resort to governmental arbitration in lieu of strikes. A concomitant reform to the Law of Professional Associations guaranteed union bosses control over the unruly rank and file.[74] The implementation of the Social Pact revealed that the government favored the "Peronist Motherland." As Perón himself put it, Peronism was "a left-wing movement. But the left that we advocate is a [J]usticialist left above all things; it is not a communist or anarchist left. It is a [J]usticialist left that wants to achieve a community where each [A]rgentine can flourish, it does not want to go beyond this."[75]

Perón's Reaction to Armed Struggle

Perón lacked only an excuse to launch his offensive against the armed organizations. This came in the form of an ERP attack against the Army Medical Corps Headquarters in Buenos Aires on September 6, 1973, in which a lieutenant colonel died. The ERP was outlawed on September 24. The following day the Montoneros killed José Ignacio Rucci, secretary general of the General Confederation of Labor, but they waited a year to claim responsibility for the attack. The government was quick to blame the ERP,[76] though this appears to have been *pour la galerie:* the day after the Rucci assassination, Enrique Grynberg, an activist in the Revolutionary Tendency, was killed by unknown gunmen; and a week later the Justicialist National Movement issued a Reserved Document, leaked to the press, describing the "infiltration of those marxist groups within the Movement . . . that state of war . . . forces us not only to defend ourselves but also to attack the enemy on all fronts and with the greatest decisiveness." [77]

Perón's offensive against the guerrillas involved legal, semi-legal, and illegal means. Left-wing publications closely associated with the guerrilla groups were closed down,[78] and in January 1974 the Criminal Code was amended and harsh penalties for terrorist offenses re-introduced. While Congress was debating these reforms, the ERP attacked the 10th Cavalry Regiment at Azul in Buenos Aires province, killing a colonel and his wife. Perón forced the resignation of the province's governor, Oscar Bidegain, a supporter of the Tendency, and the following month supported a police coup in Córdoba that resulted in the resignation of governor Ricardo Obregón Cano and vice-governor Atilio López, both Tendency supporters. Also in February, more than 30 members of the Tendency were arrested following the discovery of an alleged plot to assassinate the Peróns and Uruguayan president Juan María Bordaberry during his state visit to Argentina. But the most disquieting development was the emergence of a death squad, the Argentine Anti-Communist Alliance or Triple A. The organization was officially launched on November 21, 1973, with an assassination attempt on senator Hipólito Solari Yrigoyen. Threatening letters bearing the letter *A* were sent to personalities in artistic and political circles in the following week.[79] From then on the Triple A carried out three different tasks. First, it published death lists of prominent figures in the arts and sciences as well as in politics who were suspected of left-wing sympathies and were "invited" to leave the country. Second, it attempted to control labor militancy through repression. Third, it aimed at the physical elimination of the regime's opponents. Within a year of the emergence of the Triple A, it would be an open secret that the death squad was funded and headed by Perón's Minister for Social Welfare, José López Rega. Although there is no evidence that Perón participated in the creation of the Triple A, he was no doubt aware of the source of illegal repression.

In spite of the political setbacks they suffered following the Ezeiza massacre, the guerrilla groups increased their membership in 1973 from a few hundred to thousands, a testimony to the scope of the pre-1973 radicalization. Also during the year, guerrillas resorted increasingly to kidnappings as a source of revenue. Standard ransoms, mostly for American executives in multinational corporations, were set at one and two million dollars. To a seemingly unlimited supply of combatants and money one should add the ability to operate above ground since, as a consequence of the amnesty, guerrilla groups had become legal political organizations.

FAP and FAL were unable to profit from these opportunities. After the debate between the "obscure" and "enlightened," FAP suffered another split when some of its members started advocating a policy of assassination of corrupt union bosses, expected to produce a more combative labor movement. The debate that ensued signaled the end of FAP. The organization split into those opposing the "execution of bureaucrats" who became FAP 17 October (FAP 17 for short) and those supporting it, calling themselves FAP National Commando (FAP Comando Nacional or FAP CN).[80] In 1974 FAP CN would join the ERP and the bulk of FAP 17 joined the Montoneros. Ideological debates also destroyed FAL after the split of the CPL, which in 1974 joined the Montoneros. The previous year FAR had also joined the Montoneros, but, unlike FAP and FAL, FAR had maintained its ideological cohesion and operational capabilities. Therefore FAR did not "join" but "fused" with Montoneros, and even though the new group kept the latter's name, FAR combatants kept their ranks within the new structure.[81] Having already seized control of the Peronist Youth, the Montoneros began setting up front organizations: the Peronist University Youth, the Peronist Working Youth, the Union of Secondary School Students, and the Movement of Peronist Slum Dwellers. These organizations reinforced the Montoneros' already strong ties with a mass base and provided them with enormous mobilizing power. With time, these organizations became just a recruitment ground for the Montoneros, who also chose the leadership and dictated the policies to be followed.

The ERP suffered two splits in 1973: the ERP Red Fraction (ERP Fracción Roja or ERP FR) and the ERP 22 August, known simply as ERP 22. ERP FR, a small faction which petered out within the year, argued the PRT ought to take a more aggressive line vis-à-vis the (Peronist) labor movement. ERP 22, on the contrary, accepted the fact that the working class was Peronist and supported both FREJULI tickets at election time.[82] In 1974 some ERP 22 members returned to their parent organization while others joined the Montoneros. The ERP was further strengthened by the incorporation of FAP CN and of the surviving factions of FAL. But the ERP squandered its strength by deciding to open a rural front in Tucumán in May 1974. The decision was indefensible militarily and politically. It made no sense to try to emulate the venerated Vietnamese experience in a country where 70 percent of the population lived in urban centers, particularly when this meant transplanting city dwellers to fight in unfamiliar rural terrain.

Perón's Death and Its Aftermath

Splits and mergers within guerrilla groups in 1973–74 meant that by 1974 Perón confronted the two surviving groups, the outlawed ERP and the Montoneros. In spite of Perón's offensive, both he and the Montoneros studiously avoided an open declaration of war. The question of their relationship with Perón had produced two different answers among the Montoneros. The movementists (*movimientistas*) argued that Peronism was a class alliance which derived its strength from its subordination to the leader. The alternativists (*alternativistas*) favored the construction of a truly revolutionary party. Until Perón's death the Montoneros persisted in their movementism, albeit a hypocritical one since they continued to stage the occasional armed operation. Perón, on the other hand, seems to have believed he could work by persuasion and periodically held meetings with Montonero and JP leaders in which he insisted his young followers ought to turn to their studies and prepare themselves to become Argentina's future leaders. This stance was equally hypocritical because Perón was fully aware of the activities of the Triple A. In spite of his offensive Perón could not quite bring himself to proscribe the Montoneros just as he had the ERP. For one thing, he had lavished too much praise on them as "worthy Peronists" during the Onganiato. More important, attendance at mass rallies the Montoneros called during this period revealed that the guerrillas had the solid backing of youth sectors.

The Montoneros' break with Perón came on May Day 1974 as Perón was about to address a huge crowd on the square opposite the Casa Rosada, government house. Constantly interrupted by Montonero slogans like, "If Evita were alive she would be a Montonero," and "What is wrong, general? Why is the popular government full of gorillas?"[83] the president improvised a devastating attack on his young followers: "In spite of these stupid ones who shout . . . after twenty years there are some who are not yet content with everything we've done . . . the government is committed to the liberation [of the country], not only from colonialism . . . but also from these treacherous infiltrators who work from within, and who are more dangerous than those who work from without."[84] The Montoneros and their supporters marched off the square before the end of the speech.

Two months later Perón died and was succeeded by his wife, a frail woman given to fits of hysterics who had little formal education and was thoroughly unable to cope with the political problems she inherited from her husband. Isabel Perón did not innovate; she merely pursued her husband's policies with greater intensity. The remaining radical publications were closed down,[85] the government intervened in the University of Buenos Aires once more, and the provincial governors sympathetic to the Tendency who had not been ousted by Perón were deposed through federal interventions.[86] Isabel Perón introduced new antiterrorist legislation in September 1974, and two months later declared a state of siege. Partly as a response to the activities of the Triple A, operating without any restraint since Perón's death, the Montoneros announced in September 1974 that they were going underground, a decision that carried grave consequences.[87] Given the high visibility acquired by militants in the Montoneros' front organizations, the return to arms turned these activists into cannon fodder. This carried little weight with an organization that counted on at least 3,000 active combatants and derived financial strength from a $61.5 million ransom for the kidnapping of brothers Juan and Jorge Born in 1974. Interestingly, Isabel Perón waited a year to outlaw the organization.

By September 1974, according to one Buenos Aires daily, one death by political violence occurred every 19 hours.[88] The Triple A was of course responsible for a substantial share of those deaths. But guerrilla violence attracted most of the media's attention. What the media showed was enough to change public perceptions of the ERP and Montoneros: guerrillas concentrated increasingly on kidnappings and murders (and not on violence against property as they had up to 1973), singled out as targets groups whose deaths the public could not easily write off, like off-duty policemen or union leaders, and appeared to gloat at their military exploits.[89] Funds obtained through kidnap ransoms were no longer directed to the Robin Hood type distribution of basic staples in slums. Funds were now employed in operations against heavily guarded bases and regiments, involving more than 100 combatants and sophisticated weaponry, like the ERP's attempt to seize the 601 Arsenal Battalion or the blowing up of the Navy's *Santísima Trinidad* frigate by Montonero frogmen. The rationale behind this suicidal behavior was that finally the popular armies were fighting the regular army. This concentration on military "spectaculars" determined that the guerrillas remained uninvolved in the popular mobilizations of 1975 which occurred as economic policy veered toward the right.

1976–83: The Process of National Reorganization

On March 24, 1976, amid mounting violence and economic dislocation, Isabel Perón was deposed by a coup. Over the next seven years, Argentina was governed by three successive military juntas collectively known as the Process of National Reorganization (Proceso de Reorganización Nacional). The Proceso's avowed aims upon seizing power were to re-establish order and put an end to the activities of the guerrilla organizations; to modernize the economy; to eliminate government corruption; and to reform the educational system.[90] By 1983, when the Malvinas-Falklands fiasco forced the military to call for elections, only the first of these objectives had been achieved. The methodology employed to fight the guerrillas, which has since become known as the dirty war, involved the illegal abduction of individuals by plainclothes members of the armed and security forces. The kidnapped were taken to clandestine detention centers, tortured so that they could provide information, and then killed and buried in unmarked graves. This dirty war has been estimated to involve 8,000–30,000 such disappearances.[91]

In spite of their financial and numerical strength, the guerrillas were thoroughly unprepared for the dirty war. They simply expected another Onganía and a new dictablanda,[92] and when the scale of the slaughter became apparent, the guerrillas could not or would not adapt to reality. Disappearances of guerrillas, activists in unions or student groups, or sympathizers (approximately 4,000 per year in 1976–77) dictated a cessation of activities or a defensive strategy involving sabotage and small-scale attacks. Instead, guerrilla groups continued to expose their forces in frontal assaults, with predictable results. The PRT-ERP admitted its mistake in 1979 when it described "the inertia of the entire machine of the Party which was in the offensive. That is to say, it was impossible to stop and withdraw quickly an impulse that we carried since 1970. . . . The Party had magnificently learnt to advance, to go forward through 7 years, it could not learn to withdraw in 2 months."[93]

By the time of the 1976 coup the ERP was already considerably weakened through the attempt to maintain the rural and urban fronts. In July 1976, it was reduced to 1969 operational levels. It was at that point that, purely by chance, a detachment led by an army captain arrived at the safehouse where the ERP's top four leaders were hiding, stormed in, and killed Mario Santucho, Benito Urteaga, and Domingo Menna. Enrique Gorriarán Merlo escaped and is still at large.[94] But for the ERP, this was the end. Although it continued to carry out the occasional operation, the group went into disarray. Following the demise of the ERP leadership, the Montoneros' National Leadership went into exile. The rank and file was supposed to "hide among the masses." The masses, unfortunately, were in no position to offer protection from the paramilitary squads. By the time Argentina hosted the 1978 World Cup, the Montoneros had, by their own admission, lost 70 percent of their forces to the repressive apparatus.[95] This did not stop them from staging two final counteroffensives, one during the World Cup and one in late 1979, both abysmal failures. Thanks to the Born brothers' ransom, the Montonero leadership continued its political activities in Madrid, Rome, Mexico City, and Managua. Back in Argentina the dirty war raged on, but by 1979 the revolutionary war was over.

I

Patterns of Violence

I t is no coincidence that one of the heroes of the radicalized Argentine intelligentsia in the 1960s was General Juan Manuel de Rosas, the mid-nineteenth-century dictator who first proclaimed, "He who is not with me is against me," and had his police force, the Mazorca, dressed completely in red so that the victims' blood would not be so noticeable, for Argentina has a long tradition of political violence. Following the wars of independence, Argentines spent the better part of the nineteenth century in a state of internal war over the question of whether the country should have a centralized or federal administration. The uninformed mind tends to equate violence in twentieth-century Argentina with coups and the military. But coups have generally been bloodless affairs (1976 being the exception), which is more than can be said for other forms of political participation. A variety of social groups resorted to political violence in a multiplicity of situations, more often than not during periods of constitutional legality. The Radicals, the most democratic of Argentine parties, staged three unsuccessful rebellions (in 1890, 1893, and 1905) before attaining power through constitutional means in 1916. During the 1910s and 1920s labor unrest, influenced by European anarchism, included occupations of factories, bombings, street fights, and the murder of a chief of police. More recent history is plagued with examples of student violence, especially during the presidencies of Juan Perón (1946–55) and Arturo Frondizi (1958–62).

The coexistence of violence as a political weapon with institutional channels through which to express grievances gradually helped to legitimize the former and delegitimize the latter. But even though practice may have generated normative or instrumental justifications for violent behavior, the 1960s and 1970s represented a departure from previous patterns of violence in four ways. Whereas

45

before the sixties violence was used sporadically, after 1969 it became a constant in Argentine political life. Also, although before the late sixties violence was used by only one or two social groups at any given time, after that date every social sector resorted to it. As far as the repertoire of actions was concerned, most forms of collective violence had been tried in the past, whereas armed struggle constituted a novelty of the late 1960s, despite the three attempts to establish rural focos (in 1959, 1963–64, and 1968), which collapsed after the participants had staged one or two operations. Finally, in the past the state had occasionally over-reacted in response to collective action and infrequently used torture, yet the sixties and seventies witnessed the emergence of organized and sustained campaigns of illegal repression, first with Triple A and later under the dirty war.

The next three chapters analyze the scope and intensity of all types of political violence in Argentina during the 1969–79 period. Chapter 3 analyzes armed struggle—the actions of clandestine groups that systematically resort to military means in order to achieve political ends. The discussion will show that after 1973 political considerations ceased to rule over military strategy, and guerrilla groups came to view themselves as revolutionary armies capable of taking on the regular armed forces. Chapter 4 describes collective violent protest. Included here are all acts of collective political violence which are by and large spontaneous and unorganized, like street fights, riots, and violent strikes.[1] Chapter 5 describes violence by paramilitary squads involved in illegal repression and by certain organizations of the Peronist right that operated under police protection (or indifference) and that shared with paramilitary squads the primary objective of checking the development of the legal and clandestine left. Finally, chapter 6 discusses the joint evolution of all three types of violence to assess if collective violent protest or right-wing violence influenced the development of militarism within guerrilla groups. Analytically, it is possible to think of two such scenarios: the militarization of armed struggle could have originated in a decline in the intensity of collective violent protest or in an increase in the intensity of paramilitary violence. My analysis reveals certain feedback effects between the different types of violence. The rise in right-wing violence after 1975, for example, was a response to the increased politicization and mobilization of Argentine society during the Peronist administrations, and in turn had a sobering effect on the levels of collective violent protest. However, the evidence rules out any causal relationship between the development of militarism and variations in the intensity of collective violent protest or right-wing violence.

The data presented in chapters 3–6 are the only comprehensive statistics on all types of violence in Argentina in the 1960s and 1970s.[2] They result from my reading of eleven years of Buenos Aires daily newspapers (January 1, 1969–December 31, 1979) and recording of all incidents of violence published therein.

Relying on newspapers as a source of information has obvious limitations. First, it is conceivable that some of the violence taking place in the interior of the country did not find its way into the pages of the capital's dailies. In addition, the manner in which the press reported on violence varied considerably over the eleven-year period. Initially, violent acts were described in great detail: the number of perpetrators, the extent of damage or destruction of property, and the duration of attacks. This changed substantially with the routinization of violence. Finally, in this struggle the key parties to the conflict—guerrillas and security forces—have lied through their teeth.

After the March 1976 coup, the press obtained its information on guerrilla violence directly from the commanders of the military corps. Robert Cox, who was at the time editor of the English-language *Buenos Aires Herald,* reports,

> On the evening of April 22 [1976], all newspapers received telephone calls instructing them: ["]As from today it is forbidden to report, comment on, or make reference to subversive incidents, the appearance of bodies and the deaths of subversive elements and/or members of the security forces unless they are announced by a responsible official source.["] A second paragraph, apparently an afterthought, added: "This includes kidnappings and disappearances." . . . Those newspapers which questioned the telephone message were simply provided with an unsigned slip of paper, containing the typewritten instructions, at Government House.[3]

The armed forces could have conceivably suppressed information that highlighted the combativeness of guerrilla groups. It is unlikely that the military did this consistently, as it was in their interest to portray guerrillas as ruthless killers. The military did use its monopoly of information, however, to whitewash some of its own deeds. The official list of victims of guerrilla violence published by the armed forces includes the names of individuals who died at the hands of the military. One could cite as an example the case of diplomat Elena Holmberg. A member of a prominent family, the niece of ex-president General Lanusse, Holmberg was assigned to the embassy in Paris when, in April 1978, she witnessed a meeting between Mario Firmenich, top leader of the Montoneros, and Admiral Emilio E. Massera, a member of the ruling junta. Holmberg traveled to Buenos Aires to report to her superiors at the Foreign Ministry what she must have thought highly irregular conduct by a junta member. Before she made her report, Holmberg was found drowned in the River Plate. Massera had allegedly given the guerrillas one million dollars in exchange for a promise that they would not stage operations while the World Cup was being held in Argentina.[4] Also, after 1975, the police occasionally staged bombings and blamed them on the guerrillas, with a view to exaggerating the threat posed by armed struggle[5] while the guerrillas bombed a few of their own locales (usually offices of the Peronist

Youth or the Peronist Working Youth) and blamed the "rightist provocation."[6] In spite of these problems, newspaper information—checked against guerrilla documents, the work of the National Commission on the Disappearance of Persons,[7] and other scholarly and journalistic works produced in the almost fifteen years that have elapsed since the events portrayed in this study took place—provides as clear a picture as we are likely to get of violence in Argentina.

The typology of violent incidents used in the next four chapters is the following.

Bombings. This includes all explosives, from Molotov cocktails and pamphlet bombs to the deadlier varieties.

Attacks on property include the damage or destruction of any property, public or private—a building, park, statue, or vehicle—as long as the assailants do not use explosives. Normally, the damage is the result of stone throwing, gunfire, or arson.

Seizures. This denotes the complete physical occupation of any building or open space, irrespective of its duration.

Kidnappings involve holding a person in captivity for any period of time, from a few hours to months. The motives may vary. The assailants may want to extract a ransom or they may expect to extract certain concessions from the victim or his or her employers.

Deaths. This includes all fatalities, which is why I avoid terms like "murder" or "assassination." Though many of the victims were indeed the targets of assassination attempts, others died in the course of demonstrations or riots or guerrilla operations which clearly did not contemplate any casualties.

The analysis of guerrilla violence will also include two operations specific to such groups, *airplane hijackings,* and *thefts of arms* (wherever the theft occurs).[8] The literature on terrorism as well as the "war dispatches" by guerrilla groups normally describe other operations: the Robin Hood type distribution of foodstuffs in slum dwellings; the distribution of pamphlets and leaflets and the interception of radio and television broadcasts; and finally "requisitionings"—theft of cars, surgical materials, and wigs, as well as bank robberies. This study does not analyze these operations for several reasons. First, they were typical of the early period. None were carried out after 1971 or 1972. Second, food distribution and requisitioning operations were rarely reported in the daily press. Third, it is difficult to gauge from newspaper reports whether those responsible for incidents like bank robberies were in fact guerrillas. On occasions newspapers first reported a bank robbery by the guerrillas, and then published a police statement to the effect that they had made a mistake and realized the operation had been the work of common criminals. Finally, one could argue that the Robin Hood operation or the distribution of pamphlets was not really an armed action because the risk was minimal. If a guerrilla commando arrived at a slum dwelling with foodstuffs and household supplies, chances were it would be received with open arms. And, as one guerrilla interviewee so adequately put it, "If you jump on a public bus and yell 'We are from the ERP and we are here to sell our periodical *Estrella Roja,*' people will go nuts. They will be so afraid they'll be willing to give you their undershirt." [9]

3

Armed Struggle

his chapter first reviews some general characteristics of guerrilla operations—the location of attacks, the groups responsible, and the size of guerrilla units. The second section analyzes the relative weight of different types of operations from 1969 to 1979. The narrative highlights various indicators of militarism. One of these is the tendency for guerrilla units to become larger. The data show an increase in the frequency of large-scale attacks involving more than 20 combatants after 1973. A second indicator of militarism is the tendency to increase attacks on military installations. During these attacks, armed organizations suffered heavy losses and did not seem to derive any political capital. This suggests that whereas initially guerrillas defined their organizations as politico-military structures and armed struggle as a "tool" and used violence sparingly because they considered that a military victory over the adversary was not necessary (and was also impossible), after 1973 combatants came to believe they must prevail militarily. A third indicator of militarism is a shift from an initial emphasis on violence against property to an emphasis on violence against persons. The two operations against human targets, kidnappings and deaths, increased as a percentage of the total volume of violence from 12.17 percent in 1969–73 to 32.09 percent in 1973–76 to 45.77 percent in 1976–79. A fourth indicator of militarism is a growing disregard for the impact of armed operations on public opinion, evidenced by the high percentage of kidnappings without apparent political objectives, and by the gradual widening of the definition of the enemy to include new categories like the relatives of potential targets.

50

Some Characteristics of Armed Struggle

Table 3.1 shows the location of all guerrilla attacks between 1969 and 1979.[1] The table lists the nation's capital, Buenos Aires, the twenty-two provinces,[2] and foreign countries where attacks were staged. As the figures reveal, Argentine guerrillas by and large restricted their activity to their national turf. When foreign countries were attacked, the target was Argentine property—the embassy in Paris or Rome—or Argentine businessmen traveling abroad.

The data also reveal that attacks were highly concentrated in Buenos Aires city and the provinces of Buenos Aires, Córdoba, and Santa Fe. These four account for 81.37 percent of all attacks between 1969 and 1979 (81.87 percent for 1969–73; 77.12 percent for 1973–76; and 91.67 percent for 1976–79). This concentration of armed operations in the central region of the country could be interpreted in two different ways. It could be argued that a more equitable distribution of attacks among the provinces would have served as an indication of the local strength of guerrilla forces, and that the actual distribution makes it impossible for the guerrillas to substantiate their claims to being a national movement waging a "Second War of Independence."[3] But one could also state that the data in table 3.1 are a mere reflection of the country's demographics. According to the census of 1970, Buenos Aires city and the three provinces mentioned earlier represented 22 percent of the country's total area but housed 68.2 percent of the total population.[4] This area has also traditionally constituted the core of the country's economic activity. The guerrillas were therefore striking at the heart of economic and political power.

The only other provinces to boast more than one percent of all guerrilla attacks are Tucumán and Mendoza. Tucumán was the province chosen by the ERP for their rural guerrilla campaign, launched in May 1974 with the seizure of the town of Acheral. In February 1975 Isabel Perón signed decree S261, which directly involved the army in the fight against the guerrillas in Tucumán. This was known as "Operation Independence." It was a departure from established procedure, since internal security is normally left to the police and gendarmery, which Isabel Perón intended as a show of decisiveness. Rural guerrilla warfare in Tucumán continued through November 1976, when the army announced it had killed the last four combatants in the ERP's Compañía de Monte (Jungle Company).[5] The objective of the rural guerrilla campaign was the establishment of a "liberated zone." Urban combatants were sent to fight in a terrain with which they were unfamiliar, in a province whose economic importance was marginal and where trade union activity had petered out after Onganía closed the sugar mills in 1967. The opening of a rural front was therefore indefensible in military as well as political terms, and reflected a doctrinaire wish to emulate the Vietnamese experience.[6] The frequency of attacks in Mendoza appears to be

Table 3.1. Location of Guerrilla Attacks, 1969–79

	1969–73 (%)	1973–76 (%)	1976–79 (%)	1969–79 (%)
Federal Capital	20.70	15.92	31.64	20.37
Buenos Aires	24.50	33.75	49.44	32.58
Córdoba	16.49	17.42	2.26	14.61
Santa Fe	20.18	10.03	8.33	13.81
Entre Ríos	—	0.21	—	0.09
Corrientes	0.40	0.21	—	0.25
Misiones	0.06	0.10	—	0.07
Chaco	0.51	0.62	0.14	0.50
Formosa	—	0.77	0.28	0.39
Santiago del Estero	0.46	0.36	—	0.34
Tucumán	3.98	6.15	2.40	4.68
Salta	1.59	0.46	0.71	0.95
Jujuy	0.34	0.21	—	0.23
Catamarca	0.06	0.31	0.28	0.20
La Rioja	0.68	—	—	0.27
San Juan	0.28	0.26	—	0.23
San Luis	0.11	0.41	—	0.23
Mendoza	1.02	2.43	0.14	1.50
La Pampa	0.06	0.05	—	0.04
Neuquén	0.17	0.26	—	0.18
Río Negro	0.06	0.26	—	0.14
Chubut	0.45	—	—	0.18
Santa Cruz	0.06	—	—	0.02
Undetermined	7.68	9.66	3.96	7.95
Total, Argentina	99.83	99.85	99.58	99.81
France	0.17	—	—	0.07
Paraguay	—	0.05	—	0.02
Uruguay	—	0.10	—	0.04
Italy	—	—	0.14	0.02
Costa Rica	—	—	0.28	0.04
Total, other countries	0.17	0.15	0.42	0.19
Total	100	100	100	100
	N = 1,759	N = 1,935	N = 708	N = 4,402

Source: Contemporary press reports.

accidental, as that province was not the object of any campaign or offensive by any of the groups, even though at different times the Montoneros assigned two of their most prestigious officers, Julio Roqué and Francisco Urondo, to head the Mendoza Column.[7]

Table 3.2 shows group responsibility for attacks between 1969 and 1979. Bombings were excluded from the calculations because they represent approximately 40 percent of annual guerrilla violence for the entire period and also

Table 3.2. Groups Responsible for Guerrilla Attacks (Excluding Bombings), 1969–79

	1969–73 (%)	1973–76 (%)	1976–79 (%)	1969–79 (%)
ERP	27.32	20.75	3.25	19.89
FAL	7.30	1.78	—	3.46
FAP	3.76	0.89	—	1.77
FAR	5.75	—	—	2.09
Descamisados	1.55	—	—	0.56
Montoneros	7.75	9.53	26.25	11.98
Other	8.74	2.58	1.30	4.58
Undetermined	37.83	64.47	69.20	55.67
Total	100	100	100	100
	N = 904	N = 1,123	N = 461	N = 2,488

Source: Contemporary press reports.

boast the highest percentages of unclaimed attacks.[8] Table 3.2 only lists the six major groups. Included under the rubric of "other" are operations by splinter factions of the major groups, by short-lived groupuscules, and the infrequent joint operation.[9]

Though the ability to strike, and strike repeatedly, is not necessarily an indicator of guerrilla strength, it is usually interpreted as such by the literature as well as by government officials who confront armed struggle. Given the centralized decision-making process within guerrilla groups, the high frequency of attacks is taken to indicate that the guerrilla leadership counts on a significant body of disciplined followers. However, in the Argentine case, it is almost impossible to make conclusive statements about the relative strength of the different guerrilla groups on the basis of existing information. By October 1973 Descamisados and FAR had joined the Montoneros, and in 1974 one wing of FAP joined the Montoneros, while another wing of FAP and sectors of FAL joined the ERP. Montoneros and ERP were therefore the only two groups active throughout the three periods under consideration. The most that could be said about the decline in the operational capacity of FAL and FAP between the first and second periods is that it probably reflects the process of internal debate that led to the breakdown of the groups into splinter factions. What the table does show conclusively is the decline of the ERP, by far the most active group during the first period. This decline could not be due to a lack of funding, since, as will be discussed shortly, the group raised a fortune through kidnap ransoms; or to ravaging internal debates, because the emergence of the short-lived ERP 22 and ERP FR splinters did not significantly weaken the parent organization. The ERP's decline was probably due to the siphoning of combatants and resources to Tucumán.

Even though the information presented in table 3.2 reflects reports in the

Table 3.3. Participants in Guerrilla Attacks (Excluding Bombings), 1969–79

Number of Participants	1969–73 (%)	1973–76 (%)	1976–79 (%)	1969–79 (%)
1	0.67	0.98	12.58	3.01
2	3.87	3.21	8.24	4.38
3–5	29.09	15.85	15.84	20.66
6–10	16.48	5.79	3.69	9.29
11–20	5.42	4.45	1.52	4.26
21–50	1.22	2.67	—	1.65
51–100	0.33	2.14	—	1.09
more than 100	—	1.60	—	0.72
Undetermined	42.92	63.31	58.13	54.94
Total	100	100	100	100
	$N = 904$	$N = 1,123$	$N = 461$	$N = 2,488$

Source: Contemporary press reports.

Argentine press, it is not an accurate portrayal of Montonero strength. As stated in chapter 2, throughout the Peronist interregnum, and in spite of the fact that they had contributed to the electoral victories of Cámpora and then Perón, the Montoneros continued staging operations. Responsibility for some of these, particularly the spectacular or shocking ones (like the murder of José Ignacio Rucci, secretary of the General Confederation of Labor, barely two days after the September 1973 elections) was eventually acknowledged in the press. But given the Montoneros' half-hearted support for the fledgling democracy, it is almost certain that some significant portion of unclaimed attacks between 1973 and 1976 were Montonero actions. Because the ERP went into total disarray following the death of its leadership in July 1976, it is also likely that most unclaimed attacks during the period from 1976 to 1979 were Montonero actions.

Table 3.3 classifies guerrilla operations according to the number of participants involved in the attack. Bombings were once more excluded from the calculations, for the same reasons mentioned earlier.

The percentage of attacks with an undetermined number of participants is sufficiently high to prevent conclusive statements. Three observations can nevertheless be made. First, the preferred guerrilla unit was composed of three to five members during the three periods under analysis and noticeably so in the first two. Second, under the 1976 military government there was a significant increase in the number of attacks involving one or two combatants. Given that operating under such a repressive regime must have posed considerable problems, this would indicate a willingness to "establish a presence," to prove that in spite of paramilitary activity, the guerrillas were a force to be reckoned with. Third, during the 1973–76 Peronist administrations only attacks involving more than 21 combatants increased their frequency (except for an insignificant increase in the frequency of attacks involving one combatant). In fact, it is quite likely that the percentage of large-scale attacks was substantially higher: newspaper descriptions of "an undetermined number of combatants" do not clarify if the numbers are undetermined because there were no eyewitnesses available or because eyewitnesses did not estimate how many combatants were involved, which would point to large contingents.[10]

Evolution of Different Types Of Armed Actions Between 1969 and 1979

Table 3.4 shows a breakdown of guerrilla violence into the different types of operations described in the introduction to Part I. One of the salient characteristics of armed struggle, Argentine style, is that airplane hijacking was wholly outside the established operational repertoire.[11] Moreover, in two out of the three recorded incidents, the hijacking was executed not per se but in support of a complex operation. In 1972, in one of the few examples of a joint operation, ERP, FAR, and Montoneros hijacked the Buenos Aires-Trelew flight so that the guerrillas escaping from Rawson prison could get to Chile, and in 1975 the Montoneros hijacked a plane to transport combatants for one of their most spectacular actions, the attempt to seize an army regiment, a prison and the airport in Formosa.

A second feature that table 3.4 reveals is the preeminence of bombings. Whether one looks at the Argentine Revolution, the Peronist administrations or the eleven-year period of guerrilla activity, bombings take the lion's share of the total volume of guerrilla violence. Explosives were also used fairly frequently during the 1976 military regime, even though during that period deaths overtake bombings in importance. Several factors make bombings a favorite operation. Incidents such as Lockerbie[12] have convinced us that international terrorism avails itself of a variety of sophisticated explosives and complicated electronic devices, but it is fairly easy to make a Molotov cocktail or a number of other small-scale bombs which Argentine guerrillas generically called "pipes" (*caños*). Unlike sniping, which requires skill and practice, any high school student can manufacture simple explosives with minimal coaching. And in Argentina they did. Without having been questioned about it, four of my guerrilla interviewees mentioned having learned to make bombs while in high school. The bombs, called "trotyl loaves," were manufactured in the oven at home and with the help of simple instruction leaflets distributed by FAL and FAP.[13] Two additional reasons explain the preeminence of explosives: setting a bomb involves utilizing few of the organization's resources, since one or two

Table 3.4. Guerrilla Operations, 1969–79

	1969–73 (%)	1973–76 (%)	1976–79 (%)	1969–79 (%)
Theft of Arms	15.80	5.53	1.55	8.99
Attacks on property	11.94	12.98	15.25	12.92
Seizures	11.37	7.39	2.54	8.20
Bombings	48.61	41.96	34.89	43.49
Kidnappings	4.83	7.24	1.98	5.43
Hijackings	0.11	0.05	—	0.07
Deaths	7.34	24.85	43.79	20.09
Total	100	100	100	100
	$N = 1{,}759$	$N = 1{,}935$	$N = 708$	$N = 4{,}402$

Source: Contemporary press reports.

individuals will suffice; and it involves little personal risk.[14] These reasons could also explain why attacks on property represent a relatively stable share of the total volume of violence throughout the eleven-year period.

As table 3.4 shows, the importance of seizures declines steadily between 1969 and 1979. Seizures are by nature the most militaristic type of operation, in part because of the difficulty in physically controlling the building or group of buildings to be seized, but also because of the detailed planning and preparation required. Significantly, this most militaristic type of operation was also highly regarded: when Argentine guerrillas praised an operation which was well executed, they called it "a very *pando* operation," turning into an adjective the name of a Uruguayan town which the Tupamaro guerrillas seized in October 1969.[15] This decline in the importance of seizures after 1973 could be interpreted as a move toward less militaristic operations, but if one considers not only the number of seizures but also the objects of those seizures, the picture is different.

Whereas in 1969–72 armed organizations tended to seize schools, factories, small provincial towns, and the occasional police precinct, between early 1973 and late 1975 guerrillas attempted 15 seizures of military installations. These operations became increasingly complex, involved more and more combatants, and almost always resulted in negative consequences for armed organizations. In September 1973, when 11 ERP members attacked the Army Medical Corps Headquarters in Buenos Aires, killing Lieutenant Colonel Raúl Duarte Ardoy in the process, Perón outlawed the organization. In January 1974, 70 ERP combatants seized the 10th Cavalry Regiment at Azul in Buenos Aires province, the most important armored division in the country. The attack was repressed and the guerrillas failed to take the regiment's weapons as they had planned, but they killed Colonel Camilo Gay and his wife and conscript Daniel González, and kidnapped Lieutenant Colonel Jorge Ibarzábal, whose corpse was found eleven months later. Perón's response to the Azul operation was to depose Buenos Aires governor Oscar Bidegain, a guerrilla supporter. In August 1974, the ERP simultaneously seized the Villa María Military Explosives Factory in Córdoba and the 17th Airborne Infantry Regiment in Catamarca. The maneuvers involved a total of 130 combatants, and the guerrillas stole an important number of weapons at Villa María, but they suffered heavy losses. The August 1975 seizure of the Benjamín Matienzo airport in Tucumán by Montoneros, during which the guerrillas blew up a Hercules C-130 plane transporting 130 gendarmes, resulted in Isabel Perón outlawing the Montoneros. The two most spectacular feats occurred in late 1975. In October, 500 Montoneros seized the 29th Mounted Infantry Regiment, El Pucú airport, and Penitentiary Unit 10 in Formosa; and in December, 300 ERP combatants seized the 601 Arsenal Battalion at Monte Chingolo in Buenos Aires, the biggest arms depot in the country. Significantly, for both operations the guerrillas wore uniforms—olive green shirts and trousers for the ERP (the same as those worn by the Argentine army) and denim trousers and blue shirts for the Montoneros.[16] That these operations, designed to show that the popular armies could take on the regular army, resulted in heavy guerrilla casualties is probably the reason why their frequency declined. It should also be said that other than demonstrating a superb technical capacity, these operations had no visible objectives, at least none that could be easily discerned by the population at large. In addition, Formosa and Monte Chingolo probably went a long way toward convincing the military that the only possible response to "subversion" was the dirty war.

Another operation whose frequency declined markedly and consistently is the theft of arms. This is very easily explained. In the initial phase of the struggle, which the guerrillas defined as *pertrechamiento* (equipment), theft provided the groups with much-needed weapons. In later phases, funds obtained through different means (notably kidnappings), enabled the guerrillas to purchase whatever armament they required.

Kidnappings deserve special mention, not because they represent any significant portion of guerrilla activity or because of dramatic variations on their share of the total volume of violence in the different periods; but because Argentine guerrillas derive some of their international notoriety from this. To begin with, one of the early cases provided the basis for one of Graham Greene's novels.[17] One could add that Argentine guerrillas have broken three world records when it comes to kidnappings. First, the ERP is the only group to have kidnapped the same person twice, Anglo-Argentine industrialist Charles Lockwood, abducted in 1973 and 1975. Second, the Montoneros cashed the highest ransom ever paid for a political kidnapping, that of brothers Juan and Jorge Born in 1974. Juan Born was released almost immediately for medical reasons but his brother was held captive for months and was released in June 1975 after his company paid the guerrillas $60 million (the figure in the *Guinness Book of Records*) and gave an additional $1.5 million in supplies to slums and depressed areas.

Table 3.5. Motives Behind Kidnappings, 1969–79

	1969–73 (%)	1973–76 (%)	1976–79 (%)	1969–79 (%)
Ransom	41.18	54.29	21.43	47.70
Obtain concessions/expose conditions	22.35	10.71	28.58	15.90
Make a statement	10.59	9.29	49.99	12.13
Other/Undetermined	25.88	25.71	—	24.27
Total	100	100	100	100
	N = 85	N = 140	N = 14	N = 239

Source: Contemporary press reports.

Third, also in 1974, the Montoneros became the first group to kidnap a corpse. The organization took the coffin of General Aramburu (whom it had kidnapped and killed four years earlier) from Recoleta cemetery in Buenos Aires, to force Isabel Perón to bring Eva Perón's body back to Argentina. Mrs. Perón complied and Aramburu's corpse was returned.[18] Beyond the shocking or morbid details, kidnappings provided the guerrillas with a substantial source of revenue—not that ransom was the only motive behind kidnappings (see table 3.5).

As a general rule, when public officials, professionals, or employees were kidnapped, the objective was to extract concessions from the government or employers and/or to expose working conditions in businesses, schools, ministries, or prisons. For example, in 1972 the ERP kidnapped Oberdan Sallustro, general manager of Fiat in Argentina. The guerrillas demanded that the company rehire workers who had been laid off, but also intended to exchange Sallustro for members of the ERP's leadership who were serving prison sentences. Fiat agreed to the terms but president Lanusse refused to release the prisoners, and Sallustro was killed as members of the security forces surrounded the safehouse where he was detained. In 1973, to provide another example, FAL and a groupuscule called Revolutionary Workers' Group (Grupo Obrero Revolucionario) kidnapped Hugo D'Aquila, head of the psychiatric service at Devoto prison, in order to expose prison conditions. D'Aquila was interrogated and released, and a transcript of the interrogation was published in book form. The book contained a serious allegation, never confirmed or denied, that certain serious psychiatric conditions were intentionally induced by prison personnel.[19]

Officers in the armed or security forces, politicians, trade unionists, and foreign officials seem to have been abducted with the sole purpose of making a statement—a show of strength or a display of operational precision. The Aramburu kidnapping is a case in point. Other examples are those of former chief of Naval Intelligence Francisco Alemán, held for 60 days in 1973 until he "confessed" that the Onganiato had been a military dictatorship; and of Colonel

Table 3.6. Kidnappings with Highest Ransoms, 1969–79

Date	Victim	Company	Group	Ransom (in U.S. dollars)
5/23/71	Stanley Sylvester	Swift	ERP	$250,000
9/5/72	Jan van der Panne	Phillips	Montoneros	500,000
12/22/72	Ronald Grove	Vestey	ERP	1,000,000
12/27/72	Vicenzo Russo	ITT	Montoneros	1,000,000
3/30/73	Gerardo Scalmazzi	Bank of Boston	ERP	750,000
4/2/73	Anthony da Cruz	Kodak	FAL	1,500,000
4/8/73	Victor Brimicombe	British American Tobacco	ERP	1,700,000
5/21/73	Oscar Castells	Coca Cola	FAR	1,000,000
5/23/73	Aaron Beilinson	Babic S.A.	ERP FR	1,000,000
6/6/73	Charles Lockwood	Roberts	ERP	2,000,000
6/18/73	John Thompson	Firestone	ERP	3,000,000
10/23/73	David Wilkie	Amoco Oil	Unknown	1,000,000
12/6/73	Victor Samuelson	Exxon	ERP	14,200,000
9/19/74	Jorge & Juan Born	Bunge & Born	Montoneros	61,500,000
7/31/75	Charles Lockwood	Roberts	ERP	10,000,000
10/24/75	Enrique Metz	Mercedes Benz	Montoneros	5,000,000
Total				105,400,000

Source: Contemporary press reports. Ransom figures calculated on the basis of the dollar-peso exchange rate reported in the business section of the newspaper on the same day that payment of the ransom was reported.

Juan Alberto Pita, military overseer of the CGT after 1976, who was about to be subjected to a "revolutionary trial" for unspecified crimes when he escaped after months in captivity.[20] Significantly, this motive seems to have become outstanding in its importance after the 1976 coup. This is to say that it was once the guerrillas were being wiped out by the dirty war that they turned to such high-risk operations, against the most heavily guarded set of potential kidnap victims.

Except for the 1976–79 period, ransom was by far the most prevalent kidnap motive. By and large those kidnapped for ransom were executives in multinational corporations or in top Argentine businesses, though merchants, housewives, students, and children were occasionally targeted. It is impossible to estimate the total monetary value of kidnappings. Sometimes the press provided exact ransom figures, sometimes it merely reported that a ransom had been paid, and sometimes it omitted even that information. The 16 most profitable kidnappings are listed in table 3.6. The table provides the date of each kidnapping, the victim's name, the company paying the ransom, the guerrilla group responsible for the operation, and the ransom amount in U.S. dollars.

The ransom total of $105.4 million is impressive, considering that this represents only 16 of the 114 kidnappings between 1969 and 1979 in which there is evidence that ransom was paid. In addition, Argentine guerrillas counted on another source of revenue, the "revolutionary tax," which was extracted from companies and ensured their executives would not be abducted. It is impossible to know which companies regularly paid the tax or what the amount was. In the one case in which details were made public, ERP 22 asked the Ford Motor Company to pay a revolutionary tax of $1 million, and Ford refused. In May 1973, the guerrillas attempted to kidnap one of the company's executives on his way to work. There was a shootout, and the executive was killed and a colleague who was driving to work with him was wounded. Ford then paid its tax.[21] But even without the "revolutionary tax," the final figure provided in table 3.6 should go some way toward disproving the theory, so popular with the Argentine right, that the guerrillas were financed by the former USSR or China, with Cuba serving as an intermediary. Kidnap ransoms obviously provided Argentine guerrillas with vastly greater resources than the former Soviet Union or China could ever afford.[22]

Except for the 1976–79 period, in approximately one quarter of all kidnappings it is impossible to pinpoint a motive, either because newspapers do not report even the victim's occupation or because there was no apparent logic to the operation. The abductions of noncommissioned officers and enlisted men in the security forces, or of rural and urban workers, fall under this category. It could be argued—and the guerrillas themselves would be the first to make this claim—that armed operations must have clear political objectives that are readily understood by the mass of the population whose allegiance the guerrillas are supposedly seeking to obtain. This becomes more of an imperative when the targets of armed operations are human beings. If we assume that the first two motives listed in table 3.5 (ransom and the obtention of concessions) constitute a clear political objective, we are nevertheless left with a substantial number of cases (36.47 percent in 1969–73; 35 percent in 1973–76; 49.99 percent in 1976–79; and 36.4 percent overall) in which this is not so.

What is undoubtedly the most significant feature about table 3.4 is the steady increase in the percentage of the total volume of violence represented by deaths. It was not simply that a growing number of people fell victim to guerrilla violence. The guerrillas' growing disregard for public opinion becomes evident if one considers attacks against selected groups of persons, the accidental deaths of relatives or friends of potential targets, and the rhetoric that explained those deaths.

After 1973, armed organizations targeted for assassination campaigns certain groups whose members' deaths could not be easily justified or understood by the mass public. In August 1974, for example, following the attempt to seize the 17th Airborne Infantry Regiment in Catamarca mentioned earlier, the ERP claimed 16 of its members had been summarily shot. The government insisted the combatants had died during the getaway. The ERP then announced it would kill an equal number of officers in the armed forces. Between September and December 1974 nine officers were killed, but the campaign was called off when, along with the tenth officer, the ERP killed his three-year-old child. In 1975 the Montoneros launched a campaign to kill policemen because they were "representatives of authority." The Montonero press considered these deaths significant victories over the adversary. To the general public the deaths were inexplicable (as were the nine officers'), in particular because most of these policemen were hit while they were off duty, on public buses, outside supermarkets, or about to enter a discothèque.[23]

Equally significant, in terms of the swing in public perceptions, were the accidental deaths that resulted from operations that did not originally contemplate fatalities. When the Montoneros ambushed and kidnapped the Born brothers on their drive to work, for example, they killed the other two occupants of the car, the Borns' chauffeur and bodyguard, Juan Carlos Pérez, and Alberto Bosch, an executive in one of the Borns' subsidiaries. Individuals also died in operations in which they were not the targets. In August 1978, the Montoneros bombed the apartment of Rear Admiral Armando Lambruschini, chairman of the Joint Chiefs. Lambruschini was not home but his fifteen-year-old daughter Paula, a bodyguard, and a neighbor were killed in the blast.[24]

An additional element that developed after 1973 is the cult of death. What is striking about the guerrillas' pronouncements over the eleven-year period is the decreasing value attached to life, their own as well as their enemies'. During the early years military operations were planned with the utmost care, for two practical reasons: the guerrillas were concerned with winning public support, and the groups were small and could not afford significant losses. As FAP would explain in a letter to the police: "We had nothing against corporal Vallejos, seriously wounded by our Eva Perón Detachment. . . . But the corporal did not obey orders to stay put and attempted a futile resistance. . . . We have nothing against each one of you as individuals. . . . *Keep in mind:* that each operation we carry out is carefully planned and studied in its most minute details . . . faced with any attempt at resistance on your part there is no possible alternative: either you or us."[25]

In addition to these practical considerations there was a notion of "revolutionary morality." During the early years what mattered to the guerrillas was what differentiated them from the armed forces. The military tortured and killed; the guerrillas, on the contrary, had been forced to resort to violence, would never torture, and considered killings as a painful though sometimes unavoidable occurrence: "Armed struggle has been imposed on us as the only way out of years of oligarchical violence. . . . We are guided in this enterprise by the clean example of that great Argentine and great Latin American . . . commandant Che

Guevara . . . [the regime's] puppet generals, its torturer policemen, have staged the comedy of finding our violence scandalous . . . they are simply projecting on revolutionary combatants the image of their own methods, their own habits." [26]

With time, the notion that killing is painful was abandoned. In 1970, the Montonero communiqué announcing the "execution" of Aramburu ended with the sentence "God our Lord have mercy on his soul." By contrast, in 1976, eighteen-year-old Montonera Ana María González established a friendship with high school classmate María Graciela Cardozo for the purpose of frequenting the Cardozo home and placing a bomb under the bed of Cardozo's father, an Army general and chief of the Federal Police. The explosion resulted in the death of the general and his wife. During a press conference, González explained, "I had to make one of the militant's worst sacrifices: being in daily contact with the hated enemy. During a month and a half I had to frequent Cardozo's home as his daughter's classmate, while he supervised the kidnapping, torture and assassination of tens of comrades." [27] There was no pity for Ms. Cardozo, who must have had to fight her parents for the right to befriend González since, by the latter's own admission, her activism in the Revolutionary Tendency was known to the family.

4

Collective Violent Protest

hen Argentinians refer to the apparent breakdown of the social order in the 1960s and 1970s they allude to the guerrilla threat. This exercise in selective memory provides an excellent illustration of the pivotal role of armed struggle in Argentine politics over the past two decades.[1] For as the present chapter will demonstrate, until the 1976 coup the scope and intensity of collective violent protest were remarkable. The pages that follow analyze that protest during the Onganiato, the 1973–76 Peronist administrations, and the Process of National Reorganization.

The Meaning of Protest

Collective violence has been a permanent feature in Argentine history, but the 1960s and 1970s represented a radical departure from previous patterns of collective violent protest. First, although earlier history witnessed sporadic outbursts of protest, after 1969 collective violence was a constant. Second, whereas in the past a single constituency resorted to violence, during the Onganiato collective violence was the weapon of an increasing number of social groups. Third, in the past violence had generally been limited to a specific geographical area, but after 1969 the whole country was in flames. Finally, whereas in the past collective protest focused on specific policy decisions, what was now questioned was the basis of authority.

A central issue in the analysis of collective violent protest is whether that protest was of a revolutionary nature. The answer is affirmative in that new forms of popular organization were emerging, for example, in slums and working-class neighborhoods, and in that the rank and file in established institutions like unions and schools were challenging the existing authority structures and suggesting alternatives. But if we take the term *revolutionary* to imply a questioning of existing class relations, collective violent protest was devoid of a revolutionary character. The slogans of the period obscured this fact, however. Protesters indicated they were thirsty for violence: "Prepare the torches/prepare the tar/that the whole *Barrio Norte*/will be burnt."[2] They also showed their support for the guerrillas: "So that justice was served/and because the People wanted it/the commandos of the FAR/shot Berisso"; "They dropped by my house/some valiant boys/and then I saw that in the newspaper/they were called delinquents."[3] There were also indicators of an identification with socialism: "So that Argentina produces/workers who will lead her"; "Allende in Chile/Perón in Argentina/for the unity/of Latin America."[4]

On both sides of the political spectrum this was taken as a sign that Argentina faced a revolutionary situation. The guerrillas assumed that Peronism was passé and that in the struggle for socialism the masses would understand and support any and all guerrilla policies, joining the ranks of the popular armies in droves. This may have been true of radicalized students, but, as Samuel Huntington points out, students alone cannot make a revolution.[5] It was not true of the working class, with the exception of the *clasistas,* the workers who identified with Marxism. However, in his brilliant analysis of the ideology of the Argentine working class, Daniel James points out that *clasismo* was a minoritary current within a labor movement that has since the 1940s identified with Peronism; and that at the company level clasista leaders were respected and followed simply because they stood for honesty and provided a contrast with the corruption of the established union hierarchy.[6] On the other side of the fence, confronted with the scope and intensity of collective violent protest, the military and the bourgeoisie assumed that the ties between guerrilla and popular organizations were closer than they really were. The September 1972 issue of *Economic Survey,* an Argentine periodical, said in an editorial: "Any businessman who tries to impose some limit to the pretensions of workers, thus running the risk of turning his firm into a battlefield or of being kidnapped by terrorists, deserves a medal for heroism. . . . the military administration insists it will try to institutionalize the country, but the truth is that what it is about to institutionalize is its moral and material breakdown."[7]

The scope and intensity of collective violent protest (which in turn reflected popular opposition to specific government policies) and the occasional guerrilla intervention in labor conflicts allowed General Jorge R. Videla, who became president after the 1976 coup, to conclude that "a terrorist is not just someone with a gun or a bomb, but also someone who spreads ideas that are 'contrary to western and Christian civilization.' "[8] As this and the next chapter will show, mass organizations were to pay dearly for these misconceptions about the linkages between armed struggle and collective protest, in the form of repression and disappearances.

Protest During the Argentine Revolution

Chapter 2 mentioned that the Onganía regime was frequently called not a *dictadura* but a *dictablanda,* a benevolent dictatorship. The scope and intensity of collective violent protest after 1969 supports this characterization. A quick glance at table 4.1 reveals that during the Argentine Revolution a wide variety of social groups chose to take their grievances into the streets. This was particularly acute from March 1972 to March 1973, when all manner of disputes connected with the coming presidential elections turned violent: contending factions within the Radical and Peronist parties seized or attacked party locales, Peronists disrupted rallies organized by the Río Negro Popular party, and those advocating the blank vote placed incendiary bombs in Córdoba.[9] Collective protest was not confined to the pre-election period. In working-class dwellings the neighbors demanded official action by attacking municipal buildings; Third World (meaning radical) Catholics attacked their parishes; inmates seized a prison in order to expose living conditions[10]; and the Soviet embassy was attacked by a group advocating the independence of the Ukraine.

Students—and to a lesser extent organized labor—dominated the scene. Student protest accounted for 29.64 percent of all violence during the period. Student activism in Argentina owed something to the rebellious wave that swept campuses all over the world. Student protest in Paris, Berlin, Turin, Berkeley, and Buenos Aires had three common features: it occurred during the late sixties; it expressed legitimate grievances related to overcrowded classrooms and dormitories and outdated curricula; and it was politically motivated, as students were protesting specific government policies.[11] The more immediate catalysts for student activism in Argentina were the Night of the Long Batons and the elimination of university autonomy in 1966. Direct government control of the universities (known as intervention), the closure of the student unions, and the ban on political activities at the universities were expected to de-politicize the students, but they produced the opposite results. In spite of the intervention, student organizations continued to function in semi-clandestine fashion and surfaced again after the Cordobazo in 1969. Student grievances against the Onganiato included the price of meal tickets at university cafeterias, the size of the university's budget, and outdated curricula. But students also demanded "freedom for political, union and student prisoners" and "the repeal of all emergency legislation."[12] The key demand remained the restoration of university autonomy and student participation in the running of the universities.

In addition to marching with Molotov cocktails and seizing university build-

Table 4.1. Collective Violent Protest, January 1, 1969–May 24, 1973

	Attacks on property (%)	Seizures (%)	Bombings (%)	Kidnappings (%)	Deaths (%)	Total (%)
Students	5.30	12.91	11.31	0.12	—	29.64
Labor conflicts	3.47	4.77	2.30	0.12	0.12	10.78
Neighborhood action	0.06	0.94	0.06	—	—	1.06
Riots	35.48	5.89	5.36	—	2.06	48.79
Prison inmates	—	0.06	—	—	0.06	0.12
Intra-labor dispute	0.06	0.12	—	—	0.18	0.36
Intra-party dispute	0.12	—	—	—	0.12	0.24
Intra-Peronist dispute	0.18	—	—	0.06	0.29	0.53
Radical party members	—	0.12	—	—	—	0.12
Peronist party members	—	0.06	—	—	—	0.06
Peronist Youth	0.23	—	0.71	—	—	0.94
Third World Catholics	0.12	0.47	—	—	—	0.59
Partisans of blank vote	—	—	0.29	—	—	0.29
Free Ukranians	0.06	—	—	—	—	0.06
Unknown	0.71	0.06	5.65	—	—	6.42
Total	45.79	25.40	25.68	0.30	2.83	100
	$N = 777$	$N = 431$	$N = 436$	$N = 5$	$N = 48$	$N = 1,697$

Source: Contemporary press reports.

ings, students introduced a variety of innovative tactics to express their discontent. In Santa Fe they staged a student strike which included public trials "of all the reactionary professors who swarm in this university."[13] In Tucumán they flooded the city by opening fire hydrants.[14] In Córdoba, and in spite of the ban on political activities, students devised a system of Delegates' Committees, which other universities around the country then copied. Within each department, each class chose a delegate, and the delegates then elected an Executive Committee, which divided itself into subcommittees in order to plan and coordinate collective action.[15] In Buenos Aires the students attempted "to build dual power" at the Department of Humanities by rejecting, on political grounds, the official syllabi for certain courses and preparing for those finals on the basis of new syllabi devised by the students in cooperation with some teaching assistants, who also graded the exams.[16] In virtually every instance of student protest, the government reacted severely, thus radicalizing the situation further and involving

previously neutral actors: faculty, parents, the Catholic church, and intellectuals. At the two art schools in Buenos Aires, for example, the students initially
demanded that the administration comply with the schools' founding charter,
which mandated periodic changes in the curricula in accordance with developments in the arts. The schools' authorities brought disciplinary action against the
leaders of the protest. The students then seized the schools, demanding an end
to disciplinary sanctions against the student leaders. The authorities retaliated
by involving the police, which arrested a number of students and filed charges
against them with the Federal Penal Chamber of the Nation, the special court
created to try terrorist cases. Parents and faculty mounted a campaign in defense
of the students, and the school authorities were forced to promise to reform the
curricula.[17]

Though not as active as the students, the labor movement played an important role. Violent labor conflicts and disputes between factions of the labor movement represent 11.14 percent of all violence during the period. Labor activism
was a direct consequence of Onganía's economic rationalization plans, which
elicited two responses from union leaders. The majority, which became known
as *participacionistas,* "accepted the regime's corporatist rhetoric concerning the
need for the unions to enter a close alliance with the state." [18] A minoritarian current, the combativos, questioned labor's acquiescence to Onganía's economic
policies and the existence of union "bureaucrats," defined as "someone without
vocation, without ideals, who converts himself into a typical 'administrator' of
a union post, who uses it for his personal satisfaction and from his position starts
to 'rule' over his comrades." [19] But labor activism also owed much to certain
changes in the structure of labor organization. In the early sixties workers in certain new industries (including vehicles, petrochemicals, steel) had been allowed
to organize company unions and conduct company-level wage bargaining. This
departure from the traditional system of industry-wide national unions which
negotiated industry-wide national contracts was initially sought by the companies' management, in the hope that decentralized bargaining would weaken the
unions' response. The effect was quite the opposite. Company unions led to
greater rank-and-file autonomy from the union bosses and to increased activism.
Established in Córdoba and in the Paraná river industrial belt (from Rosario to
Buenos Aires), company unions became the epicenter of clasismo, the union
current identified with Marxism. Combativos and clasistas were key participants
in the Cordobazo and the Viborazo, as well as in the multiplicity of strikes which
frequently involved factory seizures, management hostages, and arson.[20]

Students and workers engaged in separate actions, but they were joint pro-
tagonists in what became the hallmark of collective violent protest during this
period: riots. These serious breaches of the peace of a more or less spontaneous
nature which result in substantial material damage were normally the unexpected

outcome of some other form of collective action. For example, during a rally to protest specific government policies tempers would flare up, and in no time the demonstrators would be smashing window displays and burning public buses.

The Cordobazo, the most famous of these events, also set a pattern that would be repeated elsewhere. First, the Cordobazo was a foray into "enemy territory," from the working-class districts to the city center—the upper-class neighborhoods, banking and commercial districts, and government offices.[21] Second, the protest bypassed institutional channels. The political parties, the union confederation, even the student and guerrilla organizations were notoriously absent as institutions. Following the Cordobazo there were riots in Cipolletti and Rosario in September 1969, Tucumán in November 1970, Córdoba again in March 1971 (the Viborazo), Mendoza in April 1972, and General Roca in July 1972. The motives for these riots were varied. In Cipolletti the population rose against a government decision to depose a popular mayor. In Rosario the local CGT decreed a 38-hour general strike in support of striking workers at the Mitre railroad, which also demanded the improvement of economic conditions and the abolition of repressive labor legislation, and protested excessive foreign penetration of the economy. In Tucumán the protest was mainly confined to the university budget and university conditions. In Mendoza the population protested against a 100 percent rise in electrical power rates. In General Roca the residents objected to the provincial government's decision to alter the judicial districts in the province, which they saw as an attempt by the governor to curry favor with the locals and launch his campaign for the governorship in the 1973 elections.

Irrespective of the initial motives, the riots developed along similar paths. The marchers started off peacefully, and then turned to violence. In the cases of Córdoba (the Cordobazo and the Viborazo), Mendoza, and General Roca, press coverage indicates that the protest only turned violent after the marchers were met by the police armed with tear gas and the infamous long batons. The protesters usually built barricades and set some of those on fire, burned cars, buses, and trains, destroyed shop windows, and looted shops. In Córdoba (1969 and 1971), Cipolletti, and General Roca, the rioters also seized public offices and private businesses—in Cipolletti, after seizing the town hall, the protesters threw the new mayor out the window. In Córdoba (1969) and Cipolletti there were also power cuts, a result of sabotage, and buildings were set on fire. In Córdoba (1969 and 1971), Rosario, and Tucumán, protesters used bombs, whereas in both Córdoba riots and in Mendoza, sharpshooters fired on the security forces from rooftops. In all cases except for Cipolletti and Tucumán the police was unable to contain the riots and called in the army. Press coverage of these episodes presented the image of uncontrolled hordes let loose on civilized Argentina: "A vociferous individual approaches the building with a tire in flames while the others throw stones and destroy the windows. Shortly a group of demonstrators enters the building and begins to plunder. They take all the furniture, television, refrigerator, mattresses, all of which ends in a great bonfire in the middle of the street."[22] This apparent "revolt of the masses" persuaded the guerrillas, and the military and their civilian allies that revolution was at hand.[23]

Protest During the Peronist Interregnum

With the return to constitutional rule in 1973, collective violence continued to be a weapon employed by a multiplicity of groups. And although the types of groups resorting to violence varied, their political identification did not (table 4.2). Eight of the groups listed, representing 12.34 percent of all violence during the period, are Peronist. The figure would be much higher if we take into account the probable Peronist allegiance of workers, neighborhood committees, and slum dwellers.

One obvious explanation for this is that the radicalized sectors of Peronism refused to accept the defeat that the downfall of Cámpora and Perón's turnabout represented. For after years of praising socialismo nacional from his Madrid exile, the old leader returned to power to implement a variation on his 1940s policies. That labor conflicts and disputes among factions of the labor movement account for 54.45 percent of all violence during the period suggests that workers rejected the June 1973 agreement between business and labor known as the Social Pact, which established a two-year price and wage freeze. By late 1973 businessmen were unofficially violating the pact by raising prices and hoarding basic foodstuffs. Perón obtained the cooperation of union leaders through the November 1973 Law of Professional Associations, which guaranteed the union bosses control over the rank and file. This law ratified the principle of government judicial recognition (*personería gremial*) of one union per sector of economic activity. Only unions enjoying judicial recognition could call strikes or represent workers in labor courts. Loss of judicial recognition

> deprives a labor organization of these rights and often paves the way for its "intervention," by which the government temporarily replaces the union's leaders with its own trustees, freezes its bank accounts, and confiscates its headquarters, hospitals, recreation centers, tourist facilities, and other properties. . . . parallel to the government's right to "intervene" in the CGT or in the national-level unions, the leaders of the national-level unions have the right to "intervene" in the locals (to replace local leaders with interim trustees of their own choosing) under a wide variety of circumstances.[24]

Confronted with the Social Pact and the Law of Professional Associations, militant unionism shifted the focus of strikes from pay raises to health and safety issues, back pay, job reclassification, and union democracy. At a pasta factory in San Francisco (Córdoba province), for example, workers went on strike to

Table 4.2. Collective Violent Protest, May 25, 1973–March 23, 1976

	Attacks on property (%)	Seizures (%)	Bombings (%)	Kidnappings (%)	Deaths (%)	Total (%)
Students	0.89	8.39	2.14	—	—	11.42
Labor conflicts	4.46	28.03	11.43	2.14	1.43	47.49
Neighborhood action	—	0.89	—	—	—	0.89
Riots	0.71	0.71	0.89	—	1.78	4.09
Prison inmates	0.54	2.86	—	6.25	0.36	10.01
Intra-labor dispute	1.61	0.71	1.07	0.36	3.21	6.96
Intra-Peronist dispute	0.36	—	0.18	—	0.18	0.72
Peronist Youth	0.18	1.61	—	—	—	1.79
Peronist University Youth	0.18	—	—	—	—	0.18
Rank-and-file Peronists	—	0.54	—	—	—	0.54
Revolutionary Peronist Committee	0.18	0.18	—	—	—	0.36
Commando for Peronist Resistance	—	0.18	—	—	—	0.18
Peronist militants	—	—	1.61	—	—	1.61
Popular militants	—	—	0.18	—	—	0.18
Slum dwellers	—	1.43	—	—	—	1.43
Chileans	—	0.18	—	—	—	0.18
Unknown	4.28	1.61	5.54	—	0.54	11.97
Total	13.39	47.32	23.04	8.75	7.50	100
	$N = 75$	$N = 265$	$N = 129$	$N = 49$	$N = 42$	$N = 560$

Source: Contemporary press reports.

protest pay arrears and factory conditions. When management paid no attention to their demands, the workers seized the factory and the town declared an active strike in support of the pasta workers. Active strikes were at this time the most frequent form of labor militancy in Córdoba. During an active strike, workers went to their jobs only to participate in discussion sessions about factory life and factory conditions. The San Francisco active strike was launched with a town meeting, after which workers vandalized the homes of the pasta factory owners and the owner of the local newspaper, broke into an armory, stole weapons, and burned a number of cars.[25] Active strikes, which frequently included factory seizures, bombings, and arson, were sometimes staged in self-defense. This was the case with the Tucumán sugar workers, when the Ministry of Labor withdrew the union's judicial recognition. A strike supported by the local population and the Córdoba combativos forced the government to back down.[26]

After Perón's death, and in the face of rising inflation, strikes involving wage demands became increasingly frequent. Both the government and the national union leadership agreed on the need to curb union militancy. By late 1974 the garage mechanics and the power workers in Córdoba, the print workers and the university employees in Buenos Aires, the metalworkers in Villa Constitución and the Salta CGT, all combativo and clasista bastions, had been intervened or had lost their judicial recognition. The Villa Constitución workers resisted the intervention and went on active strike. They were allowed to hold union elections, which the clasistas won. In March 1975, four months after the election, the government denounced a "subversive plot" in the Paraná industrial belt "centered on Villa Constitución" and aiming "to paralyze industrial production." No further details on the plot were offered, but more than 100 activists were arrested and the union was closed down. Elsewhere, militant unionists were forced into semi-clandestinity by the activities of the Argentine Anti-Communist Alliance. But rank-and-file discontent persisted due to the deteriorating economic conditions and exploded into massive unrest against the orthodox stabilization plan implemented by Celestino Rodrigo, Isabel Perón's third Economy Minister in eleven months. In June 1975, Rodrigo's plan prompted a series of marches, demonstrations, factory occupations, and street fights, which culminated July 7–8 in the first general strike ever staged against a Peronist government. The national level union bosses, confronting the danger of losing control over their unions, had no choice but to yield to the rank and file and side with the protesters. Virtually one month of continuous collective protest, popularly known as the July Days (Jornadas de Julio), achieved the renewal of collective bargaining contracts and the resignation of the dreaded José López Rega, Minister of Social Welfare, private secretary to the president, and head of the AAA.[27]

The contagion effect of violence was evidenced by the seizure frenzy of 1973.If riots characterized the Argentine Revolution, seizures were by far the dominant expression of collective violent protest between 1973 and 1976, in particular of the first year, when 76.6 percent of all seizures took place. A staggering 48.3 percent of all seizures in the 1973–76 period occurred between May 28 and June 30, 1973. On May 28, three days into the Cámpora administration, students, faculty, and staff seized all departments and the administration at the state-owned universities in Buenos Aires and La Plata "to prevent the [military-appointed] administration on its way out from removing compromising documents, and also to carry out an experiment in self-government." The following day Peronist activists seized a radio station in Córdoba on the grounds that it had been used by General Eduardo Lonardi during the coup against Perón in 1955.[28] In the course of the month students seized their schools and universities, workers seized their factories, employees seized hospitals, radio stations, government agencies, and banks, neighborhood committees seized town halls, and inmates their prisons. A press headline explained the motive behind a vast number of these actions: "Motto: To seize in order to depose." [29] In many of the May-June 1973 seizures collective action was geared toward the removal of authorities at the establishments being occupied, who owed their positions to the 1966–73 military regime. A small number of seizures included specific labor or social demands. Workers who seized the Astarsa factory in Tigre were protesting the absence of safety regulations which had led to the deaths of eight workers, and slum dwellers who seized the Plata food market in Buenos Aires were protesting against the housing shortage. Inmates who seized 16 prisons throughout the country protested against prison food and medical assistance, and a cumbersome judicial system under which some prisoners spent more time in jail prior to sentencing than the Criminal Code prescribed for their crime.[30] A third motivation behind the seizure frenzy of May-June 1973 appears to have been that of preventing an opposing political sector from claiming control first. Independent of the motive behind these seizures, the government took the view that the transition to democracy involved an unavoidable social dislocation and chose not to act immediately. Toward the end of June, after a joint request by the Interior Ministry, the labor confederation, and the Peronist movement, most of the seizures ended.[31]

Collective protest during this period left two lasting impressions. First, the seizure frenzy conveyed the sense of a generalized crisis of authority, that the established hierarchical order in the public and private spheres was under siege. Second, violent protest acquired a more savage character, as evidenced by the increase in incidents which resulted in deaths. The conclusion drawn here was that factional disputes among sectors of Peronism had monopolized the national political scene, and that Peronism was "ungovernable" and therefore unfit to govern. The Peronist right and left were at the time attempting to resolve by force the issue of which one would control the movement, and this struggle acquired overtones of gangsterism. As La Opinión said in an editorial in 1973, "Peronism owes more fatalities to its internal squabbles than it does to struggles against all the governments after 1955." [32] The role of the Peronist right is minimized and collective protest is considered the main culprit due to an incorrect identification of the objectives of collective protest with those of the guerrilla groups.

Protest After 1976: Chronicle of a Coup Foretold

Collective violent protest virtually ceased following the military coup. The 17 violent incidents registered in table 4.3 all occurred between September and October of 1976 and were mostly linked to a labor conflict in one of the three electrical power companies in Buenos Aires, Servicios Eléctricos del Gran

Table 4.3. Collective Violent Protest, March 24, 1976–December 31, 1979

	Attacks on property (%)	Seizures (%)	Bombings (%)	Kidnappings (%)	Deaths (%)	Total (%)
Labor conflicts	64.71	—	35.29	—	—	100
Total	64.71	—	35.29	—	—	100
	$N = 11$		$N = 6$			$N = 17$

Source: Contemporary press reports.

Buenos Aires (known as SEGBA), which then spread to the other two, Agua y Energía and Compañía Italo-Argentina de Electricidad. The other violent incidents of the period, at the state-owned telephone company, the National Savings Bank, and a post office branch, appear to have been staged in solidarity with SEGBA workers because pamphlets from a "clandestine CGT" were found at the post office.

On seizing power in March 1976 the military banned all political activity, purged the universities of "dangerous" academics, and instituted a system of university entrance exams destined to reduce the number of students. In the labor sphere the military "intervened" in the CGT and in individual unions, appointing military overseers. The military also passed a Redundancy Law allowing for the summary dismissal of state employees "who are in any way linked to subversive or dissociating activities" [33] and a Law of Industrial Security which prohibited strikes and other forms of collective action.[34] Collective bargaining agreements were abolished, and the military's economic policy led to a 43 percent drop in real wages in the first semester of 1976.[35]

Similar measures during the Onganiato had resulted in increased popular mobilization. That this did not happen after 1976 is due to the existence of widespread repression. The development of the SEGBA conflict illustrates why collective violent protest virtually ceased after the coup. The conflict started when 208 employees, "mostly former officials and leaders in the Luz y Fuerza union," [36] were declared redundant. A strike including attacks on company installations and equipment and bombings followed. Management "warned" the strikers that they should return to work and the First Army Corps announced that strikers would otherwise be dismissed and liable for criminal prosecution under the Law of Industrial Security. About 90 workers were detained and new layoffs declared at Agua y Energía and Italo, both of which joined in the strike. There were additional attacks on property and bombings while so-called police vigilance was maintained at both establishments. Three SEGBA workers disappeared and a prominent Luz y Fuerza activist was detained. Minor incidents of violence continued. When troops from the First Army Corps were assigned as "custodians" at Italo, Agua y Energía, and SEGBA, and the government stated that further action would be interpreted as "connected with subversive objectives," the strike ended.[37]

It must be kept in mind that illegal repression started well before the coup. Newspapers identified 51 murders in 1974 of activists in student, labor, and neighborhood organizations, as well as in leftist parties, and 135 in 1975. The figures do not seem high, but we must add the killing of individuals whose occupation or political affiliation the newspapers do not provide, and individuals listed as foreigners, as well as the dozens of corpses mutilated beyond possible identification and recorded as "N.N." (*nomen nescio,* name unknown). Even if the newspapers do not provide an accurate estimate of the extent of repression against popular activists, its impact on the unions, the *barrios,* and the universities was considerable. According to the National Commission on the Disappearance of Persons, appointed by civilian president Raúl Alfonsín to investigate the dirty war following Argentina's return to democratic rule in 1983, 30.2 percent of disappeared persons were workers and 21 percent were students.[38] That collective violent protest came to a halt with the coup of March 24, 1976, suggests that while the guerrillas expected General Videla to become a new Onganía, popular organizations had a clearer understanding of the situation.

5

Right-Wing Violence

his chapter focuses on violence by paramilitary squads and certain organizations within the Peronist movement or closely identified with it, known as the Peronist right or orthodox Peronism. Analysis of right-wing violence in Argentina from 1969 to 1979 reveals clear trends. Perhaps the most obvious is its increased intensity: 0.13 incidents per day during the Onganiato; 1.93 during the Peronist interregnum; and 10.18 after the 1976 coup. The data also show that the right concentrated almost exclusively on bombings, kidnappings, and deaths, and increasingly on the latter two. The Peronist right always played a secondary role, for right-wing violence was first primarily and then exclusively a state-sponsored activity. The organization of illegal repression consequently became increasingly complex. Death squad activity during the Onganiato, significant though it was, should probably be considered the result of private initiatives by members of the security forces.[1] This changed after 1973. The emergence of the Argentine Anti-Communist Alliance represented a conscious attempt to eliminate some of the regime's opponents through illegal force. Until 1976, this was a task reserved to a chosen few. After that date, the entire security apparatus was geared to that purpose.

Right-wing violence (especially after Juan Perón's death in 1974, when death squads began operating without any restraint) legitimated armed struggle by providing combatants with the justifications of self-defense and defense of unarmed militants in front organizations. Death squad activity also contributed to the development of militarism within guerrilla groups by strengthening existing tendencies toward a friend-foe view of politics, hardening the guerrillas' resolve and stimulating the view that politics is war; and by strengthening existing tendencies toward group cohesion and the stifling of dissent, as the group protected the combatants from the dangers above ground. As one of my interviewees would put it,

> [the 1974–75 period] was like the horror movie in which the room's walls are closing in. [Action] was cathartic. It demonstrated we were alive. And the Triple A hit hard. Guerrillas were used to being bank employees during the week and guerrillas during the weekend. And the Triple A got you during the weekend. The dilemma was that if you walked into a restaurant without the .45 [caliber gun] and the AAA turned up you got massacred, and if you carried [the gun] and they found it on you they massacred you anyway. We didn't have the experience or the cool judgment to react to that. After [1974–75] it was a race towards death on skateboard or bicycle. And many felt almighty with a grenade.

Discussing paramilitary squads and orthodox Peronism jointly might appear incorrect, since violence exercised from the state has a distinct nature. Some characteristics of the relationship between the Peronist right and the security forces should therefore be made explicit. Frequently the police abetted or overlooked the activities of the Peronist right. Anti-Semitic youths in a group called Tacuara, for example, were allowed to stage initiation rites at Chacarita cemetery in Buenos Aires. When evidence that those youngsters had beaten up a Jewish adolescent was presented by the victim's parents, the police tampered with the depositions and concluded that there were no grounds for prosecution. There is also evidence that members of orthodox Peronist groups joined the ranks of paramilitary squads, in particular the Triple A.[2] One could also point to a shared interest between these two sets of individuals, namely, to check the development of the left. Finally, orthodox Peronists and paramilitaries shared a world view with a proclivity toward conspiracy theories. In the 1960s and 1970s there were three different versions of an international conspiracy directed against the Argentine Republic.

The first involved the idea of a "synarchy," an ill-defined supranational entity supposedly governing the world, which Perón himself described as an alliance of capitalism, communism, Catholicism, and Zionism.[3] The second theory had its roots in anti-Semitism. The Jewish faith was seen as threatening the most cherished Christian values: "Argentina has three main enemies: Karl Marx, because he tried to destroy the Christian concept of society; Sigmund Freud, because he tried to destroy the Christian concept of the family; and Albert Einstein, because he tried to destroy the Christian concept of time and space."[4] According to what was known as the Andinia plan, the Jewish people were bent on an invasion of Argentina which would result in the establishment of a Zionist state in Patagonia.[5] Finally, the Doctrine of Ideological Frontiers, elaborated around 1959 by the Brazilian Colonel Golbery do Couto e Silva at the War College, viewed the international system as dominated by an East-West conflict in which Brazil's only possible course of action was automatic alignment behind one of the two superpowers. National security became the most important concern, but it was understood in terms of a holy war against communism. Yet because anyone who disagreed with the regime could be labeled a communist, this doctrine gave the military a free hand as far as repression was concerned. The enemy could be a Soviet, or a Brazilian, which accounts for the notions of "ideological frontiers" and "internal warfare."

In the Argentine variety of the Doctrine of Ideological Frontiers the armed forces became the moral reserves of the nation. As Onganía stated in a 1964 speech at West Point,

> obedience is due a government when its power is derived from the people, for the people. This obedience, in the last instance, is due to the Constitution and the law . . . will have ceased being an absolute requirement if there are abuses in the exercise of legal authority . . . when this is done as a result of exotic ideologies . . . or when constitutional prerogatives are used in such a way that they completely cancel out the rights and freedoms of the citizens . . . and since a people cannot, by itself, exercise this right [to resist oppression] because it is unarmed, such attribution is taken by the institutions that it has armed.[6]

Concomitant with this claim was a belief that World War III was already in progress, that it involved a proxy war confrontation between Washington and Moscow, that the struggle was of an ideological nature and that Argentina was, in the 1960s and 1970s, the favored turf.[7]

Irrational as these conspiracy theories seem, they help explain the mounting brutality of right-wing violence from 1969 to 1979, and the tendency to broaden the definition of the enemy. Between 1969 and 1973 guerrilla combatants and their legal counsel shared the brunt of right-wing attacks. As the conspiracy theories became more intricate, activists in unions, universities, political parties, factories, as well as journalists and artists, came under the right's telescopic sight.

Violence During the Argentine Revolution

As table 5.1 reveals, during the Onganiato violence was exercised by a variety of rightist groups. In spite of the high percentage of unclaimed attacks, it would be accurate to state that the paramilitaries were far more active than the Peronist groups. Paramilitary activity accounts for 22.4 percent of all right-wing violence during this period, and it is quite likely that deaths squads were responsible for a substantial portion of unclaimed kidnappings and deaths.

These early death squads seemed to have appeared and vanished with equal celerity, after staging a handful of operations. It is likely that the same individuals

Table 5.1. Right-Wing Violence, January 1, 1969–May 24, 1973

	Attacks on property	Seizures (%)	Bombings (%)	Kidnap- (%)	Deaths (%)	Total (%)
Nationalist Restorationist Guard	—	0.49	1.95	—	—	2.44
National University Concentration	—	—	—	—	0.49	0.49
Tacuara	—	—	2.44	—	—	2.44
Total, Peronist Right	—	0.49	4.39	—	0.49	5.37
Alpha 66	—	—	—	—	0.49	0.49
Anti-Communist Repression Commando	—	—	1.95	—	—	1.95
Argentine Nationalist Action	—	—	0.49	—	—	0.49
Argentine Nationalist Organization	—	—	0.49	—	—	0.49
Armed Nationalist Security Organization	—	—	0.97	—	—	0.97
Corrientes Anti-Communist Revolutionary Commando	0.49	—	—	—	—	0.49
Enough	—	—	0.49	—	—	0.49
June 30 Commando	—	—	—	0.97	0.97	1.94
Liberators of America Commando	—	—	—	0.97	0.97	1.94
Movement for National Defense	—	—	0.49	—	—	0.49
Nationalist Argentine Movement	—	—	1.46	0.97	—	2.43
National Phalanx	—	—	—	0.97	—	0.97
Nokinoto Laundry	0.49	—	—	—	—	0.49
Organized National Argentine Movement	—	—	0.97	0.97	—	1.94
Police commando	—	—	6.83	—	—	6.83
Total, Paramilitary Squads	0.98	—	14.14	4.85	2.43	22.40
Army	—	0.49	—	—	—	0.49
Navy rebellion	—	0.49	—	—	0.49	0.98
Military error	—	—	—	—	2.44	2.44
Police error	—	—	—	—	0.49	0.49
Unknown	3.90	0.97	36.10	16.59	10.24	67.80
Total	4.88	2.44	54.63	21.44	16.58	99.97
	N = 10	N = 5	N = 112	N = 44	N = 34	N = 205

Source: Contemporary press reports.

belonged to various groups at different times. And, even in the absence of concrete proof, the assumption made at the time was that these early death squads were staffed partly or wholly by active duty members of the security forces.[8] The scant information on these groups comes from their communiqués to the press, which would be normally issued after a specific attack, when the group would announce that one of its "platoons" or "commandos" (which usually took the name of a victim of guerrilla violence) had been responsible for the operation. The Peronist groups are better known, in particular Tacuara, formed in 1958. The original tacuaristas were fanatically Catholic and anti-Semitic young men from impoverished upper-class and upper-middle-class families who organized themselves in neighborhood groups called forts. Most of their early activity was geared against Jewish organizations and individuals. In the early 1960s splinter factions of Tacuara formed two orthodox Peronist groups, the National University Concentration and the Nationalist Restorationist Guard.[9]

Bombings were by far the favored operation. Kidnappings and deaths were also fairly frequent, but attacks on property and seizures were of only marginal importance. A comparison of the activity of Peronist groups and death squads reveals a certain division of labor, both in the types of operations favored and in the chosen targets. Kidnappings and deaths were by and large the preserve of paramilitaries, with the exception of the murder of one student activist in Mar del Plata by the National University Concentration. And although the Peronist groups restricted their attacks to the universities, paramilitary groups focused on three different targets. Most of those who were kidnapped and killed were left-wing activists, in some cases members of guerrilla groups. In fact, the first recorded use of the word "disappeared" in this sense occurred in connection with the kidnapping of ERP member Luis Pujals in September 1971. Bombings and attacks on property were directed in the vast majority of cases against the homes or offices of lawyers defending political prisoners, although theaters showing plays or films that the paramilitary groups considered reprehensible— including the musicals *Jesus Christ Superstar* and *Godspell* and the film *Last Tango in Paris*—were also targeted.

Also included in the tables are certain violent acts which were not the responsibility of paramilitary squads or Peronist groups. This is the case with the Army's seizure of a broadcast station in Mendoza and of a Navy rebellion which resulted in the seizure of the Navy Mechanics School (Escuela de Mecánica de la Armada or ESMA) and the death of a noncommissioned officer. There were also a number of "mistake" killings, which were to become a constant from 1969 to 1979. Mistake killings normally occurred outside military establishments and the presidential palace in Buenos Aires, and the victims would usually be driving by. In the case of military establishments, they were shot at after failing to comply with an order to stop their cars; in contrast, those killed outside the presidential palace failed to comply with the signs requesting that cars not stop on the perimeter of the compound.

Violence During the Peronist Interregnum

After 1973, violence continued to be employed by a panoply of rightist groups. As table 5.2 shows, there was an increase in the number of active Peronist organizations, even though their share in the total volume of violence decreased. This mushrooming of right-wing Peronist groups reflected two important developments within the Peronist movement: the growing importance of youth sectors and their left-wing orientation. Perón had originally structured his following around three subdivisions, called the Trade Union, Political, and Female "branches." The massive incorporation of young people into the Peronist ranks in the late sixties made it necessary to institutionalize a fourth branch for youth. Because the majority of these young newcomers to Peronism adhered to the Montoneros through the group's front organizations, it became imperative to provide a counterweight to this leftist trend. To the Peronist Youth the right opposed the Peronist Youth of the Argentine Republic. Faced with the Peronist Working Youth, the general secretary of the labor confederation created the Peronist Trade Union Youth. At the universities, the Peronist University Youth was confronted with the National University Concentration. The Organizational Command had a longer pedigree, since its members originally belonged to the Peronist Youth. In 1957, during the Resistance, the latter reorganized itself into "commands"—finances, press, organization. In 1960 all the members of this last one broke off from the Peronist Youth and adopted the name of Organizational Command.[10]

These right-wing organizations were known collectively as "orthodox youth" or "orthodox Peronist youth." It would be more accurate to think of them as shock troops. First, they were wholly unrepresentative of the youth movement, which massively supported the Revolutionary Tendency. Second, they did not evince any concern for the interests of their alleged constituents.[11] Third, there was significant cross-membership between Peronist right and paramilitary organizations. Active duty policemen were members of the National University Concentration, and prominent members of the group served as bodyguards to the head of the Metalworkers' Union. Members of the Peronist Trade Union Youth participated in the police rebellion that led to the forced resignation of Córdoba's governor in February 1974, and the top leaders of the Peronist Youth of the Argentine Republic were paid officials in the Ministry of Social Welfare. Members of these orthodox Peronist groups fired the shots that resulted in 16 dead and 433 wounded during the Ezeiza massacre on June 20, 1973. These groups' violent activities were of marginal importance, however, when compared with the death squads. The Peronist right was responsible for 1.66 percent

Table 5.2. Right-Wing Violence, May 25, 1973–March 23, 1976

	Attacks on property (%)	Seizures (%)	Bombings (%)	Kidnap-pings (%)	Deaths (%)	Total (%)
Justicialist Restorationist National Command	—	—	—	—	0.20	0.20
National University Concentration	0.05	0.15	—	0.05	—	0.25
Organizational Command	0.05	0.41	0.15	—	—	0.61
Orthodox Peronism	—	0.10	—	—	—	0.10
Orthodox Peronist Association	—	0.05	—	—	—	0.05
Orthodox Peronist Youth	—	0.05	—	—	—	0.05
Peronist Trade Union Youth	—	0.30	—	—	—	0.30
Peronist Youth of the Argentine Republic	—	0.10	—	—	—	0.10
Total, Peronist right	0.10	1.16	0.15	0.05	0.20	1.66
Anti-Guerrilla Commando	—	0.05	—	—	—	0.05
Argentine Anti-Communist Alliance	0.65	0.15	0.65	1.01	10.66	13.12
Cristina Viola Commando	—	—	0.05	—	0.20	0.25
José Ignacio Rucci Commando	—	0.05	0.05	—	0.10	0.20
Liberators of America Commando	0.05	0.10	0.20	0.10	0.65	1.10
Lt. Col. Duarte Ardoy Commando for Marxist Repression	—	—	—	—	0.05	0.05
Mazorca	—	—	—	—	0.05	0.05

Continued on next page

Table 5.2.—*Continued*

	Attacks on property (%)	Seizures (%)	Bombings (%)	Kidnap-pings (%)	Deaths (%)	Total (%)
Morality Junta	—	—	0.15	—	—	0.15
Moralizing Commando	—	—	0.05	—	—	0.05
Total, Paramilitary squads	0.70	0.35	1.15	1.11	11.71	15.02
Ezeiza massacre	—	—	—	—	0.81	0.81
Army	—	0.05	—	—	—	0.05
Police	—	0.05	—	—	—	0.05
Police error	—	—	—	—	0.41	0.41
Unknown	2.42	0.25	11.98	21.88	45.47	82.00
Total	3.22	1.86	13.28	23.04	58.60	100
	$N = 64$	$N = 37$	$N = 264$	$N = 458$	$N = 1,165$	$N = 1,988$

Source: Contemporary press reports.

of all violence during the period, whereas paramilitary operations accounted for 15.02 percent (table 5.2), a figure that could be much higher considering that most unclaimed kidnappings were probably the work of paramilitary groups, and unclaimed deaths almost certainly were. Death squads, particularly the Triple A, operated with a distinct style, which is why certain press descriptions of the state in which corpses had been found would point to paramilitary responsibility: collective graves with two or more bodies; disfigured faces; and hands cut off or fingertips burned to prevent identification.

There are only two death squads on which information is available: the Liberators of America Commando and the Argentine Anti-Communist Alliance or Triple A. The former has been alternatively characterized as "a death squad which operated in 1974–6, reputedly linked to the Army in Córdoba," "the Córdoba version of the Triple A," and "the Triple A [which] changed its name." [12] The Liberators of America Commando did, in fact, center its activity in the province of Córdoba between 1975 and 1976, but because it operated alongside the Triple A, it seems likely that the two were separate organizations. The Triple A, which was clearly the most active death squad, came into being as a result of a convergence of interests between José López Rega and Alberto Villar. López Rega had become Perón's private secretary in 1971 and was appointed Minister of Social Welfare in 1973. Villar, who had organized the Federal Police Anti-Guerrilla Brigade during the Argentine Revolution, was discharged from the force under a cloud but recalled as Chief Commissioner by Perón. [13]

Details about the membership and internal structure of the Triple A were revealed by two former members. [14] López Rega and Villar created an organization staffed by two distinct groups: active service policemen as well as former police officers dishonorably discharged on allegations of theft, smuggling, drug trafficking, and the like, and personnel attached to the Ministry of Social Welfare as advisers to the minister, bodyguards, or employees of its administrative divisions.[15] López Rega, the undisputed leader, stood at the apex of a structure divided into five sections: coordination with the police, administration, vehicles, medical services, and printing. Two sections were accountable to the minister through "links"[16]: one dealt with finances and psychological action and the other organized "the executors," the groups of three to five men in charge of the killings. Money was not in short supply, so arms were bought in Paraguay and the magazine *El Caudillo* was launched. The magazine's offices would operate as the Triple A's headquarters.[17] The organization was officially launched on November 21, 1973, with an assassination attempt on senator Hipólito Solari Yrigoyen. Threatening letters bearing the letter *A* were sent to numerous people in the following week. From then on the Triple A carried out three main tasks. First, it published death lists of personalities in the arts and sciences as well as in politics who were suspected of left-wing sympathies and were "invited" to leave the country. Second, it attempted to control labor militancy through repression. Third, it aimed at the elimination of the regime's opponents.[18]

Evidence of the participation of active service members of the security forces in the Triple A is conclusive. Of 159 alleged members,[19] 66 belonged to the security forces before participating in the Triple A's activities. After 1976, 18 of those 159 were denounced as torturers at various clandestine centers, 5 continued their careers in the armed forces, 43 in the police, and 4 went on to work for the intelligence services. The evidence also suggests that as an institution the armed forces were fully aware of the origins and activities of the Triple A.[20] Also, although death squad activity during the Onganiato should be viewed as vigilantism, the Triple A made the first large-scale attempt at illegal repression. Most important, it was the weapon of a constitutionally elected government which set the precedent that the response to armed struggle could combine the Criminal Code with paramilitary units.[21]

A look at the overall totals in table 5.2 reveals that deaths accounted for over half of all violence during the period. Once more, kidnappings and bombings were fairly frequent and attacks on property and seizures almost negligible. This is also true of paramilitary activity alone. But seizures represented the most frequent operation of the Peronist right, accounting for 69.88 percent of all Peronist violence and 62.37 percent of all seizures. A significant number of seizures by the Peronist right (14 out of 23) occurred in 1973 and coincided with the seizure frenzy described in chapter 4, indicating that at the time the tendency to resort to direct action and take the law into one's own hands was widespread throughout the political spectrum.[22]

Between 1969 and 1973 paramilitary units were responsible for most of the kidnappings and deaths, and though this was also true after 1973, the principal victims changed. Violence still focused on individuals loosely described as "leftists"—alleged guerrillas, activists in Montonero front organizations, in left-wing parties and in unions. But after 1973 journalists, artists, former officials in the Cámpora administration, and relatives of guerrilla combatants were also threatened. Another feature highlighted in connection with the 1969–73 period was a division of labor between Peronists and paramilitaries when it came to selecting the sites for their attacks. This was not the case after 1973. Between 1973 and 1976 attacks were staged against: political organizations: parties, unions, and locales belonging to the Revolutionary Tendency; the media: radio and television stations and newspapers; cultural centers including universities, other institutions of higher education, and theaters; public buildings like government offices and hospitals; private homes and offices; private businesses, and bars. The last three were targeted almost exclusively by paramilitary groups. The first four seem to have attracted equal attention from both sectors.

The Dirty War

For seven years following the 1976 coup that deposed Isabel Perón, Argentina was ruled once more by its armed forces. This period is known as the dirty war because the military introduced the methodology of disappearances, which they applied on a national scale.[23] Though the dirty war continued through 1983, when the military relinquished power to a civilian administration, 1976–79 was the height of the campaign of terror: 98.38 percent of all kidnappings and 98.3 percent of all deaths from 1976 to 1983 occurred between 1976 and 1979.[24] Following the coup, the Peronist right vanished from the scene, as did death squads like those described elsewhere in this chapter, with the exception of two kidnappings by the Triple A (see table 5.3).[25] The distinctive feature of this period is that the armed and security forces became one gigantic killing machine. To speak about death squads in this context is meaningless.

After 1976 the vast majority of right-wing attacks went unclaimed. A distinction should be made, however, between attacks on property and bombings, about which we know nothing, and kidnappings and deaths, where the only thing we do not know is what branch of the state's security apparatus was responsible for each individual act of violence. Of the 35 attacks on property and bombings during this period, 21 were staged against Jewish cultural and religious organizations, homes, and businesses. Also targeted were the universities, offices of lawyers defending political prisoners, and the homes of artists and relatives of guerrilla combatants. But the dirty war was waged primarily against persons and not property: kidnappings and deaths represent 99.75 percent of all violence during the period.

Table 5.3. Right-Wing Violence, March 24, 1976–December 31, 1979

	Attacks on property (%)	Seizures (%)	Bombings (%)	Kidnap-pings (%)	Deaths (%)	Total (%)
Argentine Anti-Communist Alliance	—	—	—	0.02	—	0.02
Military error	—	—	—	—	0.01	0.01
Unknown	0.09	—	0.16	52.32	47.40	99.97
Total	0.09	—	0.16	52.34	47.41	100
	$N = 12$		$N = 23$	$N = 7{,}342$	$N = 6{,}651$	$N = 14{,}028$

Sources: Contemporary press reports and Comisión Nacional sobre la Desaparición de Personas, *Anexos del Informe de la Conadep* (Buenos Aires: Eudeba, 1985).

The organization of the dirty war is described in a number of directives issued between 1975 and 1979—the Defense Council Directive 1/75 (Fight against subversion) and three directives by the Army Chief of Staff: 404/75 (Fight against subversion), 504/77 (Continuation of the offensive against subversion in the period 1977–78), and 604/79 (Continuation of the offensive against subversion).[26] A number of "partial orders" and "rectifications," obviously classified secret and distributed in limited numbers, delineate territorial divisions, establish a chain of command for each division, and detail the manner in which operations should be conducted.

The entire country was divided into four zones (1, 2, 3, and 5) that coincided with the jurisdictions of the different Army Corps.[27] Each zone was in turn divided into subzones, areas, and subareas. Eventually a zone 4 was created to the north of the city of Buenos Aires.[28] Within each zone, primary responsibility in the counterinsurgency effort fell to the Army. The Navy and Air Force retained jurisdiction over their bases and buildings, until and unless they received specific requests from the Army. Operations were defined as "establishing procedures to be followed according to whether one is dealing with planned targets or opportunity targets." A planned target "is the product of the gathering, assessment and processing of available information, which materializes in a concrete objective." An opportunity target "is that which is localized after an operation has begun, and which has not been previously considered, analyzed or planned."[29] There is no direct reference to the use of illegal methods in these directives, nor is there mention of the Task Forces (Grupos de Tareas or GTs). In the literature, task forces tend to refer to all personnel involved in illegal repression. Yet there were four Grupos de Tareas created shortly after the 1976 coup which operated in the jurisdiction of the First Army Corps (zones 1 and 4 in the directives).[30] GTs seem to have operated under functional specialization. GT 1 (Army) dealt with the ERP, GT 2 (Air Force) with the smaller guerrilla groups, GT 3 (Navy) with the Montoneros, and GT 4 (Federal Police) with the Montoneros and the ERP.

Illegal repression was organized around the clandestine detention centers (*centros clandestinos de detención* or CCDs).[31] A complex argot developed around the operation of these CCDs. A kidnapping or "sucking" began when the task force or "gang" took the victim to a clandestine detention center or "hole." Chained and hooded ("partitioned"), the prisoner remained in the "lion's den" awaiting interrogation. In a few cases the prisoner was held in the lion's den for several days and then freed. The vast majority headed for the "operating rooms" for their first torture session. The most popular torture method was the "machine" or electric prod.[32] The prisoner was made to lie down on a metallic board (the "grill") and electric shocks were applied with a metal prod all over his body. After torture, prisoners were moved to the cells, appropriately called "kennels." Still chained and "partitioned," they lived in the most appalling conditions. Aside from subsequent torture sessions, beatings and sexual abuse were commonplace. Prisoners made to join the "Council" enjoyed certain advantages: they dispensed with chains and partitions, they were allowed to bathe more frequently, and they were not confined to their cells. Two types of prisoners formed the "Council": those in charge of activities related to the upkeep of the camp, and those who agreed to collaborate with the repressive apparatus and "went boating," driving around with their captors in order to pinpoint former political associates in guerrilla groups or in student and labor organizations who were then seized.

The time the prisoners spent in the camps ranged from weeks to years. Their departure took place in one of three different manners. The prisoners could be placed "at the disposal of the National Executive Power," that is to say, sent to a "legal" jail. Even though legalization was supposed to be a first step toward freedom, 177 of the 5,182 persons placed at the disposal of the National Executive Power disappeared after the courts had ordered their release.[33] Prisoners were also directly released from the clandestine detention centers. Finally, most prisoners were "transferred," that is to say, eliminated. Communiqués were sent to the press stating that prisoners had been killed while attempting to escape.[34] Guerrillas supposed to have died in battles in which the security forces surprisingly suffered no casualties were seen at different clandestine detention centers before being summarily shot. Other transfer methods involved dropping drugged prisoners from a plane into the sea, incineration, and collective burials.[35]

The clandestine detention center at the ESMA deserves separate mention. It was there that the first "rehabilitation process" was launched in mid-1977.[36] Originally conceived by Captain Jorge Acosta, intelligence chief for the Navy's GT, the rehabilitation process involved the use of prisoner intellectual manpower in the service of Admiral Emilio Massera's political ambitions. Prisoners in the

"Staff" and the "Ministaff" worked in a special area of the camp known as the "Fishbowl." Ministaff members collaborated in the GT's repressive activities. Work on the Staff involved translating foreign publications, organizing a library, classifying and filing foreign press releases, and writing monographs on geopolitical issues. Staff and Ministaff members were all prominent former Montoneros whom Massera called his "left-wing advisors." When Admiral Armando Lambruschini replaced Massera as the Navy's Chief of Staff in 1978, the Staff continued to work for the latter both at the Fishbowl and at Massera's office in downtown Buenos Aires. And even though rehabilitation was not a policy that the Navy or the other two services approved of, General Leopoldo Galtieri embarked on a similar experiment in 1977–78 during his stint as Commander of the Second Army Corps. Based at the Quinta de Funes, a weekend house in suburban Rosario city, Galtieri's project was geared toward "Operation Mexico": the assassination of members of the Montonero National Leadership living in Mexico City by a commando group composed of Army officers and Montonero turncoats. As soon as the group arrived in Mexico City, Montonero Tulio Valenzuela defected and held a press conference. The plan collapsed and the Quinta de Funes experiment was terminated.[37]

6

Patterns of Violence Compared

The previous three chapters discussed different types of violence in Argentina as isolated events. Even though this was intended to facilitate the analysis, a full understanding of any one of the three types discussed must include some reference to the wider context of violence in which it took place. The pages that follow analyze the impact of any one type of violence on the other two, and in particular the effect of collective violent protest and paramilitary violence on the militarization of armed struggle.

Armed Struggle and Collective Violent Protest

Several of my guerrilla interviewees labeled themselves "the Cordobazo generation," an expression that pointed to the belief that the intensity of collective protest during the Onganiato, taken as a sign that revolution was at hand, had a considerable impact on their decision to join a guerrilla group. Guerrilla rhetoric usually posits three relationships between armed struggle and collective violent protest (or, to be more precise, mass politicization, of which collective protest is one expression). First, the guerrillas claim that armed struggle "results from the pressure of the masses," which is to say that it is a response to increased levels of collective protest. Second, guerrillas claim that armed struggle "accompanies the development of mass struggles" and is supposed to match and not supersede collective protest. Third, armed struggle is expected to work as a "motor of the masses" and produce increased levels of collective protest. Figure 6.1 portrays the evolution of collective violent protest and armed struggle. As the figure shows, the relationship between the two was not as direct as that posited by the guerrillas.

That the Cordobazo had a direct impact on the motivation of would-be guerrillas is probably true, for there was a substantial increase in the intensity of
armed struggle between 1969 and 1970. It is impossible, however, to substantiate the guerrillas' claim that armed struggle "results from the pressure of the
masses," because armed struggle and collective violent protest emerged in 1969,
and preparations to launch armed struggle had been under way for some years.
If, as the guerrillas claimed, armed struggle should "accompany the development of mass struggles," it fulfilled its purpose between 1970 and 1973, when
both types of violence develop along parallel lines. That armed struggle peaked
in 1974–76 following a decline in the levels of collective protest suggests the
guerrillas were no longer "interpreting" or "accompanying" the masses.

The idea that armed struggle spurs the masses to action seems to have been
verified between 1970 and 1973. But collective violent protest declined after
1971, whereas armed struggle rose steadily in 1972–74 and declined marginally in 1974–76. There are three likely explanations for this. First, it could be
argued that the guerrillas mistook for revolutionary fervor what was actually a
popular reaction to the Onganiato and its policies.[1] This was partly true, though
it minimizes the significance of the questioning of all forms of authority that collective protest entailed before and after 1973. Second, guerrilla intervention in
collective struggles, infrequent though it was, had a dampening effect on popular
combativeness. An activist among Córdoba slum dwellers remembers that "we
had managed to call a meeting of over five hundred inhabitants so that we could
resolve collectively the disastrous state of ditches, running water and sewage.
Suddenly, an ERP commando appeared in a truck to hand out water pumps, in
Robin Hood or charitable style. We were very angry, because that robinhoodian
attitude limited popular initiatives."[2] During a labor conflict, the kidnapping
or killing of a labor relations executive or the bombing of the factory by the
guerrillas could (and on occasions did) force management to give in to labor's
demands. In the long run, by setting the precedent that interlopers could wage
labor's battles, these actions could only damage labor's resolve and unity. Quite
probably they also weakened the position of the combativos, the labor leadership fighting the entrenched union bureaucracy. Alvaro Abós, a Peronist attorney
with lifelong experience as legal counsel and advisor to different unions, argues
that the guerrillas never understood the unions and their functioning and that
guerrilla activity connected with the union movement had an effect contrary to
the one desired, namely that of legitimizing the union bureaucracy.[3]

Finally, the theory of "the worse, the better" did not work as the guerrillas
anticipated. According to this theory, espoused by the Basque ETA as well as
by Argentine guerrillas, sustained guerrilla action would precipitate state repression, which would in turn catalyze popular combativeness and support for armed
struggle. Proponents of the theory never contemplated two likely scenarios. If,
as was the case in Spain, repression concentrated on armed organizations, there

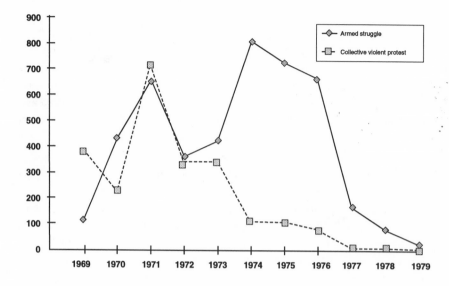

Source: Contemporary press reports.

Figure 6.1. Incidents of Armed Struggle and Collective Violent Protest, 1969–79

would be no significant increase in popular support for the insurgents. In the case of Argentina, the theory could have applied before 1974. It could not but fail once the Triple A went into action because the extralegal response to armed struggle tended to strike randomly at those within reach, at activists in mass organizations. Instead of increasing the levels of popular combativeness, the activities of the Triple A and other paramilitary squads had a paralyzing effect on all forms of collective action.

Did collective violence play any part in the militarization of armed struggle? Analysts of two other student-dominated armed organizations, the Red Brigades and the Baader-Meinhof Gang, stress the connection between a cycle of collective protest and the birth of such groups. In both Italy and Germany, armed struggle was a response to the apparent failure of collective protest.[4] This was not the case in Argentina. Both armed struggle and collective violent protest emerged in 1969 and developed along parallel lines up to 1973 (see figure 6.1). The militarization of armed struggle after 1973 cannot be explained as a response to the defeat of popular struggles. Furthermore, although the levels of collective protest declined after 1973, that protest was still significant from 1973 to 1975. The seizure frenzy of 1973, the active strikes, the combativo and clasista union militancy described in chapter 4 show that popular struggles were alive and well beyond 1973. The end of the cycle of protest (and of the acute societal politicization begun during the Onganiato) came in 1975, with the murder of activists by the Triple A and the government's intervention in the unions. The Jornadas de Julio that led to the ouster of López Rega were the swan song of collective protest. By that time, the militarization of guerrilla groups was irreversible.

Armed Struggle and Right-Wing Violence

The consolidation of democracy in Argentina will to some extent depend on the country's ability to come to terms with its recent past. A joint evaluation of armed struggle and right-wing violence is part and parcel of that effort. The administration of Raúl Alfonsín (1983–89) attempted to move in that direction when it formulated the theory of the two demons, also known as the "theory of the two terrorisms," which held that armed struggle and state terror were two sides of the same coin, and that condemnation of the latter should extend to the former, which preceded it and justified it.[5]

The theory first received official sanction a few days after Alfonsín's inaugural in December 1983, when the president ordered the prosecution of the nine junta members who had ruled the country since 1976, and of seven former guerrilla leaders.[6] The guerrillas were all living in exile and escaped immediate prosecution. The military were tried in 1985, and after the Juntas Trial, the commanders of different Army corps and some of their subordinates were put on trial, so that by 1987 about 400 officers were being prosecuted.[7] In a similar vein, the prologue to the final report by the National Commission on the Disappearance of Persons (presented to the president in September 1984) states that "during the 1970s Argentina was convulsed by a terror that emanated both from the extreme right and the extreme left, . . . to the terrorists' crimes the Armed Forces responded with a terrorism infinitely worse than the one being combated, because since March 24 1976 they counted on the power and impunity of the absolute State."[8] Alfonsín's successor, Carlos Menem (elected in 1989; term expires in 1995), also gave official sanction to the "two terrorisms." In September 1989, Menem pardoned all officers, excluding the nine junta members, who had been or were being prosecuted for human rights violations and for three military rebellions staged in 1987–89. Also pardoned were officers who had been convicted for mismanagement of the Malvinas-Falklands fiasco. The pardon was extended to the guerrillas whose prosecution had been ordered by Alfonsín, as well as to those guerrillas serving terms for convictions between 1976 and 1983.[9]

The "theory of the two terrorisms" has been hotly rejected by various sectors—the armed forces, human rights organizations, and former guerrillas. The debate hinges on whether there were two demons or one, that is to say, on how to individually characterize the behavior of guerrillas and soldiers.

Former guerrillas deny that their activity is terrorism for three reasons. First, they argue that their actions were legitimized by the fact that Onganía had eliminated all channels for legal political participation. Although this is correct, it cannot account for the continuation of armed struggle after 1973. The guerrillas also insist that their actions be analyzed in the context of generalized public contestation of events like the Cordobazo, of which, they argue, armed struggle was a part. This is once more true, but whether it should be interpreted as the guerrillas interpret it—as a sign of unrestricted popular endorsement of armed struggle—is open to debate. Finally, the guerrillas point out that their actions pale by comparison with the atrocities carried out by the security forces after 1976.[10] The military rejects a definition of its actions as terrorism on two counts. First, they argue that the constitutional government of Isabel Perón signed decree S 261, which launched "Operation Independence" in 1975, committing the armed forces to "neutralize and/or annihilate the action of subversive elements" of the ERP's Tucumán foco.[11] Because Isabel Perón was Commander-in-Chief of the armed forces, the military argue it was merely following orders. This application of the principle of "due obedience" does not, however, square with the military's decision to depose its Commander-in-Chief a year later. Second, the military insists on the idea that the fight against terrorism constituted a "war."

On this point it becomes interesting to compare official pronouncements with those of the guerrilla organizations. During the Argentine Revolution and the 1973–76 Peronist government, the guerrillas referred to their activity as the Second War of Independence.[12] As late as 1977 Mario Firmenich declared that "since October 1975 . . . we knew that the coup would occur within the year. We did nothing to stop it. . . . We made however our calculations, war calculations, and we prepared to undergo, in the first year, human losses not inferior to 1,500 units . . . if we managed not to go beyond this level of casualties, we could have the certainty that sooner or later we would win. . . . this year the dictatorship's offensive will end and finally the conditions favorable for our final counteroffensive will present themselves." [13]

That the Montonero rank and file being massacred in Argentina while Firmenich cavorted across Europe might not have shared in his enthusiasm is besides the point. The fact is that the Argentine military were getting this message from the top echelons of an "enemy" military structure. After the coup, the guerrillas changed their vocabulary and started talking about a "resistance." With the benefit of hindsight, both former guerrillas and independent analysts have argued that by 1976 guerrilla activity was in decline and that this was merely the excuse, not the reason for the coup.[14] By contrast, though official statements made before 1976 referred to guerrilla combatants as "extremists" or "terrorist delinquents" (to differentiate them from common criminals), an attempt was made to minimize the impact of guerrilla violence and stress that it could be controlled by the police.[15] After 1976, the conflict was characterized as a war. Even though the military never attempted a systematic elaboration of this notion, it is possible to discern the motives behind this characterization. In justifying the notion of war, the military argued that, according to their estimates, there were twenty-five thousand "subversives" in Argentina organized in clandestine cellular structures capable of staging full-scale attacks against military installations, and that laws sanctioned by Congress in 1973–76 and presidential decrees signed by Isabel Perón proved unable to contain their activities. The military also established a distinction between classical warfare and revolutionary warfare. In the latter, given that armed organizations were "the first to violate human rights," they dictated the tactics the armed forces were to employ, forcing the military to adopt the "previously unknown procedures" characteristic of the dirty war. In this dirty war, actions by every member of the armed forces were considered as carried out in the line of duty and only subject to the judgment of history.[16] These are post facto public rationalizations by the military, even though they constitute the principles on which the "war" was fought.

But was it a "war"? Contrary to general wisdom, the guerrillas were not in retreat by the time of the 1976 coup. In 1975 they had staged 723 operations, and in 1976 they staged 662.[17] But guerrilla operations during 1975, increasingly directed against military installations, resulted in heavy losses for the insurgents and led to their gradual isolation. By the time of the coup the guerrillas had suffered a political, not a military defeat. This could have been exploited by the military through an active propaganda campaign aimed at the general population and through infiltration of the guerrilla movement, thus making the dirty war unnecessary. This issue could be approached from another angle by asking against whom was the dirty war directed. More than 30 percent of disappeared persons are classified as "workers,"[18] which in no way represents the social composition of guerrilla groups. The Argentine military euphemistically refer to torture as "strategic interrogation." There is an obsession with "knowing where the bomb is and defusing it" and "saving lives."[19] And yet 62 percent of all disappeared persons were seized at their homes, in full view of their neighbors,[20] and clearly unable to provide any information on bombs about to explode. The "war" was directed not against the guerrillas but against society at large. The guerrillas did their utmost to provoke this reaction. As an officer explained to his Montonero prisoner, "If you attempt to deprive me of my professional role . . . I have to kill you. An army in operations is an overwhelming machine. You underestimated it. You made a mistake, nobody can destroy the Army."[21] But the guerrillas' behavior alone cannot account for the ferocity unleashed in 1976. Figure 6.2 portrays the evolution of right-wing violence and of armed struggle and collective violent protest considered jointly. The latter two are termed "agitational violence" and the former "enforcement violence," since the curve portrays right-wing Peronist as well as paramilitary violence.[22]

The dirty war was waged as a reaction to the levels of politicization and mobilization displayed by Argentine society in the 1973–76 period. The slum dwellers' movement, the student organizations, and the combativo and clasista unions constituted the "bomb" that the top brass wanted to defuse. The gears in that "overwhelming machine" were the junior officers imbued with mes-

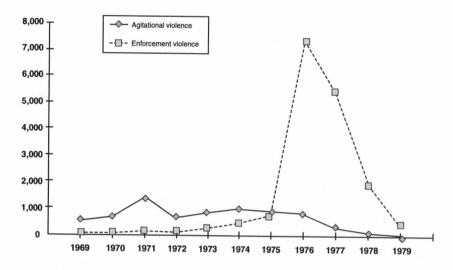

Source: Contemporary press reports.

Figure 6.2. Incidents of Agitational and Enforcement Violence, 1969–79

sianic ideas.[23] Two characteristics of that reaction were its delayed nature and its brutality. Until 1972 there is almost no response to the significant levels of agitational violence. Between 1972 and 1975, enforcement violence rises until it almost matches the steady level of agitational violence. Enforcement violence then peaks in 1976–77. These data support my earlier contention about guerrilla capabilities circa 1976. Confronted with the steep rise in enforcement violence between 1975 and 1976, agitational violence decreases marginally. Because the contribution made by collective violent protest was at this time negligible (74 out of 736 incidents in 1976), it becomes impossible to state that by the time of the coup the guerrillas had already been militarily defeated.

The greatest appeal of the "theory of the two demons" is that it blames two social groups for Argentina's ills over the last two decades. By focusing on the behavior of guerrillas and soldiers, the "two terrorisms" debate leaves out two key participants in the drama: the 1973–76 governments and civil society.

The 1973–76 Peronist governments must be brought to task for their sponsorship of the Triple A death squads. Condemnation of the Peronist administrations has so far been mild and has tended to concentrate on Isabel Perón and her strongman, José López Rega. But condemnation must extend to the revered figure of Juan Perón. Though it is true that the height of Triple A violence occurred after his death in July 1974, Perón's behavior after the Ezeiza massacre indicates that he was fully aware of paramilitary activity and condoned it.[24] In his speech the day after the Ezeiza incidents, he blamed the Revolutionary Tendency for the massacre and talked about "punishment."[25] Four months later, at a meeting with provincial governors, Perón presented a "Reserved Document" which mentioned "the infiltration of marxist groups" within the Peronist movement; and described "a state of war . . . which forces us . . . to attack the enemy on all fronts and with the greatest decisiveness."[26] Between 1973 and 1974 Perón repeatedly met with leaders of the Revolutionary Tendency. During those meetings, duly reported in the press, the Tendency elliptically referred to police repression and Perón ignored the accusations. Around this time, a joke became popular within radicalized circles: Mario Firmenich and Roberto Quieto, numbers one and two within the Montonero hierarchy, were about to be hanged. Just before the execution, one of them told the other, "this must be another of the old man's [Perón's] genialities." And, in response to the activities of the Triple A, graffito at the Department of Humanities of the University of Buenos Aires read, "Lanusse, come back."[27]

The implications of these jokes are serious. An episode of illegal repression automatically weakens the moral standing of a government battling insurgency. Illegal repression may also increase the levels of violence by encouraging retaliation by armed organizations. This happened in Ireland after the Royal Ulster Constabulary killed six Catholic men in late 1982, in circumstances which were never fully explained but which fueled allegations that the security forces had a shoot-to-kill policy. These deaths, and the subsequent acquittal of the only constabulary member tried for these events, provoked a series of attacks by Republican guerrillas, including a savage bombing at Harrods in London. The activities of the Liberation Antiterrorist Groups (Grupos Antiterroristas de Liberación or GAL), a death squad responsible for an estimated 25 deaths in the Basque region of Spain since 1983, have also driven ETA to retaliation killings.[28] But in the Argentine case there were no isolated incidents of illegal repression: the Triple A paramilitaries were engaged in a carefully planned campaign which would help legitimize the continuation of armed struggle under a democratically elected government by providing the guerrillas with the argument of "self-defense."

However, the guerrilla who in chapter 5 remembered that "the Triple A hit hard. Guerrillas were used to being bank employees during the week and guerrillas during the weekend. And the Triple A got you during the weekend," was reminiscing about 1975. The steep rise in enforcement violence after 1975 (see figure 6.2) had two negative effects on armed organizations. It reinforced the perception that the guerrillas were engaged in a "war," in which the enemy's brutality should be responded to in kind. The increase in enforcement violence also strengthened group cohesion, for the guerrilla group protected combatants from the dangers of life above ground. But the various indicators of the development of militarism, the definition of the conflict as a war, the adoption of uniforms and ranks, and the resort to frontal attacks against military installations, were all present after 1973 and well before the groups felt the impact of the Triple A and the dirty war. Although illegal repression contributed to militarism, it was not a causal factor.

Armed Struggle and Argentine Society

Above all, the "two terrorisms" thesis exonerates a radicalized civil society, which first glorified violence as an agent of social change and then justified a ruthless repression as the only means of returning to the statu quo ante. There are two dimensions of societal support for armed struggle: endorsement of the activity as such and endorsement of the objectives that armed struggle is supposed to achieve. There is an additional issue which should be kept in mind even though it might be unconnected with these two dimensions, namely the question of personal loyalties. As one guerrilla interviewee highlighted when questioned about popular support for armed struggle, "at one time everybody had a son, cousin, or friend involved in this party." [29]

In countries with an established tradition of public opinion research it is possible to ascertain whether or not there is support for armed struggle and whether support is given to the resort to violence, to the objectives of the practitioners of that violence, or to both. [30] This is not the case in Argentina. The only existing survey on public attitudes toward armed struggle, conducted in 1971, revealed that the percentage of respondents that found armed struggle "justifiable" was 45.5 in the Greater Buenos Aires area and 49.5 in the interior of the country. In Greater Buenos Aires, 43 percent of upper-class, 43 percent of middle-class, and 37 percent of lower-class respondents justified armed struggle. Support was greater in the interior: 62, 54, and 46 percent, respectively. [31] However, an estimate of the breadth of public support for armed struggle circa 1973 can be made if we consider some additional factors. First, newspaper coverage of the electoral campaign that led to the March 1973 elections does not mention a single instance in which any of the candidates condemned armed struggle. If the candidates refrained from making such pronouncements, they must have felt that the public was in no mood for them. Newspaper records of condemnations of violence by the political class appear in the last quarter of 1974, and focus primarily on the Triple A. [32] Second, it should be remembered that following Cámpora's inaugural on May 25, 1973, Congress unanimously passed an amnesty law for political prisoners, most of whom were at the time known guerrilla combatants. The amnesty was justified on the grounds that the country had suffered a period of political and normative irregularity which rendered convictions for political offenses highly questionable. The culpability of persons convicted for guerrilla activity was never in doubt. This was not an issue. What made these prosecutions objectionable was the unconstitutionality of the courts appointed to hear these cases, as well as the political context in which guerrilla actions had taken place. The congressional vote on the amnesty should also be interpreted as a reflection of the public mood at the time. In fact, according to Cámpora's Interior Minister, Esteban Righi, during preliminary debates prior to the inaugural, legislators fought over different amnesty projects because they considered that political capital was to be gained from being the author of the amnesty law.[33]

Until 1973 support for armed struggle was widespread, but was it an endorsement of the activity or of the practitioners' objectives? Support was probably given to both. There existed at the time a romantic view of guerrillas and a glorification of the instrumental nature of violence. Anyone familiar with works on Argentine politics discussing this period will have come across statements to the effect that it is very difficult to recreate the climate of opinion at the time. When I began this study I naively expected to break this pattern and convey in as lively a style as possible the radicalized atmosphere of the sixties and early seventies. The distance between my expectations and actual achievements is abysmal. I console myself by thinking that this may reflect the limitations of a mainstream social scientific approach to the topic of violence as much as it does my own shortcomings as a writer. A statistical analysis such as the one undertaken in this study was necessary, since discussions on the role of violence in Argentine politics in the sixties and seventies have for too long been based on impressions rather than facts. But a statistical analysis has certain limitations. One of the most fascinating aspects of the study of violent conflict—which the statistics cannot portray—is that an individual's evaluation of surrounding violence is inseparable from, and may be determined by, the political context in which that individual lives. This is true of any political process involving violence and in particular Argentina's in the sixties and seventies.[34]

When the Montoneros went public with the kidnapping and murder of General Aramburu in 1970, broad sectors of the population cheered. Aramburu had orchestrated the coup that deposed Perón in 1955, he had secretly shipped Evita's body to an unmarked grave in Europe, and between 1955 and 1958 he had repressed the Peronist movement. As a former guerrilla put it, the killing of Aramburu "demonstrated that the people could win at least one match."[35] Another former guerrilla remembered: "After [the murder of] Aramburu you could not go to the *barrios* to do political work and say you were a Descamisado. You had to lie and say you were a Montonero because everybody wanted 'to meet the boys in the M.' "[36] That Aramburu's death was entirely justifiable to many seems to be recognized by his own son, who in a television interview said "I have not hesitated to pardon many sectors of Peronism that applauded the death of my father. I still remember very vividly the multitudinous demonstrations by Peronists celebrating the death of my father."[37] The Aramburu case stands as a symbol of public attitudes toward armed struggle between 1969 and 1973. Support for the guerrillas was no doubt linked to the fact that they went into action against a military regime that was responsible for incidents like the "Night of the Long Batons" and the Trelew massacre. It could also be said that in those early years guerrilla operations were mainly geared toward property and not persons, but Montoneros, the guerrilla group that was to overshadow all the others, built its fame on the kidnapping and killing of someone unconnected with the Argentine Revolution and its policies.

By 1976 the public mood had changed. Guillermo O'Donnell reports on informal interviews he conducted between 1978 and 1979, in which respondents from all walks of life remembered Isabel Perón's administration as "primordial chaos" and "something intolerable, compared with which any other regime was better."[38] With the same ease with which some had found deaths like Aramburu's entirely justifiable, others (and probably some of the same individuals) now averted their look while "bolshies" disappeared. Fear was, of course, one reason why Argentinians attempted to ignore the disappearances. It could also be argued, as Robert Cox does in the case of journalists, that feelings of guilt about their radicalization during the Onganiato and after drove many to accept blindly the policies of the 1976 military administration.[39] Most important, this willingness by civil society to overlook the activities of paramilitary groups was a direct consequence of the militarization of armed struggle. It is no accident that during the "Junta's Trial" in 1985 defense counsel argued about "adequately and inadequately kidnapped" persons.[40] After 1976 many held this opinion, expressed by the cliché "the guerrillas are rightfully killed" (*los guerrilleros bien muertos están*). That to this day relatives of disappeared persons attempt to hide the guerrilla identity of the victims points to how widespread this belief must be.

II

The Guerrilla Movement

7

Guerrilla Lives

Perhaps the most fascinating questions in the study of armed struggle revolve around the combatants and their motivations. What are the determinants of violent behavior? Can we speak of a "terrorist personality"? How do the combatants deal with personal relationships? These are the least explored questions, perhaps because it is so difficult to find satisfactory answers to them. In most countries facing armed struggle, newspaper reports provide some information on the guerrillas' background; however, this information is not always reliable. Even when it is, one wonders if this information is statistically significant. The press describes captured or dead guerrillas, but what about those still at large? If providing accurate portraits of the combatants is difficult, analyzing their motivations is even more so—in this case, the guerrillas themselves are the only source to be tapped.[1]

The present chapter describes the Argentine combatants and their motivation. As one of the three factors that explains the militarization of armed struggle after 1973 is the bureaucratization of the groups, which resulted from a substantial increase in membership, the first section estimates the changing membership strength from 1969 to 1979 with a view to assessing how that membership soared after 1973. The second section describes what can be learned about the social origin of combatants through an analysis of the Argentine press. The final section of this chapter discusses my interviews with former combatants. In these life histories the reader will find a full account of the re-socialization process that contributed to the militarization of armed struggle. Combatants joined young and in the company of friends with whom they shared a previous political activism. Together, they reached adulthood and came of age politically. Together, they developed a common identity. The vicissitudes of underground life transformed the organization into a surrogate family. The other factors contributing to the militarization—the development of a manichean view of politics and the bureau-cratization of the groups—are developed more fully in chapter 8. However, these life histories also provide a description of the development of simplistic interpre-tations of reality which helped the combatants cope with political setbacks, and of the establishment of complex structures and rigid authority relations within the groups, all of which reinforced group cohesion. The interviews make clear that even though combatants had qualms about the direction the struggle took after 1973, the thought of leaving the group was almost inconceivable. The bureaucratization of the groups allowed combatants to distance themselves from operational mistakes such as accidental deaths. More important, the combat-ants' identity was tied up with the organization's, and the "friend-foe" view of politics did not leave many options—one belonged to either the revolutionary or the reformist camp.

Estimating Guerrilla Membership

Journalists and scholars have over the years estimated the membership of the Argentine guerrilla groups. Except for one analysis of the Montoneros' peak strength in 1975, these estimates have been advanced without any attempt at rationalization.[2] This "rule of thumb" method resulted in wide discrepancies among the different sources. For example, evaluating total membership for 1975, General Ramón Díaz Bessone talks about 30,000 combatants, a publication from the Center for Legal and Social Studies, a human rights organization, refers to "not more than 2,000 men," and a third source provides separate figures for ERP and Montoneros which add up to an estimated 6,000–8,000 combatants.[3] The present section attempts to provide accurate and rational estimates by rely-ing on a combination of internal guerrilla documents, guerrilla press interviews, and personal interviews with former combatants and members of the security forces.

In 1969, the four groups that coalesced to form the Montoneros counted on a total of approximately 40 members, while the Descamisados had two detach-ments, 20 members. There are no estimates on the 1969 membership of any other group,[4] However, certain inferences can be made. Chapter 2 explained that the 14 members of FAP captured at Taco Ralo in September 1968 constituted the rural contingent, and that the urban contingent, which remained undetected, went into action the following year. As the original plan contemplated the joint launching of a rural and urban campaign, one can assume that both contingents counted on a similar number of combatants.[5] During those early years FAP was the "most Peronist" of the Peronist groups, and had important contacts with union activists and veterans of the Peronist Resistance. For these reasons, I would put FAP membership in 1969 at 30. FAR and FAL were, by their own admission, originally small groups. In the course of an interview, a FAR combatant described the group's original members: "we all knew each other, we were comrades, friends in various political struggles." [6] To the interviewer's query on whether the numerical strength of FAR could be deduced from the frequency of the group's operations at the time, the guerrilla responded, "we fundamentally had audacity and a great disposition towards armed operations and a good technical capacity." [7] FAR and FAL probably started off with 20 members each. Given that the generalized impression at the time was that the ERP was the strongest group,[8] I would put the group's strength in 1969 at 30. This brings total membership in the six major groups to 160. Keeping in mind that in addition to the six armed organizations there were a panoply of groupuscules active at the time,[9] it could be said that armed struggle was launched in 1969 with an approximate 200 combatants.

It is impossible to make even informed guesses about the fluctuations in membership between 1969 and 1972, but the evidence suggests that membership did not vary dramatically during those years. The FAR combatant quoted above admitted as much and talked about "hard blows" (arrests and deaths in action), in particular toward the end of 1970.[10] A former member of FAP estimated the group's membership at 50 in 1970.[11] My interviewee was unable to provide figures for subsequent years, however, by 1971 FAP was in the thick of the "enlightened" versus "obscure" internal debate, which resolved itself when the obscure joined Descamisados and Montoneros. It is therefore unlikely that FAP underwent a rapid increase in membership at this time. The same could be said of FAL, plagued from early in its existence by internal squabbles and the emergence of dissident factions. Descamisados developed slowly but steadily. In 1970 the group had two columns with three detachments each, for a membership of 60. By the time the group fused with the Montoneros in late 1972, it had four columns and a total membership of approximately 120. As for the Montoneros, arrests and deaths following the kidnapping of Pedro Aramburu and the seizure of La Calera in 1970 decimated the organization. Montonero leader Mario Firmenich stated that in 1970, "We were reduced at one point to 20 people holed up in two flats." [12] Subsequent recruitment, inspired by security considerations, was slow. By late 1972 the Montoneros could probably count on 200 members. As the ERP was not rocked by internal debates or crippling casualties, one can assume that by late 1972 the ERP had a membership roughly equivalent to that of the Montoneros. This would put total membership in all armed organizations at 600 by late 1972.

The year 1973 brought about significant changes in membership. By the year's end all other groups would coalesce around the Montoneros and ERP. In addition, in May the Cámpora amnesty freed 371 seasoned combatants who would by and large rejoin their organizations.[13] The amnesty also indirectly facilitated recruitment by allowing the guerrillas to function above ground. It is impossible to account for year-by-year increases in membership, but a fairly accurate estimate of the Montoneros' peak strength in 1975 can be made on the basis of the number of fighting columns that the group had at the time. Daniel Frontalini and María Cristina Caiati, the only authors to provide a rationalization for their estimates, add the number of safehouses under the jurisdiction of each one of the ten Montonero columns, presume 1.5 inhabitants per safehouse, and arrive at a total Montonero membership of 1,428.[14] My calculations are also based on ten Montonero columns in 1975. My interviewees stated there were 300 combatants per column, which would result in 3,000 members. These were "territorials," combatants assigned to operate in a specific area. But in addition to the territorials the Montoneros had "professionals," individuals devoted to skills like forging identity cards, gathering intelligence, or manufacturing explosives. Estimating the strength of the professionals is very difficult, but on the basis of the limited manpower with which Rodolfo Walsh operated the Montoneros' intelligence department, it is likely that there were no more than 500 professionals nationwide, which would put total Montonero strength at 3,500.

ERP membership during this period is a matter for speculation. The "peronization" of Argentine youth determined that the ERP could in no way match Montonero recruitment after 1973. In addition, the decision to open the rural front in Tucumán in 1974 meant that the ERP had to keep siphoning combatants to that area and, to some extent, recruitment was offset by heavy casualties in Tucumán.[15] An evaluation of the ERP's peak strength in 1975, however, must take into account the combined series of operations that the group staged during the night of December 23 of that year, which involved an estimated 300 combatants. The most important of these was the attempt to seize the 601 Arsenal Battalion in Buenos Aires. The attempt failed and is said to have resulted in 100 guerrilla deaths, including summary executions, though neither the guerrillas nor the security forces have been willing to disclose details. Deducing an armed organization's numerical strength on the basis of the number of combatants involved in a given operation can be misleading. The Montoneros, on whom there exists fairly accurate information, provide a case in point. On the basis of the number of participants involved in the kidnapping of Aramburu in May 1970, and the seizure of La Calera in July, one could presume that the Montoneros were at the time a sizable group, but this was not the case. A group could conceivably decide to utilize most of its personnel in a given operation in the hope of conveying a false impression of strength. In the case of the ERP, however, the events of December 23, 1975, must be factored in, if only to point out that in spite of the constant manpower drain in Tucumán between 1974 and 1976, the group could mobilize impressive forces in 1975 and continue operating in 1976 in spite of the heavy losses. Based on this, I estimate an ERP membership of 1,500 in 1975.[16]

These two estimates combined reveal a peak guerrilla membership of 5,000 in 1975. And even though it is impossible to account for year-by-year membership increases in the 1973–75 period, the peak 1975 membership figures probably reflected recruitment taking place primarily during 1973, when armed organizations were basking in the glow of the amnesty and enjoyed the prestige of having played a vital role in the Onganiato's demise.[17] It is doubtful that the Montoneros did much recruiting after the breakup with Perón during the May Day rally in 1974, or that the ERP lured many new adherents after the rural campaign started in Tucumán, also in May 1974. Consequently we can say that armed struggle was launched with 200 combatants in 1969, that by late 1972 total membership was 600, and that even though it is possible to document a peak membership of 5,000 by 1975, that figure probably reflects mid-1974 membership levels. The bureaucratization of the groups originates in this substantial increase in membership and in the need to organize this massive following.

Evaluations on the numerical strength of the groups after the 1976 coup must be considered speculative. In a 1978 interview, Montonero Rodolfo Galimberti stated that fatalities since the March 1976 coup amounted to "70 percent of our militants, that is 4,000 deaths," and that recruitment had offset 45 percent of post-coup fatalities.[18] Even though my interviewees were reticent about providing figures on post-coup membership, three of them put the fatality rate at 80 percent, and so did a PRT-ERP document published in 1979.[19] Given the methodology applied by the security forces, these estimates appear accurate.[20] Galimberti's claim notwithstanding, it is unlikely that there was much recruitment after 1976. Therefore, speculating on 80 percent fatalities, by 1979 membership would have fallen to 1,000–700 Montoneros and 300 members of ERP.

Who Were the Guerrillas?

In order to obtain biographical data on the guerrillas I read eleven years of Argentine dailies (January 1, 1969–December 31, 1979). The information obtained is summarized in tables 7.1 and 7.2. Before turning to an evaluation of the data, a few clarifications are in order.

First, the final figure of 3,860 guerrillas captured or killed between 1969 and 1979 includes 126 names which are repeated. Some guerrillas captured during the Onganiato were amnestied in 1973 and subsequently recaptured or killed. Others escaped from prison or were released on insufficient evidence, and eventually were imprisoned again or killed. Second, the quality of the information changed over time. During the early years, press descriptions of combatants were fairly detailed, providing occupation, age, sometimes even marital status, and address. As guerrilla casualties mounted, information became scarcer. In addition, whereas originally the guerrillas' full names would be furnished, beginning in 1974 press coverage sometimes referred to "ten extremists captured"

Table 7.1. Guerrilla Casualties, 1969–79

	1969–72 (%)	1973–75 (%)	1976–79 (%)	1969–79 (%)
Outcome				
Captured	90.02	83.84	28.88	62.41
Disappeared	0.64	0.71	—	0.41
Killed in Action	9.34	15.29	71.12	37.10
Internal Execution	—	0.16	—	0.08
Total	100	100	100	100
Location				
Federal Capital	6.16	4.59	2.63	3.99
Buenos Aires	22.29	26.05	47.63	34.30
Córdoba	15.92	12.51	13.67	13.39
Santa Fe	19.11	7.26	14.83	11.76
Entre Ríos	0.21	—	0.64	0.29
Corrientes	—	0.44	0.06	0.23
Misiones	—	—	0.26	0.10
Chaco	—	5.08	2.63	3.47
Formosa	—	1.53	0.13	0.78
Santiago del Estero	1.27	1.42	0.26	0.93
Tucumán	15.08	23.10	7.70	15.91
Salta	1.06	2.89	1.16	1.97
Jujuy	—	1.69	—	0.80
Catamarca	—	0.71	—	0.34
La Rioja	—	0.98	—	0.47
San Juan	0.43	0.22	0.64	0.41
San Luis	—	0.27	0.45	0.31
Mendoza	5.10	4.81	1.80	3.63
La Pampa	—	0.66	—	0.31
Neuquén	—	—	0.32	0.13
Río Negro	—	—	—	—
Chubut	4.03	—	0.45	0.67
Santa Cruz	—	0.38	0.19	0.26
Foreign countries	—	—	0.83	0.34
Undetermined	9.34	5.41	3.72	5.21
Total	100	100	100	100
Group				
ERP	41.40	18.19	9.37	17.46
FAL	13.59	0.22	—	1.76
FAP	6.16	1.25	—	1.35
FAR	5.94	3.28	—	2.28
Descamisados	—	—.	—	—
Montoneros	11.89	8.90	43.00	23.03
Other	2.55	4.26	1.61	2.98
Undetermined	18.47	63.90	46.02	51.14
Total	100	100	100	100
	N = 471	N = 1,831	N = 1,558	N = 3,860

Source: Contemporary press reports.

or "five subversives killed." This tendency became more pronounced after the 1976 coup, when the press obtained all its information on guerrilla activity directly from the commanders of the military corps. In these cases, newspapers would normally mention the province where the "extremists" were captured or killed. Sometimes, the individuals' sex, the guerrilla group they belonged to, and their rank would also be given. The 1,492 cases of "nameless guerrillas" between 1974 and 1979 represent 38.65 percent of all combatants mentioned by the press in the 1969–79 period. It would be tempting to assume that the 1,492 "subversives" were not in fact guerrillas but merely leftists used as pawns by a government (civilian or military) interested in magnifying the threat posed by armed struggle or in justifying the incarceration of dissidents. If that were the case, given the estimates on guerrilla membership provided above, we would have to say that combatants showed a remarkable ability to remain undetected, yet this was far from true. Several guerrilla interviewees and persons affiliated with human rights groups stated that while state terror frequently struck the population randomly, it decimated the guerrilla ranks with surgical precision.[21] It is therefore likely that the "nameless guerrillas" were in fact members of armed organizations who suffered fates different from those described in the press.

In the vast majority of cases guerrillas appeared in the newspapers when they were captured or killed in combat. The press records three cases of guerrillas executed by their own organization, all ERP members turned police informers who provided the security forces with advance warnings on attacks in Buenos Aires and Tucumán, operations that resulted in heavy losses for the ERP. The organization found the culprits, staged "revolutionary trials," executed them, and notified the press. From 1969 to 1979 there may have been similar cases which were not reported to the press, but given the Argentine guerrillas' thirst for publicity this does not seem likely. Newspapers also report a few cases of guerrillas disappearing during the Onganiato and the Peronist administrations. These figures appear to be accurate. During both periods there were a number of radical weeklies which never failed to denounce disappearances, and there are no discrepancies between these weeklies and the dailies' press reports. There are no newspaper reports on guerrilla disappearances after the March 1976 coup, which is only logical given that newspapers merely transcribed communiqués issued by the different military corps. In this context, the figure of 71.12 percent of guerrillas killed in action must be seriously questioned.

After 1976, press coverage of raids on guerrilla safehouses, or of skirmishes between guerrillas and the security forces, shows one recurrent feature: while the guerrillas were dying in droves, the security forces surprisingly suffered few, if any, casualties. Since the guerrillas possessed powerful weaponry and had so far been quite adept at killing members of the security apparatus, this suddenly diminished shooting dexterity appears suspicious, given that by mid-1976 every combatant was aware of the consequences of being caught—endless torture sessions and a probable death.[22] A significant number of these combatants probably were not killed in action but disappeared, that is to say, they were kidnapped, taken to clandestine detention centers, and eventually executed. With the advent of democracy some of these cases have come to light. Norma Arrostito, a founder of the Montoneros, was reported as killed in action in early 1976. However, survivors of Admiral Massera's "rehabilitation process" at the Navy Mechanics School have said that she was taken and kept there until she was executed in early 1978.[23] Another distortion of the truth which has come to light involved the "escape law" (*ley de fuga*). In particular during 1976–77 the press reports several instances in which combatants were killed while attempting to escape, either from prison or during a transfer from one prison to another. In some of these cases it has been possible to establish that the combatants were summarily shot inside the prisons. Montonero officers Roberto Pirles and Dardo Cabo, for example, reportedly killed while trying to escape, were actually removed from their cell at Sierra Chica prison near La Plata and summarily shot on January 5, 1977. Three fellow inmates, Montoneros Horacio Crea, Jorge Georgeades, and Luis Rapaport, were killed in the same fashion several days later.[24]

If the available information were more accurate, a discussion of the ratio of captured to dead guerrillas might have provided useful evidence of a trend toward militarism in nonrevolutionary situations. In a revolutionary situation it might be advisable to take on the armed forces even if it means suffering heavy casualties. But when the long-term objective is merely to weaken the enemy's resolve and achieve a political victory, there is no place for a Tet offensive. Therefore, in a nonrevolutionary situation like Argentina's, one could argue that a high fatality rate proves the guerrillas are exposing their forces unnecessarily. Several guerrillas I interviewed claimed that unnecessary risks were taken, and increasingly so; however, given the distortions in newspaper information after 1976, one cannot consider this a reliable indicator of militarism.

Whether the combatants were killed in action as newspapers reported, or illegally abducted and killed at torture centers, after 1976 death became an everyday occurrence for combatants. The guerrilla life histories in the next section show what the ratio of captured to killed combatants in the table already suggests. Repression strengthened group cohesion in two ways. First, the underground protected the combatants from the paramilitary squads. Second, the memory of dead comrades tied the survivors to a continuation of the struggle.

A substantial portion of all guerrilla casualties occurred in Buenos Aires city and the provinces of Buenos Aires, Córdoba, and Santa Fe.[25] These four account for 63.44 percent of all guerrilla casualties between 1969 and 1979. That this should be so is only logical. These areas were the site of 81.36 percent of all attacks from 1969 to 1979 (see table 3.1). It should also be said that according to the census of 1970 Buenos Aires city and the three provinces mentioned housed 68.2 percent of the country's total population.[26] Tucumán also accounts for a sizable portion of the casualties, which also seems logical given that this is where the ERP chose to open its rural front. In all other provinces the casualty rate was negligible except for Mendoza and Chubut in 1969–72 and Mendoza and Chaco in 1973–75, which reflects arrests and deaths following isolated operations. The reason why Chubut accounts for 4.03 percent of casualties in 1969–72, for example, is the escape from Rawson prison and the subsequent execution of 16 guerrillas at Trelew. Brief reference should be made to guerrilla casualties in foreign countries, not because these were significant but, on the contrary, because they were unusual. Argentine groups operated by and large within their own country and in fact the casualties incurred outside Argentina were not a direct result of operations. All casualties in foreign countries occurred in 1977. In July six Argentines were detained by the Spanish government on the grounds that they were implicated in the kidnapping of an executive in the French subsidiary of Fiat. The French government immediately initiated extradition procedures.[27] In December a Montonero cell was discovered in Uruguay. Four combatants were captured, two committed suicide, and one was killed resisting arrest.[28]

Table 7.2 provides the biographical data on combatants as described in the press. After discussing the table I will compare my findings with those of other scholars. At the end of this section I suggest what can be stated with certainty about the social composition of Argentine guerrilla groups and what ought to be treated as speculation.

It is generally believed that women are a minoritarian component of most armed organizations, and the data in table 7.2 support this contention in the Argentine case, at any rate for the 1969–72 period. Beginning in 1973, in some instances when press reports include "nameless guerrillas," the individual's sex is mentioned: "four subversives captured, one of them a woman"; "two female terrorists and four male terrorists killed." Given the high percentage of cases in which these clarifications are not made, it would be impossible to state how minoritarian that female component was. Another statement frequently made about guerrillas is that they are young and usually recruited at university. The data presented in the table support the contention about the youthful age of combatants. The inordinately high percentages of undetermined cases after 1973 do not allow us to go much further than that. This is most unfortunate given that the interesting issue is not whether or not combatants are young but whether they get younger, or whether there is a widening age gap between leaders and rank and file. As for the notion that guerrillas are recruited at the universities, the data for 1969–72 suggest a substantial portion of members were recruited while they were students. Once more, the lack of information after 1973 makes it difficult to generalize about the guerrillas' occupation or social origin. We can, for example, state with confidence that this was not "the proletariat in arms," but we cannot say how underrepresented the working class was.[29] The data on the guerrillas' place of birth is too sparse to make assumptions.

Table 7.2. Biographical Data on Guerrilla Combatants, 1969–79

	1969–72 (%)	1973–75 (%)	1976–79 (%)	1969–79 (%)
Sex				
Female	21.02	16.71	20.15	18.63
Male	78.98	54.51	48.85	55.21
Undetermined	—	28.78	31.00	26.16
Total	100	100	100	100
Age				
16–20	6.58	4.97	0.77	3.47
21–24	19.96	9.18	1.28	7.31
25–28	16.77	7.87	1.03	6.19
29–32	6.80	3.65	1.09	3.01
33–36	3.61	1.97	1.03	1.79
37–40	1.06	0.71	0.38	0.62
41–44	0.21	0.49	0.26	0.36
45–48	0.43	0.44	0.26	0.36
49–52	—	0.16	0.13	0.13
Over 52	0.21	0.22	0.19	0.21
Undetermined	44.37	70.34	93.58	76.55
Total	100	100	100	100
Place of origin				
Federal Capital	6.37	1.37	0.45	1.60
Buenos Aires	5.73	4.75	2.56	3.99
Córdoba	12.10	0.99	0.77	2.25
Santa Fe	6.79	1.59	0.51	1.79
Entre Ríos	0.64	0.22	—	0.18
Corrientes	0.21	0.11	0.07	0.10
Misiones	—	—	—	—
Chaco	—	0.05	—	0.03
Formosa	—	0.05	—	0.03
Santiago del Estero	—	0.11	—	0.05
Tucumán	3.82	0.82	—	0.85
Salta	0.64	0.11	0.19	0.21
Jujuy	—	0.05	—	0.03
Catamarca	—	0.05	—	0.03
La Rioja	—	0.16	—	0.08
San Juan	0.21	—	0.13	0.08
San Luis	—	0.16	—	0.08
Mendoza	0.43	0.11	0.07	0.13
La Pampa	—	0.05	0.07	0.05
Neuquén	—	—	—	—
Río Negro	—	—	—	—
Chubut	—	—	—	—
Santa Cruz	—	—	—	—

Continued on next page

Table 7.2.—*Continued*

	1969–72 (%)	1973–75 (%)	1976–79 (%)	1969–79 (%)
Place of origin—*Continued*				
Foreign countries	1.91	3.12	1.41	2.28
Undetermined	61.15	86.13	93.77	86.16
Total	100	100	100	100
Occupation				
University student	21.02	4.81	1.48	5.44
High school student	—	0.16	—	0.08
Professional	10.83	3.33	1.35	3.44
Employee	10.61	3.88	1.29	3.65
Merchant	1.91	0.22	—	0.34
Technician	3.61	0.57	0.32	0.83
Urban worker	1.70	1.09	0.96	1.11
Rural worker	0.64	0.05	—	0.10
Cleric	0.21	0.39	0.13	0.26
Security forces	1.06	0.49	0.32	0.49
Housewife	—	0.05	—	0.02
Unemployed	0.43	0.05	0.06	0.11
Former public official	—	0.32	0.32	0.29
Trade unionist	0.21	0.11	0.06	0.10
Militant	—	0.05	0.06	0.06
Professional delinquent	—	—	0.19	0.08
Undetermined	47.77	84.43	93.46	83.60
Total	100	100	100	100
	N = 471	N = 1,831	N = 1,558	N = 3,860

Source: Contemporary press reports.

There have been three previous attempts to estimate the social composition of Argentine guerrilla groups on the basis of press reports. Relying on information for 1972 and September-December 1974, and without specifying the total number of cases on which his calculations are based, Pedro Barcia concludes that Argentine guerrilla groups were primarily staffed by university graduates and students, that the working-class component was minimal, and that guerrillas belonged to the middle and upper middle classes predominantly in the Buenos Aires and Greater Buenos Aires area but also in Córdoba.[30] Richard Gillespie lists 52 active combatants in FAR, FAP, Montoneros, and ERP and their occupations, in addition to 38 combatants involved in the rural guerrilla episodes between 1963 and 1969, and concludes that "the sociology of Argentine guerrilla organizations . . . suggests a dominant petty bourgeois presence with students being the largest single component."[31] Finally, Charles A. Russell and Bowman H. Miller elaborate a "profile of a terrorist" based on "published data regarding over 350 individual terrorist cadres and leaders from Palestinian, Japanese, German, Irish, Italian, Turkish, Spanish, Iranian, Argentine, Brazilian and Uruguayan terrorist groups active during the 1966–1976 time span." [32] The authors do not specify how many of these cadres were Argentine but state that the average age of Argentine guerrillas was 24, and that guerrillas were mostly single male university students from the Greater Buenos Aires area from the middle and upper classes.[33]

Given the overall estimates on the membership of the guerrilla groups presented earlier, and the total number of cases included in tables 7.1 and 7.2, the statements by these authors can in no way be considered conclusive. The data presented in table 7.2 would have been a step in this direction had the percentage of undetermined cases not been so inordinately high. But in spite of the incomplete nature of the data, a few inferences about the social composition of Argentine guerrilla groups can be made. It is likely that women were a large minority, and several former guerrillas interviewed suggested a figure of 30 percent. This seems a reasonable estimate for the period after 1973 since the evidence points to an increasing female participation: only one of eighty-eight combatants arrested or killed in the rural guerrilla episodes between 1959 and 1968 was a woman, and female participation jumped to 21.02 percent in 1969–72.

The geographical provenance of guerrillas is a matter for speculation. Given that Buenos Aires city and the provinces of Buenos Aires, Córdoba, and Santa Fe housed almost 70 percent of the country's population at the time, it would be logical to presume that a sizable portion of guerrillas came from these provinces. This was especially true of the early years since combatants joined with friends and the first generation of guerrillas was fairly homogeneous. Considering the exponential increase in membership after 1973, it would also be logical to assume that combatants were progressively drawn from other provinces, but beyond this not much can be said. In certain armed organizations like the IRA or ETA, combatants operate militarily in the same area in which they reside. However, even though chapter 3 presents fairly accurate data on the location of armed attacks, no inferences on the geographical provenance of Argentine guerrillas can be drawn from that data since combatants operated where they lived but they were also frequently transferred to other areas.

My interviews with former combatants support the data on the guerrillas' age and occupation presented in table 7.2 for the 1969–72 period. The first generation was to a large extent composed of individuals in their early and mid-twenties recruited while they were university students, though not necessarily recruited at university. Given the increase in membership after 1973, this homogeneity probably decreased. As the leadership became older (the university students of the late 1960s became the commandants of the mid 1970s), an increasing percentage was recruited in their late teens or in high school.[34] The combatants' age was an important factor in the unfolding of a manichean view of politics which presented socialism as the only alternative to the evils of capitalism, and made possible revolution in 1970s Argentina merely because it had occurred in Vietnam. The first generation was also drawn almost exclusively from the middle class.[35] However, the development of front organizations after 1973 must have resulted in an increase in the working-class component, but armed struggle remained largely a middle-class phenomenon. To a certain extent this explains why, with the development of militarism, front organizations became mere recruitment grounds and their agendas tools of guerrilla policy.

The Guerrillas Speak[36]

An analysis of guerrilla motivation must differentiate between the decision to join and the willingness to continue fighting. There are a number of situations in which armed struggle could conceivably lose some of its appeal. The group could achieve some (or all) of its objectives or, conversely, realize success is improbable. Repression might have a paralyzing effect on the group. A change in socio-political conditions might help delegitimize armed struggle. And yet guerrilla groups show a marked tendency to continue operating in spite of these changing circumstances. The distinction between these two "motivational moments" becomes particularly salient in the case of the Argentine guerrilla movement, which initiated its operations fighting against a military dictatorship and increased its activity under a constitutionally elected government. It also becomes necessary to distinguish between the first and successive generations of guerrillas, between founders and followers. The term "founders" refers to those who actually launch the organization, but also to those who join when the group is in its formative stages and has not yet become a household word. "Followers" are those who join after this has occurred. In the Argentine context, founders are the men and women recruited between 1969 and 1972.

When the founders join, they do so at considerable risk. They are entering an organization that has not yet proved its worth. The nature of the state's response to the guerrilla threat might also be unclear. By the time the followers are recruited, these questions have been settled. In the followers' decision to join there is a certain element of contagion which could not be present in the founders. This was recognized by my guerrilla interviewees. Asked to evaluate if there was any difference in the motivation of those who joined before and after the March 1973 elections, they responded with variations on the following themes:

> "Up to 1973 the motivation was political. It was the need to espouse a political project. Afterwards, you joined for appearance's sake. Eighty percent joined because it was fashionable."

"Adherence becomes more fanatical. Joining solves your life's problems. They all wanted to shoot at something."

"They joined an organization with power. We created that power."

When the followers join the founders occupy the highest ranks in the organization. To a certain extent, the founders control the organization's resources, information and money, and can therefore shape the type of follower that they want. Finally, the founders have created the group's rules and are likely to have a higher emotional involvement with the organization than the followers.

I have therefore chosen to analyze the two motivational moments with reference to the founders of the Argentine guerrilla movement. Since this is a study of the militarization within armed organizations which took place after 1973, guerrilla founders would have been the ones to develop this behavior or have observed it in others. My field work involved talks with 43 former combatants. Some of those stated from the very beginning that they would provide information or materials but were not emotionally prepared to review their guerrilla experience. Others began to tell their story and said they could not continue. The discussion below is based on extensive interviews with fifteen former combatants who spoke about aspects of their lives before, during, and after their guerrilla experience (table 7.3). These interviews took place in Buenos Aires between October 1986 and January 1988. Each one of these former combatants was interviewed between four and eight times. I have given these interviewees names that do not coincide with their real names or with their noms de guerre within their respective groups. Although the accounts that follow are not representative of the entire Argentine guerrilla movement, they provide a highly accurate and representative portrait of the founder generation.

I must be deliberately vague when it comes to the group membership of my interviewees. Some of them are now building careers in politics and the arts and this narrative should in no way lead to their identification. What can be stated is that my interviewees were members of the six major guerrilla groups. Three made their entire guerrilla careers within one organization, while seven belonged to two different organizations, four to three, and one to four groups at different times.

In addition to distinguishing between founders and followers, it is helpful to differentiate between personal and environmental components of motivation. The personal aspect refers to the characteristics of or events in an individual's life, or in the lives of close friends and relatives, that could help that individual decide to become a guerrilla. The two types of environmental influences at work in a decision to join armed struggle are the immediate (in this case, Argentine society) and mediate environment.

Table 7.3. Guerrilla Founders Interviewed

	Radicalizing milieu
Antonio	Catholicism
Bernardo	Catholicism
Carlos	Catholicism
Diego	Neighborhood
Ernesto	Neighborhood
Fernando	High school
Guillermo	High school
Héctor	High school
Irene	University
Juana	University
Karina	University
Luis	University
Miguel	University
Néstor	University
Olga	University

Source: Personal interviews.

The Decision to Join: Personal Component of Motivation

Some have attempted to delineate a "terrorist personality" by describing certain psychopathologies and/or traumatic childhood experiences that explain an individual's tendency to join violent organizations. The thesis that mental disorders or psychopathologies drive an individual to terrorism has already been discredited by others who argue that abnormal deeds can be committed by normal men and women.[37] Recent scholarship on ETA and the Red Brigades has also disputed the notion that childhood crises explain terrorist behavior. Rather, the combatants' lives prior to their guerrilla experience are described as "normal to the point of being mundane."[38] The life histories of Argentine guerrillas support this view.

It has been said that a problematic childhood can account for the violent behavior of adults, an unhappy home life or the absence of a father figure being frequent explanations.[39] This does not seem to have been the case with my interviewees. None were children of divorce. Guillermo and Carlos said their fathers died when they were young and Karina complained "there was no dialogue with my parents, before or after [I joined]," but the others reported no problems. Irene and Juana made a point of saying they had a wonderful relationship with their parents. None of my interviewees suffered economic deprivation. Karina, Bernardo, and Olga defined their families as working class, but their mothers did not work. All the others defined their families as middle class except for Carlos and Luis, who defined them as upper class.[40] In no case was there a dramatic change in the families' economic status.

In his analysis of the motivation of ETA members, Pedro Ibarra Guell emphasizes the experience of repression as a radicalizing factor.[41] This does not seem to have played an important role in the founders' decision to join. Héctor spent a short time in prison on account of his student activism and Néstor and Olga experienced repression and/or discrimination after the downfall of Perón: Néstor's family was a prominent Peronist family and Olga's father, a shop-floor activist, was accused of being implicated in the 1956 pro-Peronist rebellion led by General Juan José Valle. But following these experiences Olga, Héctor, and Néstor spent years devoted to their studies and displayed no interest in political activities. Only one person, Juana, said that there had been a particular incident in her life that had acted as a catalyst: "I went on a camping trip to Corrientes province with friends. I saw people who did not have anything to eat. When I left Buenos Aires I was an upper-class kid. In a month I had made an about-face." Luis, Ernesto, and Néstor remembered being somewhat impressed by a book they had read (*My Friend Che* by Ricardo Rojo, Guevara's *Guerrilla Warfare,* and *The Art of War,* respectively) even though they stressed this had not been a decisive influence.

It must be strongly emphasized that the decision to join armed struggle was a collective one, for the founders did not join alone, but with friends. Juana, Luis, Néstor, Olga, Miguel, and Irene joined with university friends; Ernesto, Fernando, and Guillermo with high school classmates; Bernardo, Antonio, and Diego with neighborhood friends; and Karina, Héctor, and Carlos with their spouses as well as with friends. The founders also joined at a relatively early age. My interviewees were born between 1931 and 1955. When they joined, three were 18 years old, two were 19, one was 20, four were 21, one was 23, two were 26, one was 27, and one was 37. Two never finished high school, two finished high school and went straight to work, six dropped out of university, and three completed university degrees after they had been recruited. One dropped out of the seminary and one was ordained as a priest after he had joined a guerrilla group. All but two explained the interruption of their studies through their participation in armed struggle. Fernando "didn't like high school" and Antonio dropped out of the seminary because he "realized there were two roads, the religious one and the political one. I chose the political one."

The founders not only joined young and joined with friends; they and their friends eventually became members of the same cell and were therefore expected to meet at least twice a week for discussion sessions, which Ernesto described as "a time we all remember with enormous nostalgia. . . . Everything got discussed, from politics to sex. . . . It was almost a psychotherapy group." Guillermo added: "In spite of the disasters you should stress that that generation displayed a solidarity that we have not seen in this country since and had never seen before." The result of this was the development of a common identity.

The Decision to Join: Environmental Component of Motivation

The life histories of the founders reveal that rather than talk about an evolution toward armed struggle we should be talking about an evolution toward political involvement. Before joining a guerrilla group, all my interviewees except Juana were part of a legal political organization: Guillermo, Héctor, Ernesto, and Fernando in high school; Karina, Luis, Néstor, Olga, Irene, and Miguel at university; Bernardo, Antonio, and Carlos among slum dwellers; and Diego in his neighborhood. Two of the founders had been heavily involved in the solidarity movement with political prisoners at Rawson. The abortive escape attempt which led to the Trelew massacre forced one of them to go underground. The founders became politically active at a time when Onganía was attempting to ban politics by decree. In an authoritarian context, joining any legal (or alegal but tolerated) political group could be construed as a decisive step. Becoming a guerrilla appeared like the natural follow-up. In fact, in the cases of Luis and Olga it would appear that their plans did not contemplate any political involvement, legal or otherwise. Olga explained: "I remember the Night of the Long Batons. They [the military] came into the university library where we were studying, kicking and screaming. I was very serious about school and my one goal was to study and graduate but after that I got in touch with people and became involved in student politics." Luis also experienced a changeover:

> I was the typical upper-class kid until I got to university. Even then, political events seemed not to touch me. With the Cordobazo I wasn't really fazed. [The kidnapping and murder of] Aramburu got to me. And one day I was invited to a student demonstration. Demonstrations were organized like this: suppose there were twenty guys in charge, each one had to bring ten guests, whom they agreed to meet some place. Then they all turned up at the site chosen for the demonstration, which was only known by those twenty, and the whole thing started. So I went to the appointed place, from there we all went to Pueyrredón and Rivadavia [avenues in Buenos Aires city], the place looked very peaceful and suddenly I heard this ferocious roar and two thousand got going. I was terrified. But I loved it, and next time I was carrying the molotovs. And I became totally involved in student politics and within twenty days I was an official in the student union.

Asked to pinpoint specific developments in Argentine politics, all the founders mentioned the Cordobazo. Karina also mentioned the Trelew massacre and Héctor the Night of the Long Batons as "events that shaped our generation."

Néstor said: "You should emphasize the unique characteristics of that political moment. We were impressed by what we believed was a crisis of domination. We never realized that it was a partial crisis." Héctor added: "At a given moment we believed that the revolution was at hand. This was a serious error in judgment, but it was based on the impressive mass mobilizations of the time and the movement in solidarity with political prisoners."

It is difficult to assess the influence of the mediate environment (that is to say, political developments outside Argentina) on the founders' decision to join. Asked to name a revolution or national liberation war that their own guerrilla group considered particularly important, thirteen mentioned the Cuban revolution and the Tupamaro guerrillas in Uruguay, and eight mentioned the Algerian National Liberation Front and Vietnam. Ernesto, Néstor, Carlos, and Miguel stated that "we all saw *The Battle of Algiers* five or six times,"[42] and Ernesto went as far as to imply that there was a tendency to be overly influenced by foreign developments: "We were seduced by Algeria. We never realized that the Algerians were fighting the French and that we were fighting the Argentines. We were destroyed by an excess of metaphors. Everything was 'in the manner of,' 'as if it were.' And we did not have an army of occupation. That would have legitimated us, but we did not have one." Miguel appeared to agree: "We did not discriminate because we were immature. Vietnam, Cuba, Russia, everything was seen as one step forward in the victory of socialism over capitalism." Bernardo provided a different explanation: "We admired them all [armed organizations outside Argentina]. You need that. It is a problem of conscience: 'We are many, maybe we are right.' It was a question of wisdom. If you feel alone you have existentialist doubts."

And yet when asked to evaluate how their own group viewed the Chilean socialist experience of 1970–73, they stated that Chile had been considered "relevant" only in that "it demonstrated the inviability of an unarmed revolutionary policy" (Luis), "the end of the experiment justified armed struggle" (Héctor), and "it proved [the peaceful transition to socialism] didn't work. We did not derive any other teaching" (Karina). The rest replied it had been "scarcely relevant" or "irrelevant." Carlos stated that "we were not dogmatic and we did not adopt any system of thought, like historical materialism. Our national problematique was what really counted." Antonio was more emphatic:

There were national causes for violence in the sixties. One must start in 1955 with the proscription of Peronism. . . . In fact one can go back to the nineteenth century where we start searching for an identity. . . . The 1930 coup . . . the armed forces do not escape that pattern after that. . . . In the sixties, the role of the universities, the importance of youth groups. [In Argentina] the search for an identity was part of the struggle: which development model would triumph, [the conservatives'] or ours?

The Development of a Group Ideology

Though it might be useful to distinguish between personal and environmental components of motivation, in practice the two influence each other. The interaction between a person and his/her environment implies the development of a world view. In the situation of small group dynamics in which the founders operated before and after they became guerrillas, this becomes a collective task. The outcome is the creation of a group ideology.[43] The Argentine experience suggests this is the only context in which it becomes meaningful to study the ideology of groups devoted to armed struggle. Normally ideology refers to a rational, consistent set of beliefs that provides an interpretation of reality, past and present. As the next chapter will show, the worldview of Argentine guerrillas was not very consistent. Because official pronouncements by a political group may be different from the views held by individual members, and because the individual motivation of the founders derived from a specific reading of a particular political context, two elements of that group ideology should be mentioned here.

Argentina was viewed as an example of a peripheral society, where capitalism had exhausted its capacity to generate sustained growth and socialism became the only way to escape dependency. Asked whether they would have identified themselves with reformist or revolutionary positions had they lived in Western Europe, Karina and Fernando answered that they did not know and the others stated that they would have been reformists. Luis suggested that he might even have been a conservative. Diego hastened to add that he could not imagine himself as a member of the Red Brigades or Direct Action, and Héctor was more specific: "Argentine revolutionaries had nothing in common with European terrorists."

The other key element in the development of this group ideology was a reading of Argentine history from the vantage point of the Resistance and the Onganiato. All the founders emphasized the violent nature of Argentine politics. In historical terms, this is an accurate observation. Unfortunately, Argentine history was interpreted as a long series of increasingly radical popular uprisings against the dominant sectors which started with the nineteenth-century *caudillos* and inevitably led to armed struggle in the 1960s. Carlos defined armed struggle as "a historical phenomenon going back to the nineteenth century which had to define itself one way or the other," a view echoed by Antonio, Olga, Bernardo, and Diego who all considered armed struggle in the 1960s "inevitable." Néstor was more precise: "We made an interpretation of Argentine history in which [Hipólito] Yrigoyen, Perón, and us [guerrillas] were the same thing. It was too heroic a vision. The people-versus-oligarchy confrontation did not occur as we thought it did. We did not capture the dimension of the change that we brought about."

In this evaluation of violence there was a strong ethical component, no doubt linked to the participants' age. Karina explained: "I was moved by a rebelliousness and a need to do things. I could have joined the Montoneros, FAP, any organization. . . . Young people turned to politics in an unheard of way. Nobody has studied why an entire generation was ready to die, and that is why what you are doing is important." Luis said, "What happened to me happened to many in my generation. You wanted to study and couldn't. You were kicked out of every place. You looked at your parents' generation and you saw hypocrisy everywhere. Violence was institutionalized, and you should stress that. . . . We did not want to be accomplices, and you should stress that, too. Ours was a story of people who were very much alive." For Hector, "There was no room for anything other than armed struggle." According to Miguel: "Guerrilla warfare was a youth phenomenon. This gave it strength but also meant inexperience and immaturity. You got to the conclusion that the system wasn't working and had to be changed. It was the 'This is it. We must do something different.' "

Life Within Guerrilla Groups Until 1973

Membership in armed organizations involved considerable change in the founders' lives, even if this did not invariably mean leading a clandestine existence. During the early years groups were small and short of funds, so the general rule was that guerrillas only went underground when it became absolutely necessary. One of the founders who had collaborated with the escape from Rawson prison was forced underground after the Trelew massacre. Another of my interviewees had to go underground when the spouse was arrested. But on the whole, during these early years the founders were, in the words of Ernesto, "weekend guerrillas." Even so, there were necessary behavior changes. Néstor explained that "you had to pretend to be apolitical. If you had been involved in something [political] you had to fake a loss of interest. You also had to develop a hobby which helped justify your spending two or three days away from home and your inviting new people home." Irene said: "I was told I had to move out of my parents' house because it was a bourgeois habit to live with your parents. And I didn't want to, because I got on very well with my parents. But I did it." When Miguel first arrived at a café for an interview, he remarked: "Never sit with your back to the door. You always should be able to see who's coming in. That was one of the first things they taught you."

The founders' accounts reveal that the different armed organizations had a common recruitment and training policy. Juana recalled, "You first did political work. Then came the irons." The lapse of time before the new recruits became familiar with the "irons" (*fierros*), guerrilla jargon for weapons and military action, varied from one group to another—two months for Luis, six for Néstor, and a year for Juana and Irene. But involvement appears to have been increased gradually, as Luis stated: "The policy was, you had to do everything. I spent two months doing neighborhood work, then you got military instruction and you did small things like auto theft. That always came first. After that yes, military operations."

Also common to all groups during the early years was the emphasis on combined political and military activity. According to Miguel, "It was all political, union work, logistics. You had to do everything. That was lost with specialization"—meaning with the emergence of the professionals. This was a view echoed by most of the founders. Diego described the early years as "the ability to be involved in 30 things at the same time and do them well." The founders were all expected to keep up their militancy in mass fronts: Carlos and Bernardo in slums; Antonio, Juana, Fernando, Olga, Miguel, and Ernesto in working-class neighborhoods; and Guillermo, Luis, and Karina in student organizations. Diego did both union and neighborhood work, Héctor was involved with one union and one neighborhood group, and Néstor and Irene were active in student and neighborhood groups. Whether mobilizing slum dwellers to demand particular government services, helping to organize a strike, or establishing a neighborhood day-care center, the idea was, as Olga put it, to "establish pockets of consciousness." In addition to their activism in mass organizations and their regular jobs or studies, the founders participated in weekly discussion sessions, distributed leaflets (*volanteadas*), covered walls with graffiti (*pintadas*), and guarded safehouses. They also participated in military operations, though, as Irene explained, "You could choose not to grab the irons." Guillermo and Olga never participated in an armed action, even though they were required to undergo periodic training (*práctica de tiro*), and Bernardo, a priest, "never participated in an operation in which people could die. In the organization the kids fought among themselves about participating in military actions, so when operations were being planned I was immediately left out because I was a priest." Eight of the founders stated that "I was more of a political than a military cadre." Ernesto's involvement in military action is typical of my interviewees' attitude toward violence: "I did most of my military operations before [late 1972]. After that, I participated in only one operation where I was being shot at. In other operations I was armed, but no one was shooting at me. Besides, before each operation I [urinated] in my pants. A little, but I did." This de facto division of labor within the groups, which allowed Guillermo and Olga to stay out of armed action and most of the others to stay out of operations resulting in deaths, allowed the founders, and I suspect many others, to displace responsibility onto others when the groups changed their focus from violence against property to violence against persons.

Because the founders were weekend guerrillas, there was no need to put families or friends outside the group in the know. In this respect my interviewees did not follow any clear pattern. Guillermo chose to tell his mother but not his brother, Antonio and Ernesto told their siblings but not their parents, everyone in Carlos' family knew, and Bernardo kept his family in the dark but dropped broad hints to his fellow seminarians. Sometimes siblings joined, usually as followers. Karina, Ernesto, and Fernando each had one brother join their groups, and Antonio and Carlos each had two brothers join.[44] Reflecting on the attitudes of the relatives who were told or found out, Héctor said: "Militancy tended to separate you from your family either because the militant didn't accept that they didn't approve, or because they didn't approve. And because it was also a vertiginous life in which what one lived and what one thought were out of phase." But this appears to have been an exception, and as a rule, the families accepted the involvement. Luis's parents "found out by themselves. One day I came home and found my mom with a Molotov that I had in my room, studying it. They didn't like it one bit, but as with everyone's folks, they accepted because I was the son." Guillermo said, "Mom knew and the only thing she said was 'take care of yourself.' She also gave some money to the party and joined the relatives' association when I went to jail." Fernando's parents "realized what was happening. I didn't have to tell them. They didn't approve of armed struggle but I was their son. Dad said everything was fine as long as I didn't bring stuff home or use the car for operations. I did both." Miguel's mother was suspicious, "but she didn't say anything. Parents on the whole didn't punish you for it."

Founders remembered with nostalgia the period from 1969 to 1973, when armed organizations were fighting a military dictatorship. Néstor spoke of "a double radicalization, of armed organizations and civil society." Miguel elaborates: "Until 1973 support was widespread in different sectors. The popular sectors understood and supported 'the boys.' Almost everything we did resulted in political capital. The middle class was divided but did not condemn us. It provided more general support. It was all linked to a certain romanticism and the youthful phenomenon. It was clear that violence was transformative. Nobody distinguished between guerrillas and militants." Ernesto said, "we were seen as a charming movement," and Irene complained, "the middle class from which guerrilla cadres were drawn is a crappy class. Without conscience. Nobody's realized that they made mistakes, that at the time they all supported armed struggle."

Life Within Guerrilla Groups After 1973

In 1973 the guerrilla groups suffered a sudden and significant increase in membership, known in guerrilla jargon as "the fattening process" (*engorde*). Néstor, Carlos, and Fernando stated that the fattening process hurt their groups. Most of those who joined were "parsleys" (*perejiles*), naive, politically immature individuals. Juana voiced similar complaints: "We recruited and recruited but did no political work." Organizational development led to increased complexity and to the emergence of the professionals, guerrillas who performed very specific tasks like forging documents. It also led to the introduction of military ranks and uniforms and the establishment of rigid authority relations. The change was very noticeable to Ernesto and Guillermo, temporarily separated from their groups while they complied with compulsory military service. Ernesto recalled: "While I was a draftee I started seeing the militarization. And inside the barracks I wore a uniform and saluted but outside I didn't feel like it . . . uniforms and ranks were introduced here, not in exile. [The 29th Mounted Infantry Regiment in] Formosa was attacked wearing uniforms. By the time I finished military service there were already ranks and you had to salute when a superior came into the room and call him 'usted.' "

During this period the guerrillas steadily lost their ties with the outside world. Clandestine life was now generalized since the Peronist government had outlawed the ERP in September 1973 and the Montoneros in September 1975. The Montoneros had in fact outlawed themselves in September 1974 by deciding to return underground when they were still a legal political group. Clandestine life and the emergence of the Triple A death squads made contacts with families and friends outside the guerrilla group extremely difficult. Romantic involvements were possible only with fellow guerrillas and in fact likely to develop only with someone in the same organizational structure. Karina, Héctor, and Carlos were already married when they joined; Antonio, Ernesto, Néstor, and Irene met their spouses within their groups. Fellow guerrillas came to act even more as a surrogate family. As Ernesto put it, "life was lived to the fullest because you could die tomorrow. Besides, you had people around you whom you knew would be ready to die in order to save you. All our emotions were very intense because there was no time." It could be said that no definition of identity became possible outside the group, as Miguel recalled: "Everything was linked to our age. We were all twenty or twenty-one. The organization provided you with an identity. We argued, we fought, but we felt one and the same."

Strong affective ties linked the guerrillas with dead comrades as much as with those who were still alive. Ernesto explained:

People will deny this, but if your wife or your girlfriend got killed beside you, the only thing you wanted was revenge. It happened to me after my best friend died. It is very hard to see someone die. Or you don't see him but you find out he has died. . . . There is no way I can describe to you what it is like when you are at home and you get a telephone call and someone asks if you have seen so-and-so and you say "no," and they tell you "he is sick" or "he has broken a leg," which meant he was dead, and you are overcome by impotence.

That the dead should carry such weight in a situation of small group dynamics would be only natural. But this was also fostered by the groups. Official pronouncements after 1973 glorified those who died in combat. For example, under the heading "I don't want to give myself up alive," a combatant described in *Evita Montonera* how he and his girlfriend attempted to resist arrest: "Moni tells me she is wounded . . . she says she doesn't want to give herself up alive, that I should help her kill herself . . . her love for the people and the Organization . . . determined that I should comply with what she asked." The description ended with an official commentary: "Comrade N. was promoted to officer and decorated for his distinguished action in the observance of the revolutionary duty. Comrade Moni demonstrated, with her attitude in the face of the enemy, sufficient political understanding and ideological solidity to integrate our Organization (our party), as a full member."[45]

It must be pointed out that official sanction of this cult of death became possible only through the rank and file's readiness to die. According to Fernando, "[In the early years] as a rule we canceled an operation unless we all had a 95 percent chance of coming out alive. In 1975 I had to carry out an operation where I only had a 50 percent chance of surviving. I told myself, 'this is not for me.' . . . By that time we had developed a conception of heroism. What counted was no longer life but death. He who did not die was worthless." Diego recalled that "when the Triple A became serious [my cell] suggested we should hide a bit. You couldn't keep staging a military operation here and a distribution of leaflets there, exposing yourself," and Ernesto stated that by 1974 armed organizations "were playing with people's lives, they were running unnecessary risks, like sending you unarmed to plaster the neighborhood with 'Long live . . .' posters while the Triple A was operating and you could disappear for much less than a stupid poster." But none of them ever refused to carry out an order, whatever the cost.

After 1973 the environment increasingly lost its relevance as the guerrilla group became the only meaningful environment. I asked my interviewees if the evidence of popular support, or lack thereof, had any effect on their group's morale. Héctor, Bernardo, and Fernando said this was "decisive," and Juana qualified it, "up to 1973." Antonio, Luis, and Diego said popular support was important "only insofar as it helped us do our political work," and the rest said it played no role. Ernesto went beyond this: "What was important was what we thought about ourselves. I admired my superiors and others admired me."

Two distinct but interrelated developments took place within guerrilla groups: armed organizations became more concerned with politics within the groups than with the groups' role in Argentine politics; and the groups lost touch with political realities. This process may not have been willed, but it was obvious to some at the time. Talking about his group's formulation of policies, Carlos said: "We were no longer intuitively responding to reality as we had done before. We were constructing our own abstract reality. Hence the disaster." Héctor expressed similar views on a more specific aspect, his group's sexual mores:

"There was a lot of ambiguity, because on the one hand ours was the generation of the sexual revolution and there was a lot of that in the group, but on the
other hand you had these extremely rigid revolutionary codes describing what
the morals of the 'new man' we wanted to create should be. And that was fine,
but you had to be more flexible in the face of reality."

I asked my interviewees if they thought that armed operations resulting in
unplanned deaths had any impact on the public's evaluation of armed struggle.
Their responses are indicative of this increasing loss of touch with reality. Ten
of the founders stated that "there were almost no accidental deaths"; that "it
hardly happened until 1973" or that "it hardly happened until 1975." However,
descriptions of guerrilla operations in the Argentine daily press reveal that the
rate of accidental deaths was high from 1969 to 1979.[46] The combatants' isolation made them unaware of the cumulative effect of their group's military action.
I also asked my interviewees if they considered that accidental deaths had any
impact on the evaluation of armed struggle made by members or sympathizers
of guerrilla groups. Only Héctor, Fernando, and Antonio suggested a possible
negative impact. Diego said: "Sympathizers disagreed [with accidental deaths].
Members questioned them but accepted them. Even justified them. Politics has
objectives and consequences. One has to see which of the two was considered
more important."

What came to be known as the "hedge theory" (*teoría del cerco*) provides
the best illustration of this inward-looking attitude. According to this theory,
which became popular after Perón returned to the country and to power in 1973
and changed his policy toward armed organizations, Perón still supported the
guerrilla groups but was driven to a confrontation with them because he was
influenced by Isabel Perón and other representatives of the Peronist right. Perón's
entourage was viewed as the hedge, preventing any meaningful contact between
the leader and his radicalized young followers. Néstor explains the reasons why
such theory was formulated: "Here our policy changed. Up until the 'hedge'
the organization's development was subordinated to the development of a mass
policy. With the 'hedge' the organization was, for the first time, elaborating a
policy for internal consumption. The 'hedge' was meant to explain to the rank
and file that the old man [Perón] was betraying us." Juana concurred: "By that
time what was said and what was being done were two different things. The
'hedge' was for the 'parsleys.' " Even though it represented a policy for internal
consumption, the hedge theory was indefensible in that it did not square with
Perón's behavior and with the official sponsorship of the Triple A death squads.
Néstor, Karina, Juana, and Luis stated they did not believe it. Yet many did:
Miguel stated, "I didn't, but the [Revolutionary] Tendency believed anything.
[Guerrilla] officers half-believed it." According to Irene, "the leadership didn't
believe it, but it spread like fire." Three founders confessed to believing in the
"hedge": Fernando "believed it . . . we reacted like the husband who's found

out his wife is unfaithful." Diego said that "at first I did. I think everyone did. Even though we knew [the truth]." For Antonio, "deep down I didn't believe it because I knew. We were blaming the AAA for bombs in Peronist Youth locales but a lot of those bombs had been placed by us. On the other hand I cursed Perón's 'hedge' and sometimes I even believed it."

Implicit in some of these comments on the hedge theory is the idea that the guerrilla rank and file were lied to by their leaders. Former combatants and analysts of the guerrilla phenomenon call this phenomenon "the divorce between the leadership and the rank and file," and it has been used to explain the continuation of armed struggle after 1973 as well as the emphasis on spectacular attacks against military establishments and on indiscriminate killings. The clearest formulation of this argument is provided by two former participants[47] who contend that, through its control of financial resources and information (and given the cellular organization known as "compartmentalization," which is typical of guerrilla groups), the leadership was able to obtain the compliance of the rank and file.

Compartmentalization did not work as it was supposed to. As Guillermo explained, "you were recruited with all your friends whom you knew since high school, so it was a joke, you were told you were not supposed to know anyone's name, and during meetings we all knew each other's names, addresses, and all that." All the founders also made it clear that at the time they had substantial knowledge of what went on in other organizational structures within their guerrilla group, and frequently mentioned contacts with combatants from those other structures. This would indicate that the leadership did not have a monopoly on information. My interviewees were not members of the top echelons of their organizations, but they were not rank-and-file members, either. All except Karina, Héctor, Guillermo, and Miguel were officers, where such a rank existed, or occupied positions of similar responsibility. Asked whether they agreed with the notion of the divorce between the leadership and the rank and file, only Bernardo, Antonio, and Ernesto said they did. Bernardo did not elaborate further; Antonio said "this was due to the conception of 'popular army' "; and Ernesto said: "After 1973 I wrote several papers for my superiors criticizing certain policies. Nobody responded. Besides, people simply obeyed." Karina stated the divorce existed only insofar as " 'democratic centralism' was more centralized than democratic," an idea which Luis, Néstor, and Héctor voiced in almost the same words. But Karina also added, "I disagree with the thesis that the rank and file were wonderful individuals and the leadership a bunch of degenerates," a view echoed by Luis, Carlos, and Néstor.

A more probable explanation is that the powerful emotional bonds with the organization led to an obliteration of the individual conscience. Combatants ended up obeying policies decided within the upper echelons without voicing their opposition even though they might have considered those policies erroneous. Carlos admitted, "Mistakes were made both by the leadership that elaborated a policy and by the rank and file that obeyed it." Karina explained, "You obey without questioning because life within the organization creates a militant who says, 'I am opposed to this but it must be right.' "

The bureaucratization of guerrilla groups was undoubtedly a contributing factor. But when an individual defines his or her identity only in connection with a reference group, the pressure to conform is enormous, and it becomes difficult to conceive of an identity outside that group. Asked whether they had at any given time felt they wanted to leave their guerrilla group, eight of the founders said "never." Guillermo said: "Not when things turned sour but in 1971. I had an attack of pacifism. It lasted for six months." Juana, Antonio, Olga, and Ernesto said they first had doubts "after mid-1973"; and Bernardo "when it became clear that our policy was at odds with Perón's political project." Miguel reported that leaving the group was "no big deal" except in the case of informants: "The key issue was, how much did you know and how much would you reveal if apprehended?" Juana, Bernardo, and Carlos described the process of requesting permission to leave as "cumbersome," but Guillermo said that if there was any pressure at all, it was emotional. It is significant that Ernesto waited for two years before deciding to leave, whereas Juana left immediately but continued working for the group as a salaried employee for another two years. Antonio and Bernardo tried to garner support among their comrades so that they could create a significant split in the organization they both belonged to, but although many apparently shared their grievances, the others had second thoughts and eventually Antonio and Bernardo were the only ones to abandon the group.

Diego provides a revealing comment: "Yes, I had doubts. But with my friends we thought we could change the organization from within. . . . After Formosa [the 1975 attack against the 29th Mounted Infantry Regiment], it was erroneous to keep thinking you could change anything from within." The top leadership had no need to withhold information from the militants. Rather, the militants lied to themselves. The founders had a term for it: in guerrilla jargon, "to melon" (*melonear*) is to try to recruit and/or persuade someone, through deception if necessary. After 1973, armed struggle became an exercise in self-meloning.

Life Within Guerrilla Groups Revisited, 1986–88

During the 1976–83 military government the guerrilla founders suffered various fates. Eight served prison sentences, varying in length from two to nine years. One was taken to a clandestine detention center. Three went into exile, and the remaining three managed to stay at large, inside Argentina, undetected by the security apparatus. In the case of the founders who were married, the spouses shared their fate. In addition, Karina and Antonio each have one brother and

Carlos two brothers who disappeared. The brothers of Ernesto and Fernando spent years in prison and one of them was first taken to one of the most notorious torture centers.

The founders who went to prison regarded imprisonment as a favorable occurrence. As one of them explained, being captured early on "saved us, because after 1976 no more prisoners arrived at the jails." Most guerrillas caught after the coup were taken to clandestine detention centers, and most of those were eventually killed. Not that prison life was without hardships. As one of the founders recalls,

> The army kept us well informed. Periodically they held meetings to bring us to date, so you might say we knew more than those outside. But it was a horror. I remember one guy who used to tell us that he was happy where he was because he'd previously been [involved in the army's counterinsurgency effort] in Tucumán where he'd been cutting people in slices and he didn't like it all that much. In 1979, when the Inter-American Commission [on Human Rights] visited the country they were debating whether to kill us before the commission arrived. They kept going back and forth.

The founders' prison experience involves executions disguised as applications of the "escape law," beatings, torture, and mock executions. The combatants who remained at large, including those who eventually went abroad, describe the post-coup situation as "the horror" and "the disbandment."

> I didn't have a place to sleep in. I had to get money so that my wife and I would be able to sleep in an assignation hotel. . . . I also slept in a lawyer's office, a policeman's house. . . . There were people who slept in public buses. . . . And you saw what happened around you and it was a horror. People said they didn't know [about the dirty war] but they knew. On Corrientes [avenue in downtown Buenos Aires] I saw a guy being summarily shot, and raids on bars where they came in with Itakas and picked up people.

Another combatant said staying at large meant "having no money, no identity papers, no one to take care of you." A third recalled, "With the disbandment I got a job and [hid in the provinces]. I slept with the door open so that they wouldn't break it when they came for me."

According to Néstor the combatants, whether in prison, exiled, or at large, "could be divided into two categories: the 'exiles,' those who said 'here I am, I might as well make the most of this situation,' who were also called the 'broken ones,' and the 'combatants,' those who refused to accept the facts and were still politicking, only that instead of being in Villa Martelli [in Greater Buenos Aires] they were in Madrid or Rome."

Olga and Diego resorted to the same description, which must have been in the minds of all the founders at the time. By and large they remained, as

Néstor stated, "combatants." Group solidarity, developed over a period of years through the process of resocialization described, was reinforced by repression. In the midst of the "disbandment," not letting the others down became a driving consideration and stifled dissent. This was true in particular of the case of the imprisoned founders, who kept (or reorganized) their command structure inside the prisons, "socialized" food and supplies, protested against prison conditions, and attempted to publicize human rights violations.

Following Argentina's return to democratic rule in 1983, my interviewees faced for the first time since the late sixties the prospect of leading a normal life. Five of the founders remain on the closest of terms with their former comrades. According to Fernando, "we have a long common history," and for Juana, "we are all godparents to each other's children." Nine of my interviewees still "see some of them," although as Irene explained, "many old timers are dead." According to Miguel, "daily life separates you from your former comrades. We're all engaged in a struggle for subsistence." Three of the founders are no longer in touch with anyone.

The founders' interest in politics has diminished considerably. Two of my interviewees remain actively involved: Fernando hypothesizes that he "might even think of running for city councillor or congressman in a couple of years," and Luis explains, "even though I'm repulsed by [contemporary Argentine politics] I do not resign myself to letting others decide for me what kind of a country I want. The day I resign myself is the day I leave the country." However, six of the founders only report "some contacts" and the other seven have no political activity whatsoever. The political scene seems to them rather gray: "I cannot identify with this" was Olga's comment; Juana felt that "this is a circus"; for Antonio, "everything's rotten"; and Carlos found that "if you lived through that [period] it is difficult to become interested in this." Karina felt that she "lost touch with my first daughter because of my militancy. I enjoy watching my second daughter grow up. Sometimes I feel I'm slime because I'm no longer involved but everything's the same and I don't see a way out."

The founders are not overly optimistic about Argentina's future. Interviewed in 1986–88, eight believed that as a consequence of the radicalized sixties and the repressive seventies, Argentines would settle for a democratic system which does not appear to eliminate any of the existing economic inequalities. Ernesto described this as "decadence, Colombian style," and Héctor believed that "Peronists and Radicals are in agreement, and the popular camp has been defeated." Diego believed Argentina's economic crisis would result in a new outburst of collective violence, a view echoed by Antonio, Bernardo, Fernando, and Miguel. Carlos and Olga considered a military coup "a distinct possibility."

Asked if they would consider taking up arms against the state once more, Guillermo, Bernardo, and Luis said that they did not know if they would. Karina, Olga, Héctor, and Miguel categorically rejected the possibility, while Néstor,

Juana, and Irene said they would not enlist but might support armed struggle. "Under certain conditions," Ernesto, Diego, Fernando, and Carlos said they might join, and Antonio was certain he would. This is no doubt linked to the founders' balance sheet on their guerrilla experience. Héctor no longer believes in it: in Argentina "armed struggle doesn't provide an answer to the problems it is supposed to solve. What alternative does it present?" Fernando, on the contrary, still considers it "the highest level of political struggle. Politics always represents violence, particularly [in Argentina]." The others are ambivalent: "up to a certain point," "depending on the situation," "at a given time and place," armed struggle is "a necessary process," "a valid method," "an avenue for change." To some extent, the founders are still engaged in self-meloning. In 1987 they continued to haunt the same cafés they had frequented in the sixties, yet my interviewees referred to the guerrilla groups they had belonged to using the third person: "what they should have done at that stage"; "they were running unnecessary risks"; "when they started killing off-duty policemen." And although they describe their groups' actions after 1973–74 as "the disaster," "the foul-up," and "the delirium," they composed the following guerrilla epitaphs: "We were the generation that kicked the board and said 'this is it' "; "in spite of the things I hate I still feel a Montonero"; and simply "when you write about us, say that we loved each other deeply."

8

Ideological and Organizational Somersaults

The present chapter discusses the remaining two factors that contributed to the militarization of armed struggle: the development of a manichean world view and the bureaucratization of guerrilla groups. The analysis of the ideology of armed organizations is not always productive, for a variety of reasons. First, ideological pronouncements by such groups frequently lack consistency. One example of inconsistency was the decision by a Marxist organization like the ERP to refrain from attacking the Cámpora government in 1973 while reserving the right to harass its armed forces. Second, armed organizations frequently burst into splinter factions engaged in byzantine ideological debates which mask power struggles within the groups. Finally, armed organizations—much like political organizations in general—sometimes preach one thing and practice another. For these reasons this chapter analyzes ideology and internal organization jointly. A discussion that juxtaposes ideological formulations and their practical application around certain organizational principles should be able to shed more light on the behavior of Argentine guerrillas: ideological formulations from 1969 to 1979 may have maintained a half-hearted commitment to certain political objectives, but organizational changes show beyond doubt that after 1973 the guerrillas had ceased to consider armed struggle as "politics by other means" and were bent on emulating the Argentine army.

The groups' attitude toward mass action exemplifies why a joint analysis of ideological pronouncements and organizational changes is useful. After 1973, internal documents of the PRT, the political wing of the ERP, proclaimed the need for an anti-imperialist front and extensive party involvement in factory struggles. At the same time, however, the PRT decreed that its political cells

should be employed in military operations in support of the ERP. The Montoneros professed a greater interest in mass action than the ERP. Through the
Peronist Youth they were the driving force in Cámpora's electoral campaign in
1973, and after his inaugural the guerrillas undertook the organization of various
social groups. But the leadership positions in these "fronts" went to guerrilla
officers, who used their ability to mobilize these social groups as a means to
enhance their standing within the guerrilla organization. The Montoneros also
selected (and changed) the issues around which mass fronts would be mobilized.
This is indicative of the role that Montoneros assigned to them, namely, that of
tools of Montonero policy.

The pages that follow describe the guerrillas' key organizational and ideological principles during the 1969–73 period and show how these were modified
with the restoration of Peronism and the advent of the dirty war. The narrative
emphasizes common themes. Therefore, unless a group is specifically mentioned, the reader should assume that generalizations apply to the entire guerrilla
movement.

The chapter describes the groups' simplistic, almost dichotomic view of
reality: all capitalism was evil, and socialism was the solution; the only principled opposition to bourgeois reformism was revolution. Because the guerrillas
viewed armed struggle in the 1960s as a continuation of the nineteenth-century
struggle for independence from Spain, they concluded that politics was equivalent to war. Ideological pronouncements by the groups were based from the start
on an incorrect characterization of Argentine society. When the guerrillas stated
that the oligarchy and the masses had been locked in combat since the wars of
independence, they were not only ignoring the existence of a strong middle class
in Argentina, they were rewriting history, as the middle and working classes did
not become politically organized until the twentieth century. Whenever reality
threatened to intrude, guerrilla rhetoric resorted to the theme of "illusion versus
reality": elections were a trap that the guerrillas knew better than to succumb
to; politicians and union bureaucrats disguised themselves as Peronists; Perón
appeared to favor the masses while he pursued bourgeois policies; the masses
adhered to Peronism because they had not yet been offered anything more in
agreement with their class interests.

The manichean worldview helped the combatants deal with the uncertain-
ties of life in the underground and reinforced group cohesion. Since politics was
equivalent to war, since the enemy was fundamentally evil and the guerrillas the
incarnation of everything that was good, dissent with guerrilla policies was tantamount to identification with the enemy. Organizational changes also resulted in
a reluctance to question orders. The growth in membership after 1973 led to the
increasingly complex organizational structures described below. The division of
labor within the groups helped diffuse responsibility and guilt for the violence.
Bureaucratization also gave birth to careerism within the groups, as promotion

and status became rewards for conformity. If dissent appeared in spite of all this, the formalism of salutes, uniforms, and standard operating procedures could absorb it.

International Influences on the Ideology of Argentine Guerrillas

The Cuban revolution enjoyed an enormous prestige among progressive sectors of Latin America in the early sixties. As an American journalist wrote at the time, Castro "is a symbol to Latin American Nationalists, not to Communists. He is opposed to our investments, and to our pressure. . . . Other Nationalists are hoping to do the same in every country of Latin America." [2] Before and after Castro announced he was a Marxist-Leninist, what was admired was the simple act of defiance of the United States. The Cuban example also persuaded certain sectors of the Latin American left that revolution could be successful, and for a decade after Castro's victory revolutionaries across the continent attempted, without success, to copy the Cuban insurrectionary model and establish rural focos, the guerrilla nuclei expected to create the conditions for revolution in developing countries where such "objective" conditions did not exist. [3] The attempt to emulate the Cuban model was due to two factors. First, there was an incorrect analysis, within and outside Cuba, of the conditions which had led the Sierra Maestra guerrillas to victory: their role was overemphasized and that of the urban resistance groups minimized; and the revolutionary rewriting of history failed to distinguish between the Oriente *precaristas* and the bulk of the Latin American peasantry. Second, the writings of Che Guevara and Régis Debray, which became extremely influential, provided an insurrectionary recipe which was to be followed ad nauseam. The recipe stated that popular forces could defeat a professional army; that it was not necessary to wait until objective conditions for revolution were present in Latin America, since the nucleus of armed insurrection or foco could create them; that the revolutionary struggle should be waged in the countryside; and that it should be continental in scope. [4] By late 1967, when Guevara died attempting to establish a foco in Bolivia and the theory's failure became apparent, the only lessons to be derived were geographical—action merely moved from the countryside to the urban centers (and from northern to southern South America), but no attempt was made to evaluate the viability of this revolutionary dogma. [5]

Until 1968, and for roughly the same period that the Guevara-Debray thesis was applied in its original form, Castro's foreign policy also stressed the exportability of the Cuban revolution. This policy began with Castro's Second Declaration of Havana in 1962, promising support for the liberation struggles in Latin America, and continued with the meeting of the Tricontinental Conference in 1966, endorsing the *fidelista* line of armed struggle. During this period Cuba also provided arms and training for various Latin American guerrilla groups. But the greatest encouragement for continental revolution came with the creation of the Organization of Latin American Solidarity (OLAS) by Latin American delegates attending the Tricontinental. At its first meeting in Havana in August 1967, OLAS issued a twenty-point declaration that stated:

1) that making the revolution constitutes a right and a duty of the peoples of Latin America. . . . 5) that armed revolutionary struggle constitutes the fundamental course of the Revolution in Latin America; 6) that all other forms of struggle must serve to advance and not to retard the development of this fundamental course which is armed struggle. . . . 8) that the countries in which this has not yet been undertaken will regard it as an inevitable sequence in the development of revolutionary struggle in their countries.[6]

What is generally known as the "OLAS period" marked the decline of the established Communist parties of Latin America and the emergence of ultraleftism. With the exception of Venezuela, Communist parties categorically rejected armed struggle and, in cases such as Argentina, were so committed to electoral politics and the existing political system that sympathizers came to view them as regressive forces. The OLAS ultraleft, on the contrary, appeared as the true defender of revolution, and the foquismo it preached a shortcut toward that end.

Early guerrilla efforts in Argentina benefited from Cuban material support. This support became irrelevant in the late sixties since kidnappings were supplying Argentine combatants with more cash than Castro could ever advance. A handful of Argentine guerrilla cadres are also known to have received training in Cuba: Roberto Quieto, Marcos Osatinsky, Carlos Olmedo, and Arturo Lewinger from FAR; Fernando Abal Medina and Norma Arrostito from Montoneros; and Mario Roberto Santucho, Luis Pujals, Antonio del Carmen Fernández, and Joe Baxter from ERP. Beyond this, the foco theory influenced the Argentine guerrilla groups in several ways. Early statements by all six major groups paid homage to the "revolutionary moral stature" of Guevara. In addition, all the groups emphasized the continental nature of their struggle and specified that, the 1959–68 experience notwithstanding, they contemplated opening up rural fronts in the future. The ERP was the only group to do so. In early 1976, once the failure of the ERP's foco was more than apparent, Montoneros briefly sent a jungle force to Tucumán (Fuerza de Monte del Ejército Montonero). The force's first casualty was officer Juan Carlos Alsogaray whose father, General Julio Alsogaray had, as Army Chief of Staff, been one of the organizers of the 1966 coup. But the foco theory's greatest legacy was the notion that action creates revolutionary consciousness. Stated explicitly during the early years, this idea would be implicit in the behavior of Argentine combatants from 1969 to 1979.[7]

A second influence on the emergence of insurrectionary ideas in Argentina was the *aggiornamento* of the Catholic church. This began with the Second Vatican Council (1962–65), which brought about significant changes in the organization of the church, the liturgy, and communal activity. The Latin American clergy attempted to adapt these reforms to the continent's particular conditions. The underlying concern, expressed at various meetings, was about political and economic oppression in the different countries. Pope Paul VI's *Populorum Progressio* raised the issue around which two divergent opinions would emerge. The encyclical defended the rights of the underprivileged but condemned violence "except where there is a manifest lasting tyranny that harms the fundamental personal rights and represents a danger for the good of the country."[8] The church hierarchy restricted the idea of a "manifest lasting tyranny" to the political field. The priests, whose parish work inevitably confronted them with social realities, adopted the view that economic oppression meant institutionalized violence, and that violence should be fought with violence. This more radical view, which became known as Liberation Theology, was an attempt to blend Catholic thought with Marxist analysis:

LATIN AMERICA HAS, FOR MANY CENTURIES, BEEN A CONTINENT OF VIOLENCE. It is the violence of a privileged minority . . . against the vast majority of the exploited people. It is the violence of hunger, of helplessness and underdevelopment. The violence of persecution, of oppression and ignorance . . . We call this "violence" because it is not the fatal and inevitable consequence of a technically insoluble problem, but results from a situation [which is] voluntarily sustained . . . one cannot condemn an oppressed people when it is forced to use force to liberate itself, or one would incur a new injustice . . . one cannot compare the UNJUST VIOLENCE of the oppressors who sustain this "nefarious system" with the JUST VIOLENCE of the oppressed. . . . These peoples have a right to their legitimate defense. Christians throughout the continent must be firmly and clearly urged to opt for all that contributes to liberation. . . . Christians must be given a wide berth in their election of the best means to obtain that liberation."[9]

Priests not only preached this new catechism, but in some cases joined the guerrillas—father Camilo Torres, killed in action in 1967 while fighting for the Colombian National Liberation Army, became the most famous. His death turned him into a hero, second only to Che Guevara, and his message that "the Catholic who is not a revolutionary is living in mortal sin" would push many to a similar fate.

These changes within the church were particularly noticeable within Argentina, where over 90 percent of the population is baptized Catholic. Two men played a vital role in the development of this new Catholic doctrine: Father Carlos Mugica and Juan García Elorrio. García Elorrio, a former seminarian, became the editor of *Cristianismo y Revolución,* a periodical propagating Camilo Torres' views. Mugica, a Jesuit priest, was founder member of the Movement of Third World Priests, which originated in Buenos Aires in 1968 but quickly spread throughout Latin America.[10] He was also professor of theology at the University of our Savior (Universidad del Salvador), and spiritual advisor to the Catholic Student Youth branch at the National Buenos Aires School (Colegio Nacional Buenos Aires), the most prestigious state high school in the country. Both institutions became notorious for providing guerrilla cadres. Three of the founder members of Montoneros—Mario Eduardo Firmenich, Fernando Abal Medina, and Carlos Gustavo Ramus—were Mugica's pupils at the Nacional. In addition, several of the remaining founder members of the organization militated in Catholic Action, the Catholic Student Youth, and the Catholic Worker Youth. Radical Catholicism was also a driving force for the original Descamisados, most of whom were members of the youth wing of the Christian Democratic party, and FAP counted with several ex-seminarians and priests.

Ideology and Organization During the Argentine Revolution

The Argentine Situation

Most guerrilla pronouncements during the early years inevitably referred to the first Peronist era (1946–55). Perón was viewed as the initiator of a struggle for national liberation, and events following his downfall in 1955 were taken as proof that the dominant sectors were bent on preventing the continuation of that struggle: "the disappointment, the bewilderment provoked by the fall of a government with wide popular support, nevertheless deposed with an amazing ease. . . . The new regime was based on an attack against the union movement, which it attempted to destroy, in political proscriptions, preventing the participation of those who represented the working class and the popular sectors in general." [11] The continued proscription of Peronism provided an indictment of the groups that abetted it. Foremost among these were the union leaders, called "bureaucrats," who had repeatedly betrayed their rank and file, and the politicians who had agreed to participate in fraudulent elections. "Because many times our people has been betrayed by the old politicians and the union delinquents." [12] "As you well say the leaders who call themselves peronists have betrayed the masses, have switched to the side of the oligarchy and imperialism. In this way they have ceased to be peronists even though they disguise themselves as such." [13]

At the same time, Argentina was considered a classic example of a dependent Third World country exploited by industrial nations, in particular the United States. The "imperialist offensive" launched with the ouster of Perón had become more pronounced under Onganía, "a military dictatorship in the service of monopoly capital." [14] While political events since 1955 served to condemn parties and liberal democracy, economic conditions in Argentina provided an indictment of capitalism and pointed to the need for a socialist transformation.

The Second War of Independence

Socialism in Argentina was to be attained through violence. Two arguments seemed to support this view. First, guerrillas pointed not only to the violent nature of the country's politics but to the continuous presence of that violence. From the vantage point of their 1960s radicalization, guerrillas interpreted Argentine history as a series of confrontations between the oligarchy and the masses:

> We feel part of the last synthesis of an historical process that begins 160 years back. . . . Throughout this historical process there have been in the country two political currents, on the one hand that of the liberal *Oligarchy,* clearly anti-national and traitorous, on the other hand that of the *People,* identified with the defense of its interests that are the interests of the Nation, against the imperialist assaults of each historical circumstance[15]; . . .
>
> This struggle, this action, [is] the continuation of the struggle staged by rural workers, by industrial workers. . . . We are also the continuators of general San Martín, because we are in the second independence for the liberation from yankee imperialism and for the construction of the socialist motherland.[16]

Therefore, if the first War of Independence had brought about the collapse of Spain's empire in América, only a second War of Independence would rescue Argentina from its neo-colonialist situation.

The second argument made in support of armed struggle was that the experience of the Peronist Resistance and other spontaneous outbursts like the Cordobazo proved that mass struggles were insufficient. Unarmed, the people inevitably suffered repression. The intensity of the "counter-revolutionary offensive" in the 1960s determined the need for armed struggle:

> [The Cordobazo] is a fundamental event but also demonstrated that spontaneity is not enough. That what is needed is the organization of the people's armed vanguard. We believe this has been understood and expresses itself in the way that popular sectors have assimilated the revolutionary struggle; . . . those who accuse us . . . of dismissing the importance of political struggle because we have chosen the road of arms, of armed struggle, forget that this struggle is nothing but politics by other means and not any other means, but efficacious means. Our people resorted to other possibilities, to all those at hand and [those other channels] were blocked.[17]

The Strategy

Having established the need for a socialist transformation of Argentina, and having characterized the struggle as a Second War of Independence, the guerrillas defined their strategy. This was popular war, described as "total, because it supposes the destruction of the Capitalist State and its army . . . national, because it aims for the emancipation from foreign domination . . . prolonged, because we must organize the Popular Army." [18] However, armed struggle was not considered the only form of struggle, merely the most efficacious. During those early years all guerrilla groups made repeated, though vague, references to the need to coordinate mass struggles and armed struggle. Two reasons for this were advanced. First, armed actions were supposed to be "understood and accepted" by the masses and were also expected to match and not supersede the intensity of class confrontation. Second, guerrillas knew it would take considerable time before they found themselves in the position to challenge the regime openly.[19]

The analysis described in this entire section was shared by all guerrilla groups. However, there were two issues on which ERP and FAL disagreed with the other groups. The former were Marxist-Leninist and believed that a revolutionary party must guide and control the revolutionary process. Because Montoneros, Descamisados, FAR, and FAP adhered to Peronism, they did not see the need to create such a party. The second disagreement arose over the characterization of Peronism. All the groups agreed that it was a multiclass alliance. ERP and FAL (clinging to what had been the Argentine left's traditional view of Peronism until the Resistance) concluded that this resulted in a perpetuation of bourgeois ideology within the movement for which Perón was responsible. Yet they accepted and praised the left-wing sectors of Peronism and seemed to advocate a "Peronism without Perón." Peronist guerrillas distinguished between the national bourgeoisie and the bourgeoisie linked to monopoly capital, for in their view, the process of internationalization of capital created common interests between the national bourgeoisie and the working class and awarded the former a role in the national liberation struggle.[20] These differences of opinion between Marxist and Peronist guerrillas did not appear to be very important during this period, for the groups' intellectual production was very limited. In addition, the groups (and the rest of Argentine society) believed that the military would be in power for a considerable period of time. When Lanusse called for elections the groups started talking about "the electoral trap," with the conviction that the elections would be canceled. Finally, it should be pointed out that in spite of these ideological differences relations among the different groups were cordial and frequently led to loans of money and materiel, to the sharing of technological developments, and occasionally to joint operations.[21]

Organization

Armed organizations adopt a cellular structure according to the principle of compartmentalization, where an individual only knows the identity of the mem-

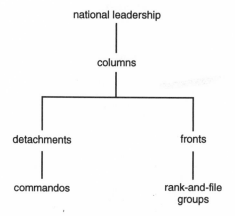

Sources: Interviews with former combatants; communiqués to the press after individual operations; guerrilla documents not for citation.

Figure 8.1. Initial Guerrilla Structure

bers of his or her own cell, and that of a member of another cell who acts as nexus. Decisions are communicated in two different manners: the organization can adopt a pyramidal, decentralized structure in which decisions made at the top are communicated downward, or it can adopt a centrifugal structure resembling a wheel in which decisions made at the hub are communicated out.[22] Throughout the period 1969–79, Argentine groups adopted variations on the former. Figures 8.1 and 8.2 exemplify the standard guerrilla structures adopted during the Onganía regime.[23]

Initially, the fighting unit was the commando. Several commandos formed detachments, which formed columns. Members of these fighting units were expected to do political work as well as to participate in military actions (see chapter 7). In addition, the organization counted with members devoted exclusively to political work, operating in rank-and-file groups (*grupos de base*). All the groups devoted to work in the same milieu constituted a "front"—the union front, the student front, and so on.[24] Members of mass fronts still belonged to a specific column but were "compartmentalized" from the combatants. Columns (sometimes called regionals or zones) had a territorial basis, normally corresponding to a province. Provinces of marginal importance were sometimes clustered together, as with the ERP's Salta-Jujuy regional. The organizing principle was a loose version of democratic centralism, or, to use the guerrillas' jargon, "strategic unity and tactical decentralization," where the national leadership set broad policy goals and individual columns were free to implement those goals as they saw fit.

There were no military ranks within the groups, and the head of a fighting

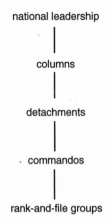

national leadership

columns

detachments

. commandos

rank-and-file groups

Sources: Interviews with former combatants; communiqués to the press after individual operations; guerrilla documents not for citation.

Figure 8.2. Guerrilla Structure Circa 1972

unit was simply addressed as the *responsable* (responsible person). The national leadership of each group was theoretically collegiate. But in the cases of FAR, Montoneros, and ERP, one man was recognized as the leader. Fernando Abal Medina was the first leader of Montoneros. He and Gustavo Ramus were ambushed and killed at a pizza restaurant in Buenos Aires province on September 7, 1970, thereafter known as the "Day of the Montonero." Abal was succeeded by José Sabino Navarro, who was killed in an ambush in Córdoba in July 1971. Mario Firmenich then became the group's leader. Mario Roberto Santucho was Commandant of the ERP from 1969, and after his death in 1976, Luis Mattini took his place. Carlos Olmedo led FAR until his death in action in 1971. He was succeeded by Roberto Quieto, who negotiated the fusion with Montoneros in 1973 and became the Montoneros' second in command.[25]

As figure 8.2 shows, by late 1972 this structure had been revised. Members of the commandos were still expected to engage in political work as well as military action, but, significantly, the fronts lost their autonomy and rank-and-file groups came under the supervision of the responsible person in the commandos. Members of these rank-and-file groups now received military instruction and were also expected to provide logistical assistance and support for armed operations, and this at a time when the country was preparing for the March 1973 elections. This was the first intimation of what would become apparent after 1973, namely, the subordination of political work to military activity.

The ERP's structure, shown in figure 8.3, was slightly more complex. This was due to the fact that the ERP had been created by the Workers' Revolutionary Party (Partido Revolucionario de los Trabajadores, or PRT). Closely following

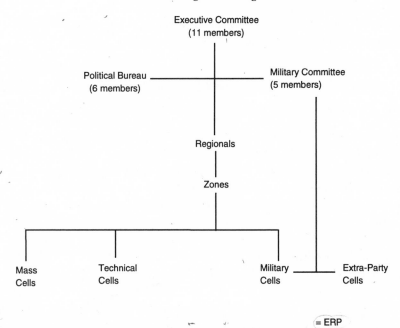

Sources: Interviews with former combatants; Partido Revolucionario de los Trabajadores, *Resoluciones del V Congreso y de los Comité Central y Comité Ejecutivo Posteriores* (Buenos Aires: Ediciones El Combatiente, 1973).

Figure 8.3. Structure of the PRT-ERP

the Vietnamese experience, the PRT believed in a strict control of the party over the army.

The party was headed by an Executive Committee of 11 members which were divided into a Political Bureau and a Military Committee. The latter also constituted the ERP's direction. The party then branched into seven regionals subdivided into zones. Each zone had three different types of cells. Mass cells were supposed to do political work, and within a zone, mass cells engaged in the same type of work also constituted a front. Technical cells were in charge of propaganda and general administrative work. Military cells constituted the ERP. The ERP's statutes also contemplated the existence of a small number of cells formed by individuals who were not party members, as long as they were willing to subordinate themselves to the party's Military Committee. In other aspects the ERP's organization was similar to the one described above. The army was organized into commandos, brigades, and columns, and there were no military ranks. The PRT's direction was in fact exercised by the Political Bureau, the Military Committee, the Executive Committee, and two additional organs, the Party Congress, which met every three years, and the Central Committee (selected at the Party Congress) which met every six months. But the Executive Committee was in charge of the day-to-day running of the party.[26]

The Peronist Interregnum

"Why and Against What the ERP Will Continue Fighting"

One month before Cámpora's inaugural, the ERP sent the president-elect a long letter explaining that the organization respected the popular will and would not attack his government, but it would continue to attack foreign businesses and the army. The police, subordinate to the executive through the Ministry of the Interior, would not be attacked "as long as it remains neutral." [27]

The decision is justified by ERP leader Mario Roberto Santucho in a booklet entitled *Bourgeois Power and Revolutionary Power*.[28] Santucho states that the Argentine bourgeoisie asserts its domination through two forms of dictatorship, parliamentarism and bonapartism. In the former, "apparently all the people elect those who will govern them. But in reality this is not the case because as we all know candidacies are determined by the power of money." [29] In the latter the bourgeoisie "openly affirms the government on the armed forces, which are presented as saviors of the nation." Santucho then analyzes Argentine history after the 1943 military coup as a cyclical alternation of parliamentarism and bonapartism, and concludes that the 1973 Peronist government is, in spite of appearances, "bourgeois and pro-imperialist." Perón, an experienced politician, could defend bourgeois interests while appearing to favor the popular sectors. Writing shortly after Perón's death in July 1974, Santucho suggests this is no longer possible and states that Argentina is at the brink of a revolutionary situation. The pamphlet proposed, and the PRT's Central Committee adopted as policy, the establishment of liberated zones which would lead to the development of dual power. In order to achieve this, the PRT aimed for the gradual transformation of the ERP into a regular force. Because this would be possible only with "the broadest unity and mobilization of the popular masses," [30] the party resolved to increase its presence in the factories and to sponsor the creation of an Anti-Imperialist Democratic Front.[31] The other Marxist organization, FAL, declared a truce with the Cámpora government but stated that "today, like yesterday, we affirm that we will win with our weapons . . . the present is one of struggle and the future is ours." [32] But FAL was at this time crumbling into different factions. By the end of the year it had ceased to exist and a portion of its membership had joined the ERP.

The Hedge Theory

Unlike the ERP, Peronist guerrillas had reasons to feel satisfied, as they had achieved the return of Perón to the country and of Peronism to power. Yet between Cámpora's inaugural in May and Perón's inaugural in October 1973 the guerrillas suffered a series of political setbacks: a reformist economic policy; the Ezeiza massacre on June 20 and Perón's speech blaming the Revolutionary Tendency; the forced resignation of Cámpora in July; and the nomination of Isabel Perón as vice-presidential candidate for the September elections. As one radicalized periodical put it, "a notorious disappointment reigns today within the peronist youth and the revolutionary sectors of peronism . . . Perón returns to Argentina . . . and destroys one by one, carefully, the youth's dreams." [33]

The guerrillas attempted to explain Perón's about-face through the hedge theory, according to which Perón still supported the radicalized youth wing of his movement but took unpopular measures because he was influenced by his wife, Isabel, his private secretary José López Rega, and representatives of the Peronist right, notably the union bosses. The first formulation of this theory appeared in a communiqué issued by the Montoneros the day after the Ezeiza massacre: "they wanted to prevent the meeting [between Perón and the people] so that they can maintain the hedge they have built around our Leader . . . lying to Perón about what the people say and think and lying to the people about what Perón says and thinks." [34] The youth's answer to the situation was to organize a march attended by 80,000 people to Perón's house on July 21, 1973. Perón agreed to speak to four Peronist Youth representatives and promised to keep in permanent contact with his radicalized young followers. The cover of *El Descamisado*'s next issue would proclaim "The Wizard López Rega's Hedge is Broken." [35] The exultant mood was broken when the guerrillas and their sympathizers found out that the man Perón had appointed to act as liaison between them and their leader was none other than the hated López Rega. In the months that followed, the Revolutionary Tendency would return to the theme of the hedge every time that Perón's actions or speeches indicated that he no longer favored armed organizations. [36] But Perón's behavior made it clear that the hedge did not exist and, in fact, pushed the guerrillas to reappraise his role as leader.

Movementism Versus Alternativism

The polemic between movementists and alternativists started within FAP in 1971–72 [37] and spread to other sectors of the Revolutionary Tendency in 1973. The debate centered around contending views on the course of the national liberation struggle. Both parties to the debate agreed that Peronism had, since its origins, been a multiclass alliance. The movementists believed that it should continue to be so, given that national liberation preceded social liberation. During the first (or national) phase the principal contradiction was between the nation and imperialism, whereas the contradiction between the bourgeoisie and the proletariat was secondary:

> The slogan "Liberation or Dependency" marks the terms of the principal confrontation. On the one hand, imperialism and its allies; on the other, the peronist people and its allies. The People, formed by the working class . . . small urban and rural producers, the great majority of students and intellectuals . . . middle urban and rural producers . . . On the other hand, imperialism . . . and its native allies, the industrial, financial, commercial and landowning oligarchy.[38]

Alternativists claimed that movementism served to disguise class struggle and rejected the division of the struggle into two phases:

> It is typical of movementism, on the one hand to mask class struggle, and on the other, to divide the process into two phases, in the first of which there would be a national liberation, led by the movement, and then social liberation (socialism). . . . The only consistently anti-imperialist class is the working class. . . . But the struggle of the working class is not only anti-imperialist but pro-socialist and therefore the first national liberation phase does not exist.[39]

Although movementists believed in complete obedience to the revolutionary leadership of Perón, alternativists claimed that Perón was not a revolutionary and proposed what they called "the *revolutionary* working-class alternative *independent* of bourgeois, bureaucrats, and traitors."[40] This slogan, which was repeated constantly but never explained much further, translated into suggestions for permanent rank-and-file organization and mobilization in factories, neighborhoods, slums, and Peronist party locales.

The Montoneros were the main proponents of movementism, and FAR and Descamisados, which by late 1973 had fused with Montoneros, were also movementist. FAP defended alternativism, yet one wing of the alternativist FAP ended up joining the movementist Montoneros, as did an ERP splinter (ERP 22) and two FAL splinters (CPL and FAL 22) which, from a Marxist perspective, also defended alternativism.[41] In fact, the ideological confusion that surrounded the movementism versus alternativism debate was rampant. At the same time that they expressed their desire for a socialist transformation of Argentina and stated that Perón was not a socialist, the alternativists claimed they were not challenging the leadership of Perón.[42] The movementists professed their faith in the undisputed revolutionary leadership of Perón at the same time that they viewed their role as that of monitoring the government's deviation from original goals. Those responsible for these deviations were the "traitors" who attempted to influence Perón, while the Montoneros were the only ones displaying "loyal" behavior: "either obsequiousness or loyalty . . . those who hide their treason behind their obsequiousness. . . . Are the spokespersons for all that which opposes [the country's] liberation. We already know that many of them are linked directly to imperialism."[43]

The Montoneros persisted in their movementism until Perón's death in July 1974, when they adopted the slogan "Isabel is not Perón" and became committed alternativists. Whether the Montonero leadership ever believed in movementism is highly debatable. In late 1973, while the Montoneros publicly accused the alternativists of failing to grasp the truly revolutionary nature of Perón's leadership,[44] Mario Firmenich gave a lecture for a select group of Montonero officers which came to be known as the "Perón is a bourgeois leader talk" because that was, in essence, the message.[45] That the Montonero rank and file believed in movementism is more than likely.

Socialismo Nacional

Ultimately the movementism/alternativism polemic was spurious in that neither faction overruled the possibility of a continuation of armed struggle under democratic conditions. Interviewed immediately after a meeting with Perón in September 1973, and asked about Montonero strategy, Firmenich answered:

> Guerrilla warfare . . . is the highest level of political struggle. This method is developed when political objectives cannot be attained through non-armed forms of political struggle . . . We define ourselves through the resort to this form of struggle as politico-military organizations, our fundamental end is and always has been a political objective, . . . power springs out of the barrel of a gun . . . if we abandoned our weapons we would retreat in our political positions . . . As long as the power of imperialism and the oligarchy has not been destroyed we must prepare ourselves to endure and face the next confrontation.[46]

Therefore while ERP and FAL did not even wait until Cámpora's inaugural to state that they would continue fighting, Peronist guerrillas publicly explained that they might have to return to arms if Argentina's transition toward national and social liberation was interrupted. In fact, only one wing of FAP ceased military operations after Cámpora's inaugural.

The attainment of this national and social liberation was defined as *socialismo nacional*, literally national socialism. But even though the meaning of socialismo nacional was never fully explained, what was stated beyond any doubt was that it did not entail a nazification of Argentina (national socialism, in any case, translates as *nacionalsocialismo*). What was also repeated was that socialismo nacional was an adaptation of the principles of socialism to Argentine conditions. Scholars have studiously (and understandably) avoided discussions of this term because it is difficult to rationalize Montonero thought on this issue. No Montonero document, official or unofficial, explains the meaning of socialismo nacional. Speeches and articles in radicalized periodicals assumed that the readers understood what the concept meant, which was not the case. In fact, when asked to explain what the difference between Marxism and socialismo nacional was, each guerrilla interviewee provided me with a different answer.[47] Since socialismo nacional was equated with the abolition of private property and the establishment of the dictatorship of the proletariat, it is not easy to see what specific adaptation to Argentine conditions this entailed. References to socialismo nacional often highlighted the redistributive policies of the first Peronist government (1946–55), implying that socialism was "national" because it built on an earlier populist experience. Considering that discussions of socialismo nacional also referred to the two stages of national and social liberation and specified that the working class would build socialism, a second interpretation could be that what made socialism "national" was a transitional phase and the fact that the abolition of classes would be dictated by the levels of class consciousness displayed by the masses. A third, more cynical (but probably correct) interpretation might be that socialismo nacional was at best a naive and mistaken view of Peronism and the Peronist masses and at worst a dishonest attempt to find legitimation within the Peronist movement.[48]

Organization

The gradual transformation of the ERP into a regular force, decided by the PRT in 1974, involved the introduction of military ranks and uniforms and the organization into larger fighting units. Luis Mattini states that when ranks were awarded, "the squadron '*presented arms*' . . . with rigorous military salute, the pertinent speeches and closing with a toast. The graduate had to swear according to regulations drafted by Santucho himself in the juridico-military Castilian used officially . . . combatants took all this formalism very seriously and patiently explained [these rituals] to new recruits, sympathizers and adherents who wondered what the difference with the fanfare of the bourgeois army was."[49]

The ERP's new structure is presented in figure 8.4.

The smallest unit was the squadron, led by a sergeant. Squadrons were grouped into platoons, led by a lieutenant, and platoons formed a company. Companies were led by a captain assisted by a General Staff formed by the lieutenants commanding the companies' platoons. The largest unit was the battalion, formed by various companies. Battalions were led by a commandant and a General Staff formed by the different company commanders. The heads of battalions formed the ERP's Central General Staff, theoretically the supreme command even though Commandant Santucho, a member of that body, was also consid-

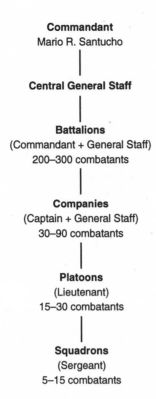

Commandant
Mario R. Santucho

Central General Staff

Battalions
(Commandant + General Staff)
200–300 combatants

Companies
(Captain + General Staff)
30–90 combatants

Platoons
(Lieutenant)
15–30 combatants

Squadrons
(Sergeant)
5–15 combatants

Sources: Interviews with former combatants; Mario R. Santucho, *Poder Burgués y Poder Revolucionario* (Buenos Aires: N.p., 1974); Luis Mattini, *Hombres y Mujeres del PRT-ERP* (Buenos Aires: Editorial Contrapunto, 1990).

Figure 8.4. Structure of the ERP, 1974

ered Commandant of the ERP.[50] The structure of the PRT described in figure 8.3 theoretically remained the same, the only modification being the decision to employ the members of mass and technical cells in combat and combat support roles occasionally. After 1973, in fact, those wanting to join the party were expected to take an "entrance course." This did not entail, as might be expected, instruction on Marxist texts, but rather basic instruction on the use of firearms.[51] Even though the PRT was still supposed to direct the ERP by 1974 the leadership of the ERP was also the leadership of the PRT. Santucho was both Commandant of the ERP and General Secretary of the PRT; and all the members of the PRT's Executive Committee (those in the Political Bureau as well as those in the Military Committee) were commandants in the ERP. In practice, by 1974 the PRT was subordinate to the ERP and, as the decision to use mass and technical cells in combat reveals, political activity was subordinated to the development of a regular force.[52]

Along with the military reorganization, the PRT employed two "political tools"[53] during this period: the Anti-Imperialist Pro-Socialist Front (Frente Anti-Imperialista y por el Socialismo or FAS) and the Rank and File Union Movement (Movimiento Sindical de Base or MSB). These were not strictly speaking the ERP's front organizations because the PRT helped launch both (assisted by other political forces), but the ERP had a leading voice in both. The FAS, launched in 1973, grouped activists in student, union, and neighborhood organizations of socialist extraction. The MSB grouped rank-and-file combativos and clasistas. In addition to its participation in the MSB, the PRT apparently intensified its activism in factories of the Buenos Aires-Córdoba-Santa Fe industrial belt. Though various party documents make this claim, there is no way to estimate the strength of the PRT's shop-floor presence.[54] The FAS and the MSB held several congresses in 1973–74, but they were doomed to failure from the start. The PRT's characterization of Peronism as "reformist" turned them into sectarian organizations. The MSB, for example, was expected to provide "an alternative of democratic trade unionism,"[55] which was impossible given that the majority of the union movement adhered to Peronism, and the PRT-ERP rejected it as a tool of bourgeois domination. In addition, the PRT-ERP's strategy of dual power determined a concentration on military action and reduced the FAS and the MSB to sources of recruitment.[56] Proof of the PRT-ERP's lack of a serious commitment toward mass action is provided if one considers the "July Days" (Jornadas de Julio) of 1975, the series of strikes and mobilizations that led to the ouster of the hated López Rega, Minister of Social Welfare and creator of the Triple A death squads. Tucumán and Villa Constitución, the epicenters of the PRT-ERP's FAS and MSB activity, were uninvolved in those events.[57] That Tucumán was also the province where the ERP was conducting its rural guerrilla campaign should have alerted the guerrillas to the fact that military action does not create revolutionary consciousness.

The new structure adopted by the Montoneros is portrayed in figure 8.5. The group, which now called itself "Politico-Military Organization Montoneros," reverted once more to what in guerrilla jargon is known as the "double pyramid," with the military structure and the mass fronts compartmentalized.

The military side of the organization was still structured into ten columns. The territorial basis was maintained and combatants were still expected to perform political work as well as participate in military action. Three innovations were implemented during this period. First, military ranks were introduced: aspirant, officer, second officer, first officer, and major officer. Second, the old commandos became combat platoons, now joined by a structure of combat militias expected to perform paramilitary functions in support of the platoons. While

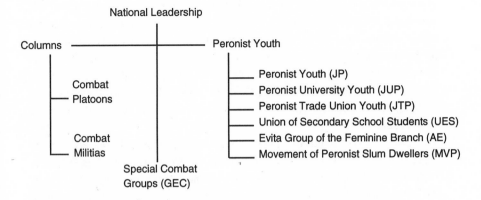

Sources: Interviews with former combatants; "Hacia la construcción del Ejército Montonero," *Evita Montonera*, 8, October 1975, pp. 25–26; Partido Montonero, "Critica y Autocrítica," *Vencer*, 2/3, 1979, pp. III–XXXII. National Leadership is now capitalized because that was the name given to the collegiate executive.

Figure 8.5. Structure of the Politico-Military Organization Montoneros, 1974

the platoons staged an operation in a given neighborhood, the militiamen (a rank below that of aspirant) could be asked to stage a demonstration and throw a few Molotovs nearby to create a diversion for the security forces. Finally, elite troops known as Special Combat Groups (Grupos Especiales de Combate or GEC), not affiliated with any given column, were created. The GECs could be called upon to operate anywhere in the country. This was the beginning of the distinction between territorials—which belonged to a specific column, operated politically and militarily within a given geographical area, and obeyed orders from the leadership of their column—and professionals—which were not ascribed to any geographical area, did not perform political work, and were accountable directly to the National Leadership.[58]

On the political front, the Montoneros came to control the Peronist Youth (Juventud Peronista or JP). Though the JP had been in existence since 1957, by the late 1960s "Peronist Youth" was a generic term used to describe a myriad of unconnected small groups. In 1970, as these groups approached one another with a view to establishing a unified structure, the Montoneros, decimated by arrests and deaths following the kidnapping of Aramburu and the seizure of La Calera, turned to mass political work. In a two-year maneuver devised by Montonero Carlos Hobert, the organization would recruit members within each of the JP groups and smear the reputations of the leaders of the other groups, who were accused of being reformists, opportunists, and so on. The strategy was called *entrismo*. The youth groups, completely ignorant of the maneuver, were doubly manipulated: first, because they were being controlled by the Montoneros; and second, because the individual Montonero who established the contact used his or her influence with the youth groups as a tool to enhance his or her power within the Montoneros.[59] Through this strategy of divide and rule, by the time these youth groups had coalesced to form a nationwide JP in mid-1973, Montoneros controlled its leadership. The unified JP would be organized into seven, and later eight, regionals, which were to the JP what columns were to the military structure. The collegiate executive was composed of the heads of all the regionals.

In the first six months of 1973 the Montoneros established a variety of front organizations: the Peronist University Youth (Juventud Universitaria Peronista or JUP), the Union of Secondary School Students (Unión de Estudiantes Secundarios or UES), the Peronist Working Youth (Juventud Trabajadora Peronista or JTP), the Movement of Peronist Slum Dwellers (Movimiento de Villeros Peronistas or MVP), and the Evita Group of the Feminine Branch (Agrupación Evita de la Rama Femenina or AE). The names of most of these organizations are self-explanatory. The JTP operated at the factory and union level and the Evita Group was created for work within the Peronist movement, which since the 1940s had been organized around a Political, a Trade Union, and a Feminine branches. Each of these five organizations constituted a different front, yet generically they were known as either Peronist Youth or Revolutionary Tendency. Each one had its own nationwide executive, and the JUP, the JTP, and the UES were also organized into regionals.

These front organizations channeled an entire generation's impetus toward political participation. Young people involved in these organizations engaged in projects like building schools and health units, sporting activities, and community organizing. An example is Operation Dorrego, in which 8,000 militants in these front organizations joined 5,000 soldiers of the First Army Corps in reconstruction and building work in depressed areas of Buenos Aires province.[60] But they were undoubtedly the tools of Montonero policy. The experience of working-class organization in the JTP is particularly revealing. The emergence of a group that questioned the bureaucratic nature of unions was an extremely healthy thing. However, as long as the Montoneros subscribed to movementism, the maneuverability of the JTP was seriously limited. The JTP could challenge the corrupt leadership at the factory level, but it could not attempt any change in the national level union organization as Perón supported the union hierarchy and the Montoneros' movementism prevented any challenge to Perón's leadership. When the guerrillas switched to alternativism around the time of Perón's death, the JTP was employed to fight the Law of Professional Associations, which guaranteed the union hierarchy's control over the unruly rank and file and was the cornerstone of the Peronist government's economic policy. Two months after Perón's death the guerrillas decided to return underground, and the JTP activists, who had acquired considerable visibility, were easy prey for the Triple A. The same could be said of activists in all Montonero front organizations. The guerrillas handpicked the leadership of each organization and, as Hobert's JP strategy described above reveals, some of the leaders of these front organizations were at the same time Montonero officers. This is why in Montonero circles the distinction between those who belonged to the military structure and those who did not was not as important as that between those who were *encuadrados* (a nearly untranslatable term, although in English "aligned" comes close) and those who were not. Encuadrado derives from *cuadro,* that is to say, cadre, and encuadrados were all those who belonged to the Montonero ranks. Every member of a column was an encuadrado, but only a minority within the front organizations was. That encuadrados were leading the mass fronts need not have been a crippling factor. However, since the Montoneros viewed political influence in numerical terms, they repeatedly used their ability to put hundreds of thousands of activists in the streets to pressure Perón. This was recognized by Father Carlos Mugica, the Montonero founders' erstwhile spiritual advisor. Celebrating mass for Alberto Chejolán, a slum dweller and MVP activist killed during a demonstration organized by the guerrillas, Mugica said: "The death of Alberto Chejolán is lamentable. . . . So is the fact that outsiders come into the slums to attempt to manipulate the dwellers. . . . That is why there are two guilty of brother Chejolán's death: the irresponsibility of the police, yes, but also those who control the comrades and use them for their own interests." [61] In addition to the fact that they were persistently mobilized in aid of Montonero policy, front organizations were expected to furnish the personnel for the combat militias.

The Dirty War

Pronouncements by ERP and Montoneros following the military coup of March 24, 1976, are reminiscent of the early years. Guerrillas equated General Videla with General Onganía and expected the masses to display the same combativeness that had led to the Cordobazo. Shortly after the coup, under the slogan "Argentinians, to arms," Mario Santucho would editorialize in the pages of *El Combatiente:* "In our first war of independence the rebel armies twice attempted to advance through Bolivia towards Perú and failed; then they discovered the triumphant road through Chile. . . . This is what is happening and will happen in our revolutionary war. With advances and retreats we will escalate the abrupt and glorious path that leads us to the much desired national and social liberation of our motherland and our people." [62]

Santucho's initial enthusiasm could be somewhat forgiven, but in May, while the ravaging effects of the dirty war were more than apparent, the Montoneros ascertained that "the working class will unify the totality of classes and social sectors in a National Liberation Front which will be able to vanquish definitively the power of imperialism in our motherland." [63]

While they were still applying their Second War of Independence logic, there were three basic differences between 1969 and 1976 that the guerrillas did not appreciate. First, while Onganía's regime had been considered a *dictablanda*, Videla inaugurated one of the most repressive regimes in recent history, responsible for an estimated 8,000–30,000 disappearances. Second, given this repression, it was highly unlikely that any significant measure of popular resistance would materialize. Finally, guerrilla performance during the Peronist interregnum had so antagonized Argentine society that rather than support the guerrillas as it had done in 1969–73, it vigorously supported their elimination.

After 1976 there were no ideological changes. There was no need, as the struggle was characterized as the continuation of that begun in 1969.[64] At a meeting of the PRT's Central Committee in March 1976 the party predicted that the military dictatorship would fall through a general mass insurrection supported militarily by the ERP. It was decided to "militarize the party" by devoting a "significant portion" of the membership to permanent military action.[65] The entire national structure of the PRT was placed under the command of the ERP's Central General Staff. In practical terms, of course, this had already taken place after the 1974 reorganization that followed Santucho's *Bourgeois Power and Revolutionary Power*. Unlike the early years, the PRT-ERP did not even contemplate it had a role to play in the process leading to the expected mass insurrection. As the dirty war raged on, the Central Committee of June 1976 ruled that reverses were due to "lack of technico-military preparation" and "insufficient assimilation of marxism-leninism."[66] The Committee also decided that Commandant Santucho should leave the country for safety reasons, but Santucho was killed on July 19, the day he was scheduled to go into exile.[67] During 1977 the ERP devoted itself to careful military planning of future campaigns, an increasingly futile activity given that the PRT and the ERP were being annihilated.[68] In May 1977 the Executive Committee decided that the party's members should leave the country. "The decision was largely obeyed with military discipline (since this was the spirit in which it was ordered) . . . in fact, the PRT ceased to exist as an organized political force, save inside the prisons."[69]

While the ERP viewed its shortcomings in terms of insufficient "technico-military preparation" Montoneros regretted "the emergence of bureaucratizing tendencies, of de-militarization" within its ranks.[70] The group apparently thought it could resolve this by adopting a complex organizational structure (figure 8.6). The old politico-military organization turned itself into a party (Partido Montonero or PM) given that "Perón died and today we can ascertain that the only organization capable of leading the peronist masses is Montoneros."[71]

The highest party organs were the National Leadership (four members) and the five National Secretaryships. The party then branched off into six regionals, among which the ten columns were distributed. Columns were divided into cells devoted to political, trade union, or military activity. In addition to these

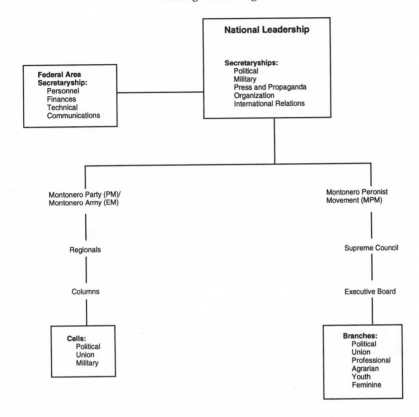

National Leadership

Secretaryships:
Political
Military
Press and Propaganda
Organization
International Relations

Federal Area Secretaryship:
Personnel
Finances
Technical
Communications

Montonero Party (PM)/
Montonero Army (EM)

Regionals

Columns

Cells:
Political
Union
Military

Montonero Peronist
Movement (MPM)

Supreme Council

Executive Board

Branches:
Political
Union
Professional
Agrarian
Youth
Feminine

Sources: Interviews with former combatants; "Entrevista al Comandante Firmenich: Poder Sindical o Destrucción Nacional," *Vencer*, 1, 1979, pp. 4–10; Partido Montonero, "Crítica y Autocrítica," *Vencer*, 2/3, 1979, pp. iii–xxxii; Francisco Cerecedo, "Los montoneros se explican," *Cambio 16*, 245, August 16, 1976, pp. 40–43; "Montoneros en dos frentes," *Cambio 16*, 295, August 7, 1977, pp. 36–38.

Figure 8.6. Structure of Montoneros After 1976

territorial structures, the party counted on another four professional secretary-ships providing specific services, known collectively as the "Federal Area."[72] On paper, this was how things were supposed to work, but in practice all the members of the National Leadership except for Mario Firmenich held National Secretaryships. And though Firmenich was both First Secretary of the Party and First Commandant of the Army (Ejército Montonero or EM), and official documents referred to "party and army," the army did not exist as a distinct entity. Rather, all party members were at the same time members of the army and held military ranks. With the creation of the party a new rank structure was adopted, roughly copied from the Argentine Army: second lieutenant, lieuten-ant, first lieutenant, captain, major, second commandant, commandant. Though uniforms had been used since the attack on the 29th Mounted Infantry Regiment in 1975, its use was officially regulated in 1978.[73]

Mass action was structured around the Montonero Peronist Movement (Movimiento Peronista Montonero or MPM), modeled on the traditional Peronist organization into branches. The MPM's executive organs were the Executive Board (ten members) and the Supreme Council which was comprised of, in addition to the Executive Board, eight representatives from each branch. These changes were considered "a qualitative transformation of the [Peronist] movement,"[74] though the only apparent change was that the Montoneros replaced Perón in the leadership role. Above the Supreme Council stood the "strategic leadership"[75] of the party with Firmenich as General Secretary of the MPM. But party and movement were designed as separate structures. The MPM represented "the massive political alignment of the Argentine people"[76] and the PM was defined as "not a mass party but a party of cadres, since the fact that the working class is subordinate to the dominant ideology generates as a consequence the existence of different levels of consciousness within the working class itself."[77] Simply put, "Lenin for the leadership and Perón for the plebes."[78] The Montoneros were not very consistent on the issue of the separation of party and movement, however, as members of party cells were expected to "fight for internal hegemony" within the movement's branches "but as the movement's activist, not as a member of the party."[79] Again it becomes necessary to distinguish between theory and practice. The separation of party and movement was artificial in that the vast majority of members of the MPM's Supreme Council and Executive Board, as well as those in the leadership of the different branches, were also PM members. In addition, rank-and-file members of the movement, militants of the old fronts of 1973–76, were the first victims of the dirty war. Thanks to repression, soon there was no following behind the MPM's elaborate command structure. One could also wonder what the point of creating a movement was, since "resistance" to the military government was only viewed in terms of military action.

In December 1976 the Montonero leadership went into exile. The logic behind this decision was the same one employed by the ERP when it decided to send Commandant Santucho abroad: an army never exposes its generals.[80] In exile, the PM and MPM leaders held conclaves, adopted resolutions that the rank and file left behind were expected to obey without questioning through the principle of democratic centralism, and planned further military campaigns.[81] Beyond their regular "Military Campaigns," of which there were four in 1976–78, the Montoneros staged two major counteroffensives. The first took place during the World Cup in Buenos Aires in mid-1978. It was a short and very successful operation (at least insofar as it demonstrated the ability to operate in "enemy territory") in which the EM mainly targeted military and police installations with sophisticated weaponry. It was also ignored by the Argentine press.

This was followed in late 1979 by the "Popular Counteroffensive," a disastrous adventure in which an undetermined number of top PM and EM cadres, including Commandant Horacio Mendizábal, Military Secretary of the Montonero party, met their deaths. In preparation for this offensive the Montoneros restructured themselves once more, eliminated secretaryships, and added new ones. As far as Argentina was concerned this was of no import. Back home there was no one, and nothing, for the Montoneros to lead.[82]

9

The Lost Patrol Revisited

his study began by introducing the idea that armed organizations resort to violence in order to promote certain political objectives, and
that these objectives are gradually forgotten as the struggle is defined
purely in military terms. Militarism within Argentine guerrilla groups mani-
fested itself in several ways. At the level of operations, chapter 3 showed how the
initial emphasis on attacks on property and not persons gave way to indiscriminate killings and frontal attacks against the armed forces, employing increasingly
larger units. At the organizational level, chapter 8 described the introduction of
ranks, uniforms, and insignia, the attempt to mimic the Argentine armed forces
in any way possible, and the manner in which, though guerrillas took advantage
of the opportunities opened by the 1973 amnesty to establish a variety of mass
fronts, these were employed in the service of military structures as a source of
recruitment or as a political complement to a military strategy. Ideological formulations tended to equate politics with war, to glorify death in combat and to
dehumanize the enemy. Free elections and Perón's return to the country became
tactical objectives in a war strategy. Political negotiations typical of democratic
processes were considered squalid, whereas armed struggle represented the only
principled course of action. Finally, at the level of individual motivation, the
life histories of guerrilla founders described in chapter 7 showed that the initial
heated debates—the "psychotherapy sessions" that interviewees remembered
with such nostalgia—gave way to complete subservience to the whims of the
groups' leaderships.

Barbara Tuchman's study of the coming of the First World War contains an
anecdote that every reader remembers. At the eleventh hour, scared by the prospect of a war on two fronts, the Kaiser considered a negotiation with France that

156

would have left Germany free to concentrate on the eastern front. His Chief of Staff replied this could not be done. The German General Staff's strategy (the so-called Schlieffen plan), organized even to the last train schedule, involved a massive westward mobilization and a quick defeat of France that would leave Germany free to fight Russia. A change of course, or an alteration in the rigid mobilization schedules, were deemed impossible.[1] This anecdote condenses what analysts of civil-military relations have described at length, namely, the differences between the military mind and the civilian mind. Soldiers favor order, hierarchy, and planning; politicians improvise and negotiate. Soldiers favor the group over the individual; politicians are great individualists. Furthermore, these two mind-sets result from the performance of very different functions.[2]

Armed struggle in Argentina became militarized because, to begin with, guerrillas provided military responses to political situations. Nothing exemplifies this better than the manner in which guerrillas chose to confront the Triple A. Opposition to illegal repression made Ricardo Balbín, leader of the Radical party, a natural ally. Balbín enjoyed an excellent relationship with officers in the armed forces, to whom the Triple A represented a challenge on their monopoly on violence. During the last year of Perón's life Balbín also developed a strong friendship with him and was generally viewed as the only politician who could influence Isabel Perón. But before joint action could prosper, the guerrillas undertook the execution of known paramilitaries, a policy Balbín could never approve of or condone. After the Montoneros killed Arturo Mor Roig—formerly Lanusse's Interior Minister, a prominent Radical politician, and a close friend of Balbín's—the Radical leader broke all contact with guerrilla groups.[3] In addition, the struggle became militarized because it displayed "a vast array of customs, interests, prestige, actions and thought associated with armies and yet transcending true military purposes."[4] The guerrillas' response to the 1976 coup makes this clear, for the guerrillas viewed Videla as another Onganía, and the 1976 military government as a repeat performance of the Argentine Revolution. Yet when it became clear that the armed forces took Isabel Perón's order "to neutralize and/or annihilate the action of subversive elements" literally,[5] armed organizations should have turned to a defensive strategy involving sabotage and small-scale attacks. Instead, guerrilla groups continued to expose their forces in frontal attacks, with predictable results. Rodolfo Walsh clearly outlined the need for a defensive strategy in his *Papers*,[6] as did others. At the time, guerrilla jargon referred to these options as "shots or papers" (*tiros o papeles*), that is to say, military offensives or armed propaganda. The groups chose the former course of action and, like the German General Staff, were unable to reverse it.

The strategic choices of armed organizations can be considered a product of both extrinsic and intrinsic factors. The extrinsic factors that could have explained the militarization of Argentine guerrilla groups include: the failure to mobilize support; the competition from rival underground organizations; the harsh state response to violence; and the existence of international pressures and/ or examples. Donatella della Porta and Sidney Tarrow resort to the first explanation when they argue that left-wing terrorism in Italy was a response to the apparent failure of the first cycle of protest in the late sixties.[7] This explanation would not fit the Argentine case because collective violent protest and armed struggle occurred simultaneously, and the militarization of armed struggle took place at the time when guerrilla groups were enjoying widespread popular support and had achieved a number of their objectives—the restoration of democracy, the return of Peronism to power, and the advent of the most progressive administration Argentina had ever had. In fact, by the time the cycle of protest ended in 1975, the militarization of armed struggle was a fait accompli. The notion that the behavior of armed organizations can be explained through the existence of rival groups, and that any armed organization will make strategic choices aimed at differentiating itself from its rivals or at preventing defections to rival groups, probably applies to the Palestinian Liberation Organization. Scholars have, for example, viewed escalation by such factions as the Popular Front for the Liberation of Palestine, Black September, and the Abu Nidal group as a means to radicalize the struggle, to obtain support from Arab states, or to challenge Yassir Arafat's leadership. Others have explained the intensity of violence in Northern Ireland in terms of ideological differences between the Irish Republican Army and the Irish National Liberation Army.[8] But this could not explain the militarization of armed struggle in Argentina because relations among the groups were amicable and not competitive (leading to exchanges of technological know-how, loans of materiel, and occasional joint operations), and factional activity was of no consequence. In fact, though factionalism is the norm among armed organizations, Argentina was the exception to the rule, and by 1973, when the process of militarization emerged, the six major groups and the smaller groupuscules had all coalesced around ERP and Montoneros. And, to the extent that there were major ideological differences among the groups, these became minimal as militarization developed.

As for the idea that government repression may influence the guerrillas' behavior, in Northern Ireland and the Basque region of Spain the existence of illegal repression and maltreatment of prisoners has helped legitimize armed struggle and has occasionally encouraged retaliation by armed organizations. In Argentina there is no doubt that the Triple A and the dirty war contributed to the militarization process. As the life histories of the combatants made clear, illegal repression strengthened group cohesion because armed organizations protected combatants from the dangers of life above ground, and the memory and the example of those who fell hardened the resolve of the survivors. In addition, illegal repression reinforced the organizations' view that they were irregular armies engaged in a struggle against the regular armed forces—an all-out war in which anybody who did not side with the guerrillas automatically became an enemy.

But because the Triple A death squads were launched in late 1973 and only operated openly after Perón's death in July 1974, and the dirty war was launched in 1976, illegal repression may have contributed to the militarization, but it did not cause it. Finally, the notion that international pressures or examples determine guerrilla behavior does not apply to the militarization of armed struggle in Argentina. To the extent that Argentine combatants received any encouragement or aid from Cuba, this took place only during the decade immediately following the Cuban revolution (1959–68) and had ended when the militarization began. The only experience of armed struggle that made any impact on Argentine combatants—that of the Tupamaros in Uruguay—was over by 1972. It could also be said that although guerrilla pronouncements occasionally paid homage to certain national liberation struggles, notably Algeria and Vietnam, combatants were largely impervious to political developments in the sixties and early seventies like the Chilean experience with socialism. As one of my interviewees said, "what mattered was our national problematique."

It is for these reasons that this study's explanation of the militarization of armed struggle focused on factors intrinsic to the groups. This has also been—albeit implicitly—the path followed by scholars and former participants, who have explained the guerrilla debacle in Argentina through the notion of "the divorce between the leadership and the rank and file." The argument runs as follows: through its control of financial resources, of rewards in the form of military promotion, and of information, and given the compartmentalized organization into cells, the leadership was able to obtain the compliance of the rank and file.[9] Similar theses have been advanced to describe the evolution of above ground, legal political organizations. Frances Fox Piven and Richard Cloward have described what they view as a paradox in the development of social movements in the United States: popular organizations make up for their lack of financial resources through membership strength, but increases in membership lead to divergent interests among leaders and followers. In addition to, or even in opposition to, the movement's initial goals, the leadership has as its objective the maintenance of its position of power. In pursuit of its own agenda, the leadership may sacrifice the interests of its following. Robert Michels provided the original formulation of this argument, the "iron law of oligarchy," in connection with European political parties.[10] There is some plausibility to the divorce argument, in that democratic centralism within Argentine guerrilla groups meant that decisions taken at the top had to be discussed, but eventually obeyed. Guerrillas termed this "bringing the line down" (bajar línea). In the case of the Montoneros it must also be said that the key decision to return underground in September 1974, a decision that placed activists in the mass fronts directly under the Triple A's telescopic sight, was never discussed within the organization. The rank and file, and the militants in front organizations, found out about it through the morning press. Mario Firmenich's statements made from the comfort of his Cuban exile, coldly evaluating his army's fatalities, also support the divorce argument: "we turn the organization into a weapon, simply a weapon, and therefore, we sacrifice the organization in combat in exchange for political prestige. We have five thousand cadres less, but, how many masses more? This is the point." [11]

Yet the divorce argument is too simple. The Montonero and ERP leadership allocated funds to the various columns or regionals and maintained the ability to reward conformity with military promotion, but they did not control information. The guerrilla founders, all mid-level cadres, repeatedly stressed that they had substantial knowledge of what went on in other organizational structures within their groups and were in contact with combatants in those other structures. The ease with which paramilitary squads destroyed the guerrilla organizations on a column-by-column (Montoneros) or regional-by-regional (ERP) basis during the dirty war indicates that captured combatants could provide substantial information under torture, beyond detailed knowledge of their individual cells. [12] In order for the guerrilla leadership to issue orders, someone had to obey them, and the leadership could not have sent hundreds to their deaths unless those individuals were willing to die or had lost the individual will to resist such orders. The leadership was not, as the divorce argument suggests, deceiving the rank and file. Combatants deceived themselves.

The explanation for the militarization of armed struggle advanced here focused on the interplay of three factors: the resocialization process, the development of a friend-foe ideology, and the bureaucratization of guerrilla groups. The life histories of guerrilla founders made clear that combatants joined very young and in the company of friends, political fellow travelers, and relatives with whom they embarked on a guerrilla "career." The new experiences in the underground, the learning process that becoming a guerrilla involved, reinforced these affective ties developed during an earlier militancy in legal organizations, to the point where the guerrilla group became a combatant's surrogate family and sole reference point. Several of the guerrilla founders made it clear that they had qualms about the direction the struggle had taken after 1973, yet the thought of leaving the group was almost inconceivable since their identity was so tied up with the organization. Ideological formulations that centered on the war analogy did not leave many options. One belonged either to the revolutionary or to the reformist camp. As former ERP member Hernán Invernizzi recalls, "many comrades (militants, leaders, intellectuals) were aware of the mistakes. The majority kept their mouths shut. *They were scared*. Scared they would be accused of being reformists." [13] This manichean war analogy viewed Argentine history as a constant confrontation between oppressors and oppressed, between friend and foe, good and evil. Any deviation from orthodoxy was tantamount to betrayal, the worst-epithet that guerrilla rhetoric reserved for the enemy's behavior. Ideological formulations thus reinforced the centrifugal tendencies of the re-socialization process. In addition, the phenomenal increase in membership after 1973 made some kind of hierarchical organization necessary. It did not require the introduction of military ranks, uniforms, and discipline, nor the gradual involvement of the legal fronts in combat, even though that was the outcome. And, if affective ties linked combatants to each other and ideology condemned dissent, the organization rewarded conformity with a position of power. Bureaucratization also allowed the combatants to distance themselves from the consequences of their group's actions. Statements by the guerrilla founders about being "more a political than a military cadre" point in this direction.

The unfolding of campaigns of armed struggle in other countries replicates several of the characteristics emphasized in this book.[14] At the operational level, according to Donatella della Porta, the Italian Red Brigades and the German Baader-Meinhof Gang initially emphasized "violence against property, not persons." This was reversed as the cycle of protest of the late sixties came to an end, the groups became more isolated and felt the impact of repression.[15] Radicalized German periodicals of the mid-seventies showed the same widening definition of the enemy seen in Argentina, as not only members of the security forces, but also politicians and bureaucrats were listed as "creatures that deserved to be killed."[16] Even greater parallels can be drawn between the Basque ETA and the Argentine groups. In both cases, armed organizations derived wide societal support from the fact that they went into action against an authoritarian government; and squandered their support by intensifying their violent repertoires with the advent of democracy. As Francisco Llera, José M. Mata, and Cynthia Irwin point out, ETA carried out most of its murders after the death of Francisco Franco in November 1975 and in particular during the key phase of the transition to democracy, while the referenda on the Spanish constitution (1978) and the Basque Autonomy Statute (1979) took place.[17]

More important, analyses of the membership of Spanish, Italian, Irish, and West German groups highlight aspects of the resocialization process described here. In the Italian and West German cases, combatants frequently joined following a period of political involvement in legal organizations in key radicalizing milieus of the "New Left"—the University of Trent, the Metropolitan Political Collective in Milano, the Berlin "counterculture scene," and the German Students for a Democratic Society. The decision to join was usually made in the company of friends or relatives. *Etarras* usually met at mountaineering clubs, a frequent source of recruitment for ETA. In describing Irish hunger striker Bobby Sands, Padraig O'Malley states, " many young people like Sands, who had just turned eighteen, didn't make decisions to join paramilitary organizations—they simply drifted into them with consequences out of all proportion to the level of motivation that led them to join in the first place. It seemed like the thing to do. . . . Even the knowledge that friends or neighbors had joined up was sufficient."[18]

The phenomenon of "guerrilla dynasties" in Argentina was also seen elsewhere. Describing West German combatants, Klaus Wasmund mentions that "the number of couples, and brothers and sisters is astonishingly high." Of the ten Irish combatants who went on hunger strike in March 1981, three had seen family members interned without trial, and three had brothers serving sentences in the Maze/Long Kesh prison.[19] The socialization of Italian and German combatants also reveals that, like their Argentine cousins, the choice of going underground was made comparatively quickly but brought about significant changes in the combatants' lives. Terms like "party," "fun," "family," and expressions such as "I had such a good time" and "sense of the group," are all reminiscent of the nostalgia with which the Argentines described the early phases of their involvement and of the strong affective ties which determined that commitment to the others became such an important component of motivation.[20]

The adoption of a simplified friend-foe view of politics also seems to have been widespread. According to Baader-Meinhof leader Ulrike Meinhof, the world was divided into "human beings and pigs," and in the case of ETA, Pedro Ibarra Guell explained that commitment can only be sustained "as long as I convince myself that outside my community of struggle there are only groups with which it is not even worth speaking."[21] While one Italian combatant remembered that "outside the organization there was only evil," another one stated, "We lived the problem of death inside a grand ideology. . . . For me it was a routine job. And this is the very aberration of the ideology; on one side, there are your friends; and on the other, there are your enemies, and *the enemies are a category, they are functions, they are symbols. They are not human beings.* And so they have to be dealt with as absolute enemies; so that you have a relation of absolute abstraction with death."[22]

The war analogy served three functions: it lowered the combatants' inhibitions about violence by de-humanizing the enemy, reinforced individual commitment, since dissent became equivalent to betrayal, and introduced the imagery of heroic behavior. This allowed Rodolfo Walsh to rationalize the death of his daughter Vicki by positing that, although she could have chosen to serve others in ways "that were different without being dishonorable" she had chosen death, "the fairest, the most generous" road. Faced with their increasing isolation, the Italians combatants developed a similar exalted view of self-sacrifice. This cult of the hero received official sanction from the guerrilla groups: in Italy and Argentina (and sporadically in Germany) it became customary to name specific platoons and companies after fallen combatants, while the IRA buries its dead draped in the republican flag, with a cortege of uniformed combatants in attendance and a gun salute.[23]

Finally, Italian and West German groups modified their self-image in a fashion similar to that of Argentine guerrillas. In both countries armed organizations initially considered themselves as part of a broader social movement but eventually came to view themselves as armies. With the transition to democracy that followed the death of Franco, ETA confronted the same dilemma facing the Argentine groups in 1973—the choice between involvement in mass action or continuation of armed struggle. Within ETA, this led to the split between the "politico-militaries," who abandoned armed struggle in 1981, and the "militaries," who operate to this day. The relationship between the ETA militaries and radicalized but legal organizations in the Basque country is not unlike that which existed among ERP, Montoneros, and their mass fronts—legal organizations sympathetic to ETA have been forced "to accommodate the better part of their plans and actions to ETA's short-term projects . . . the subordination of all [their] activity to a project which is not even strategic but a basic necessity of ETA's: *its own survival as an armed organization.*"[24] A similar relationship exists between the IRA and its political wing, Sinn Fein. The latter functions as a legal political party, but its integrity as such is compromised by the need to express solidarity with the combatants. The more intense IRA violence becomes, the greater the need for Sinn Fein to justify it, and the less it can appeal to voters in the Republic of Ireland as well as the north.

All of the above suggests that militarization was not a process restricted to Montoneros and the ERP. The political contexts in which armed struggle emerged in Spain, Italy, Ulster, Germany, and Argentina were different. Yet in all cases armed struggle acquired a logic of its own, independent of its environment. What made the Argentine experience more dramatic was the financial and numerical strength of the groups, which allowed the guerrillas to stage such spectacular operations.

It could be said that armed struggle, Argentine style, consisted of an "is" and an "ought to." Guerrilla groups transformed themselves into a parody of the armed forces they were seeking to destroy. In their obsession with becoming a regular force, combatants copied all the vices and none of the virtues of military action. They never realized that the fact that in the eyes of Argentine society they increasingly resembled an army represented their political defeat. The political objectives that had originally animated the fight were sacrificed to military considerations, and the groups that were supposed to bring national and social liberation to the country developed into bureaucratized structures consumed by the cult of personality. In analyzing the behavior of Argentine guerrillas, however, one must not forget the societal context in which they operated. In Argentina the distance between political theory and political practice has always been enormous.

After 1976, from the television screen, the military asked parents: "It is 10 P.M. Do you know where your children are?" The underlying assumption was that the lack of strong parental authority and control turned children into guerrillas. That the military should take this view is quite remarkable considering that their own offspring had joined the enemy's ranks: General Julio Alsogaray's son, General Alberto Numa Laplane's son and daughter-in-law, the daughters of General Bernardino Labayru and Brigadier Laureano Landaburu, and Admiral Emilio Massera's niece, to name a few notorious cases, were all known guerrillas. In addition, counterterrorism was not the holy war it was made out to be. Repression proved profitable, as participants derived economic advantages in the form of the "war booty," which involved stripping an apartment bare after its occupants had disappeared, and selling children born in clandestine detention centers. The fact that over the eleven-year period in which armed struggle was a permanent feature of Argentine politics an array of legislative and judicial reforms were introduced to meet the guerrilla threat should allow for interesting comparisons with other countries. The Federal Penal Chamber of the Nation, introduced under Onganía and abolished by Cámpora, was not unlike the "diplock" or juryless court used in Northern Ireland; and after 1976 the Argentine military offered reduced prison sentences in exchange for public repudiations of the guerrilla organizations, though unlike the Repentance Law employed against the Italian Red Brigades, the Argentine bargaining was unofficial and was never legislated on. However, serious analysis of the effectiveness of antiterrorist legislation in Argentina is nearly impossible because right from the start armed struggle was fought with a combination of the Criminal Code and illegal repression.[25] The Montoneros and ERP share many traits with other organizations like ETA or the Red Brigades, but the singular role of illegal repression in Argentina cannot be overemphasized. Emotional bonds with fellow fighters and a manichean view of politics produced an inward-looking attitude within the groups. But an explanation of militarism must take into account the threat posed by the death squads. Guerrilla groups acted as substitute families because of the affective ties between combatants but also because the organizations protected their members from the Triple A, or so the combatants felt. Moreover, the theory of the two demons or two terrorisms, which considers armed struggle and state terror as two sides of the same coin, allows Argentine society to forget that at one stage it supported armed struggle unequivocally. The two demons theory also allows the political class to forget that the 1973 amnesty law received a unanimous vote in Congress, and that party leaderships failed to condemn armed struggle or illegal repression until late 1974.

The question that guided this book—why guerrilla groups chose to intensify their violent activity and emulate the regular armed forces—should perhaps be turned around: could the combatants have done otherwise? It was generally believed that following the 1973 amnesty guerrillas would turn to conventional political action en masse, and no doubt this is what they should have done. However, since conventional political action was something they had barely witnessed in their lifetime, combatants could hardly be expected to develop a taste for it. Theirs was a generation whose first political experience was made gun in hand. For them, to engage in political activity was "to militate," an activity one undertook in "fronts." Presented the options of "shots or papers," guerrillas chose the shots.

Notes

Chapter 1. The Lost Patrol

1. Rodolfo Walsh, *Operación Masacre* (Buenos Aires: Ediciones de la Flor, 1984); and *Quién Mató a Rosendo?* (Buenos Aires: Ediciones de la Flor, 1986). Juan Perón was deposed by a coup in 1955, and the repression of the Peronist movement that ensued motivated the 1956 rebellion. The information on Walsh's life is taken from *Caras y Caretas*, 85:2210, May 1984, pp. 2–8; and "Escritos Póstumos: Rodolfo Walsh y los Montoneros," *Unidos*, 3:5, April 1985, pp. 151–159.

2. *Los Papeles de Walsh*, published in two installments as "Escritos Póstumos: Rodolfo Walsh y los Montoneros," *Unidos*, 3:5, April 1985, pp. 151–159, and 3:6, August 1985, pp. 178–193.

3. The letter is reprinted in *Operación Masacre*, pp. 205–213.

4. *Clarín*, July 5, 1970, p. 30. See also "El Calerazo y las Guerrillas," *Confirmado*, VI:264, July 8, 1970, pp. 16–17.

5. To this day, many Argentines vindicate the dirty war on the grounds that it saved the country from "the subversive threat." This belief cuts across social classes. See Carlos Gabetta, *Todos Somos Subversivos* (Buenos Aires: Editorial Bruguera, 1984), passim; Guillermo O'Donnell, "Argentina: La Cosecha del Miedo," *Alternativas*, 1, September 1983, pp. 5–14; and a three-page paid advertisement in *La Nación*, June 20, 1989, pp. 11–13. In the latter, I counted the names of 5,352 citizens arranged in alphabetical order under the heading, "GRATITUDE AND SOLIDARITY. We express our gratitude and solidarity to the totality of the Armed, Security and Police Forces which defended the Nation in the war started by subversive aggression and defeated the terrorist organizations that expected to impose on us a marxist regime." Emphasis in the original.

6. I do not not mean to imply that this is the first work on Argentine guerrillas. Chapter 2, nn. 28, 35, and 42, cite the major books and articles which deal directly or indirectly with the topic. But the only in-depth scholarly work is Richard Gillespie, *Soldiers of Perón: Argentina's Montoneros* (Oxford: Clarendon Press, 1982). Although Gillespie has produced a masterful history of the Peronist guerrillas, this study discusses all armed organizations and uses them as a springboard to theorize on the internal mechanics of guerrilla groups.

7. Martha Crenshaw, "Reflections on the Effects of Terrorism," in Martha Crenshaw (ed.), *Terrorism, Legitimacy, and Power* (Middletown, Conn.: Wesleyan University Press, 1983), p. 2; Ted Robert Gurr, "Some Characteristics of Political Terrorism in the 1960s," in Michael Stohl (ed.), *The Politics of Terrorism* (New York: Marcel Dekker, 1988), p. 33;

Chalmers Johnson, *Revolutionary Change* (Stanford, Calif.: Stanford University Press, 1982), pp. 152–153; Walter Laqueur, *The Age of Terrorism* (Boston: Little, Brown, 1987), pp. 144–145, and *Terrorism* (Boston: Little, Brown, 1977), p. 79; Thomas Perry Thornton, "Terror as a Weapon of Political Agitation," in Harry Eckstein (ed.), *Internal War: Problems and Approaches* (New York: Free Press of Glencoe, 1964), p. 73; Eugene V. Walter, *Terror and Resistance: A Study of Political Violence with Case Studies of Some Primitive African Communities* (New York: Oxford University Press, 1969), p. 5; Paul Wilkinson, *Political Terrorism* (London: Macmillan, 1974), p. 11; and *Terrorism & the Liberal State* (New York: New York University Press, 1986), p. 51.

8. On state terror see Walter, *Terror and Resistance*.

9. The IRA understands this only too well, which is why over the past 30 years it has occasionally attempted to "take the war to the mainland," and has recently targeted London repeatedly. On this issue see Conor Gearty, "What Is Terror?" *Times Saturday Review*, March 9, 1991, pp. 10–12; Roger Faligot, *Nous Avons Tué Mountbatten: L'IRA Parle* (Paris: Editions Jean Picollec, 1981); Tim Rayment, John Davison, and James Darlymple, "IRA devastates heart of the City," *Sunday Times*, April 25, 1993, pp. 1, 24; and William E. Schmidt, "Bombed Again by IRA, London Goes to Work Undaunted," *New York Times*, April 27, 1993, p. A3. But in order to terrorize the inhabitants of mainland Britain the IRA would have to carry out a campaign of violence of considerable intensity, which is well beyond the operational capacity of the Provos. Though I have cited the IRA as example, this is true of most terrorist groups.

10. Martha Crenshaw, *Terrorism and International Cooperation* (New York: Institute for East-West Security Studies, 1989), p. 8; Johnson, *Revolutionary Change*, pp. 146–150; Laqueur, *The Age of Terrorism*, pp. 147–148, and *Guerrilla: A Historical and Critical Study* (Boston: Little, Brown, 1976), pp. viii–xi; Wilkinson, *Terrorism & the Liberal State*, p. 54.

11. Conor Cruise O'Brien, "Terrorism under Democratic Conditions: The Case of the IRA," in Crenshaw (ed.), *Terrorism, Legitimacy, and Power*, p. 91, emphasis in the original. O'Brien's article is interesting because it introduces the notions of consent and participation as criteria for defining terrorism. The author argues that while in a number of situations it is impossible to characterize adequately the activities of armed organizations;, when this activity takes place under democratic regimes in which there are established channels for nonviolent political participation, it should be called terrorism. This argument is implicit in Edward S. Hyams, *Terrorists and Terrorism* (London: J. M. Dent, 1975). Unfortunately, in dealing with terrorism democratic states have sometimes been their own worst enemies. By resorting to illegal repression, however infrequently, democracies weaken their moral standing on this issue and provide terrorists with an excellent argument about "self-defense." This was made more than evident by the attempted government cover-up of the murder of six Catholic men by the security forces in Ulster in late 1982, which became known as the "Stalker Affair." Juan Linz discusses the importance of adequate government responses to violence in *The Breakdown of Democratic Regimes: Crisis, Breakdown, and Reequilibration* (Baltimore and London: Johns Hopkins University Press, 1978), pp. 36–37, 56–61. See also John Stalker, *The Stalker Affair* (New York: Viking Press, 1988).

12. Robert P. Clark, *The Basque Insurgents: ETA, 1952–80* (Madison: University of Wisconsin Press, 1984), p. 132; Richard Gillespie, "A Critique of the Urban Guerrilla: Argentina, Uruguay and Brazil," *Conflict Quarterly*, 1:2, 1980, pp. 39–53: 39; Walter, *Terror and Resistance*, pp. 6–7; Wilkinson, *Terrorism & the Liberal State*, pp. 64–65.

13. Clark, *The Basque Insurgents*, p. 123; Crenshaw, *Terrorism and International Co-*

operation, p. 6; Gillespie, *Soldiers of Perón*, p. 147 fn. 56; Johnson, *Revolutionary Change*, chapter 8; Wilkinson, *Terrorism & the Liberal State*, p. 55.

14. These are assumptions made pervasively in the literature. See for example Gurr, "Some Characteristics of Political Terrorism in the 1960s." For a critique of this tendency toward generalizations see Martha Crenshaw, "An Organizational Approach to the Analysis of Political Terrorism," *Orbis*, 29:3, 1985, pp. 465–489.

15. On the Baader-Meinhof Gang see Jillian Becker, *Hitler's Children: The Story of the Baader-Meinhof Terrorist Gang* (London: Michael Joseph, 1977), and Klaus Wasmund, "The Political Socialization of West German Terrorists," in Peter H. Merkl (ed.), *Political Violence and Terror: Motifs and Motivations* (Berkeley and Los Angeles: University of California Press, 1986). On the Red Brigades see Alessandro Silj, *Mai più senza fucile! alle origini dei NAP e delle BR* (Florence: Vallechi, 1977), and Leonard Weinberg and William Lee Eubank, *The Rise and Fall of Italian Terrorism* (Boulder, Colo.: Westview Press, 1987). For a comparison of West German and Italian organizations see Donatella della Porta, "Social Movements and Terrorism in Italy and West Germany: Strategic Choices and Escalation Dynamics in Underground Organizations," paper presented at the XII World Congress of Sociology, Madrid, July 9–13, 1990. On ETA see Clark, *The Basque Insurgents;* Juan J. Linz, *Conflicto en Euzkadi* (Madrid: Espasa-Calpe, 1986); and Francisco J. Llera, José M. Mata, and Cynthia L. Irwin, "ETA: From Secret Army to Social Movement—the Post-Franco Schism of the Basque Nationalist Movement," *Terrorism and Political Violence*, 5:3, 1993, pp. 106–134. On the IRA see Faligot, *Nous Avons Tué Mountbatten;* and Tim Pat Coogan, *The I.R.A.* (London: Fontana, 1982). On the FLQ see Ronald D. Crelinsten, "The Internal Dynamics of the FLQ During the October Crisis of 1970," in David C. Rapoport (ed.), *Inside Terrorist Organizations* (New York: Columbia University Press, 1988); and on Direct Action see Xavier Raufer, *Terrorisme: Maintenant la France? La Guerre des Partis Communistes Combattants* (Paris: Garnier, 1982).

16. Pedro Ibarra Guell also uses the term "armed struggle" in his discussion of ETA, for reasons related to those mentioned here. See his *La Evolución Estratégica de ETA* (San Sebastián: Kriselu, 1989), pp. 10–12, 27–28. The actions of the Argentine and other groups are sometimes described as urban guerrilla warfare. I have avoided the term because it is polemical. There has always been a debate among the field's specialists on the accuracy of this term. Those who use it argue that guerrilla warfare can take place in both rural and urban settings. Those who reject it argue that the urban setting is not conducive to two features which they consider distinctive of guerrilla warfare: the irregular force's development into a popular army and the military victory over the adversary. The arguments are developed in the works of Paul Wilkinson and Walter Laqueur (already cited). The greatest theoretician of urban guerrilla warfare, Abraham Guillén, argued that "revolutionary war is never decided by arms but rather by winning the political support of the people" (Donald C. Hodges [ed.], *Philosophy of the Urban Guerrilla: The Revolutionary Writings of Abraham Guillén* [New York: William Morrow, 1973], p. 250]. Guillén is right in that the military victory is not a distinctive feature of guerrilla warfare, but the military nature of the targets is, which is why the term "urban guerrilla warfare" should be avoided.

17. Alfred Vagts, *A History of Militarism Civilian and Military* (New York: The Free Press, 1959), p. 13. For a review of the different meanings assigned to the term "militarism," see José Enrique Miguens, "El Militarismo como Patología en la Milicia y en la Política," paper presented at the conference "Armed Forces, State, Defense and Society," Buenos Aires, October 26–28, 1988; and Kjell Skjelsbaek, "Militarism, its Dimensions and Corollaries: An

Attempt at Conceptual Clarification," in Asbjorn Eide and Marek Thee (eds.), *Problems of Contemporary Militarism* (London: Croom Helm, 1980).

18. Sometimes, they explicitly do so. There is the example of ETA's split into a "Politico-Military" and a "Military" wing. In fact, recent discussions of the internal dynamics of ETA refer to the development of militarism with an analysis analogous to the one made here. See Ibarra Guell, *La Evolución Estratégica de ETA,* especially pp. 157–180, and Fernando Reinares, "La violencia política civil y organizada en un contexto de democratización: consideraciones para una interpretación del caso vasco," paper presented at the III Congress of Sociology, Donostia-San Sebastián, September 1989.

19. Consider Rodolfo Walsh's "Letter to my friends" reflecting on the death of his daughter: "I have asked myself if my daughter, if all those who die like her, had other options. The answer springs from the bottom of my heart and I want my friends to know it. Vicki could have chosen other roads that were different without being dishonorable, but the one she chose was the fairest, the most generous, the most reasoned. . . . She did not live for herself: she lived for others, and those others are millions." The letter is reprinted in Horacio Verbitsky (ed.), *Rodolfo Walsh y la Prensa Clandestina, 1976–1978* (Buenos Aires: Ediciones de la Urraca, 1985), pp. 119–120.

20. For a detailed description of life in guerrilla safehouses see Sir Geoffrey Jackson, *Secuestrado por el Pueblo* (Barcelona: Editorial Pomaire, 1974). Jackson was British ambassador to Uruguay when he was kidnapped and held for nine months by the Tupamaro guerrillas.

21. Ibarra Guell, *La Evolución Estratégica de ETA,* p. 165. The original description of the "friend-foe" view of politics was provided by Carl Schmitt's *Concept of the Political* (New Brunswick, N.J.: Rutgers University Press, 1976).

22. The classic analysis of how organizational development leads to bureaucratization remains Robert Michels' *Political Parties* (New York: The Free Press, 1968). See also Frances Fox Piven and Richard A. Cloward, *Poor People's Movements: Why They Succeed, How They Fail* (New York: Vintage Books, 1977), passim; and Envar El Kadri and Jorge Rulli, *Diálogos en el Exilio* (Buenos Aires: Editorial Foro Sur, 1984), chapter 9.

23. Albert O. Hirschman provides similar arguments about the organization of firms in his *Exit, Voice, and Loyalty: Responses to Decline in Firms, Organizations, and States* (Cambridge, Mass., and London: Harvard University Press, 1970).

24. Lenin went on to say that a revolutionary situation is followed by revolution only when "the above-mentioned objective changes are accompanied by a subjective change, namely, the ability of the revolutionary *class* to take revolutionary mass action *strong* enough to break (or dislocate) the old government" (V. I. Lenin, *Collected Works* [Moscow: Progress Publishers, 1964], vol. 21, p. 214. Emphasis in the original).

25. The newspapers consulted for statistics-gathering purposes were *La Nación,* January 1969–December 1971 and January 1977–December 1979; *La Prensa,* January 1969–December 1972 and January 1976–December 1979; *Clarín,* January 1973–December 1975; *La Razón,* January 1974–December 1975; *La Opinión,* May 1971–December 1976. For every year in the 1969–79 period I consulted two different newspapers to ensure greater accuracy of information.

Chapter 2. Politics in Argentina After 1955 and the Development of the Guerrilla Movement

1. On the Radical administrations see David Rock, *Politics in Argentina 1890–1930: The Rise and Fall of Radicalism* (Cambridge: Cambridge University Press, 1975), and on the Peronist era, Peter Waldmann, *El Peronismo, 1943–1955* (Buenos Aires: Editorial Sudamericana, 1981). Two seminal works that span Radical and Peronist administrations are Carlos Waisman, *Reversal of Development in Argentina: Postwar Counterrevolutionary Policies and Their Structural Consequences* (Princeton, N.J.: Princeton University Press, 1987), and Peter H. Smith, *Argentina and the Failure of Democracy: Conflict Among Political Elites, 1904–1955* (Madison: University of Wisconsin Press, 1974).

2. On political and economic developments in post-1955 Argentina see Marcelo Cavarozzi, *Autoritarismo y Democracia, 1955–1983* (Buenos Aires: Centro Editor de América Latina, 1983); Carlos F. Díaz Alejandro, *Ensayos sobre la Historia Económica Argentina* (Buenos Aires: Amorrortu Editores, 1983); Carlos S. Fayt, *El Político Armado: Dinámica del Proceso Político Argentino, 1960–1971* (Buenos Aires: Ediciones Pannedille, 1971); H. S. Ferns, *La Argentina* (Buenos Aires: Editorial Sudamericana, 1973); Marcos Kaplan, "50 Años de Historia Argentina (1925–1975): El Laberinto de la Frustración," in Pablo González Casanova (ed.), *América Latina: Historia de Medio Siglo* (Mexico: Siglo Veintiuno Editores, 1982); Félix Luna, *Argentina de Perón a Lanusse 1943–1973* (Barcelona: Editorial Planeta, 1972); Guillermo O'Donnell, "Permanent Crisis and the Failure to Create a Democratic Regime: Argentina, 1955–66," in Juan J. Linz and Alfred Stepan (eds.), *The Breakdown of Democratic Regimes: Latin America* (Baltimore: Johns Hopkins University Press, 1980); Joseph A. Page, *Perón, A Biography* (New York: Random House, 1983); Robert A. Potash, *The Army and Politics in Argentina 1945–1962: Perón to Frondizi* (Stanford, Calif.: Stanford University Press, 1980); David Rock, *Argentina 1516–1987: From Spanish Colonization to Alfonsín* (Berkeley and Los Angeles: University of California Press, 1987); and David Rock (ed.), *Argentina in the Twentieth Century* (Pittsburgh: University of Pittsburgh Press, 1975); Alain Rouquié, *Radicales y Desarrollistas en la Argentina* (Buenos Aires: Schapire Editor, 1975); Miguel Angel Scenna, *Los Militares* (Buenos Aires: Editorial de Belgrano, 1980); and Peter G. Snow, *Political Forces in Argentina* (New York: Praeger, 1979).

3. Rock, *Argentina 1516–1987*, p. 262.

4. Waldmann, *El Peronismo*, p. 123.

5. Alain Rouquié, "Le Vote Peroniste en 1973," *Revue Française de Science Politique*, 24:3, 1974, pp. 469–499: 474.

6. Cavarozzi, *Autoritarismo y Democracia*.

7. Daniel James, "The Peronist Left, 1955–1975," *Journal of Latin American Studies*, 8:2, 1976, pp. 273–296: 273 n. 1. On repression under Aramburu and the Resistance, see James William McGuire, "Peronism without Perón: Unions in Argentine Politics, 1955–1966," Ph.D. diss., University of California, Berkeley, 1989, pp. 86–117; and Daniel James, *Resistance and Integration: Peronism and the Argentine Working Class, 1946–1976* (Cambridge: Cambridge University Press, 1988), Part Two.

8. James, "The Peronist Left," p. 275.

9. On the party system see Snow, *Political Forces in Argentina*, chapter 2.

10. The situation was analogous to what Samuel P. Huntington described as "mass praetorianism" in *Political Order in Changing Societies* (New Haven and London: Yale University Press, 1968), chapter 4.

11. Cavarozzi, *Autoritarismo y Democracia*, p. 11.

12. See *Gallup Polls*, 1965.

13. On the "moderator pattern" see Alfred Stepan, *Brasil: los militares y la política* (Buenos Aires: Amorrortu Editores, 1974), especially pp. 73–84. On the difference between 1966 and previous coups see Guillermo O'Donnell, *1966–1973 El Estado Burocrático Autoritario: Triunfos, Derrotas y Crisis* (Buenos Aires: Editorial de Belgrano, 1982), pp. 95–99. On the Onganía regime see Natalio R. Botana, Rafael Braun, and Carlos A. Floria, *El Régimen Militar, 1966–1973* (Buenos Aires: Ediciones La Bastilla, 1973); Mariano N. Castex, *El Escorial de Onganía* (Buenos Aires: Ediciones Hespérides, 1981); Andrew Graham-Yooll, *Tiempo de Tragedia (Cronología de la "Revolución Argentina")* (Buenos Aires: Ediciones de la Flor, 1972); Andrew Graham-Yooll, *Tiempo de Violencia: Cronología del "Gran Acuerdo Nacional"* (Buenos Aires: Granica Editor, 1973); Roberto Roth, *Los Años de Onganía: Relato de un Testigo* (Buenos Aires: Ediciones La Campana, 1981); and Gregorio Selser, *El Onganiato* (Buenos Aires: Hyspamérica Ediciones, 2 vols., 1986).

14. *Ayuda Memoria. Motivaciones. Justificación. Alcance.* Document circulated among top army officers before the coup, quoted in Alain Rouquié, *Poder Militar y Sociedad Política en la Argentina* (Buenos Aires: Emecé Editores, 1983), vol. 2, p. 253.

15. Frederick C. Turner, "The Study of Argentine Politics through Survey Research," *Latin American Research Review*, 10:2, 1975, pp. 73–116: 93; and O'Donnell, *El Estado Burocrático Autoritario*, p. 66. See also John M. Goshko, "Onganía Given Dictator Power," *Washington Post*, June 30, 1966, p. A21; and "Few in Argentina Yearn For Politics," *New York Times*, August 27, 1967, p. 15.

16. See François Gèze and Alain Labrousse, *Argentine: Révolution et Contre-révolutions* (Paris: Editions du Seuil, 1975), pp. 99–108, 126; and Ernesto Laclau, "Argentina—Imperialist Strategy and the May Crisis," *New Left Review*, 62, 1970, pp. 3–21: 4–8.

17. Cavarozzi, *Autoritarismo y Democracia*, p. 38.

18. O'Donnell, *El Estado Burocrático Autoritario*, pp. 167–256. For a detailed analysis of dissatisfaction with the economic policy among different sectors of society, see Juan Carlos Portantiero, "Economía y Política en la Crisis Argentina: 1958–1973," *Revista Mexicana de Sociología*, 77:2, 1977, pp. 531–565: 550ff.

19. Guido di Tella, *Argentina under Perón, 1973–76: The Nation's Experience with a Labor-based Government* (New York: St. Martin's Press, 1983), p. 35.

20. Guillermo O'Donnell, "State and Alliances in Argentina, 1956–1976," *Journal of Development Studies*, 15:1, 1978, pp. 3–32: 4.

21. Kenneth F. Johnson, *Argentina's Mosaic of Discord, 1966–68* (Washington, D.C.: Institute for the Comparative Study of Political Systems, 1969), p. 47.

22. For a complete list of banned publications see Graham-Yooll, *Tiempo de Tragedia* and *Tiempo de Violencia*, passim.

23. H. J. Maidenberg, "4 of 8 Rectors Quit Posts," *New York Times*, August 1, 1966, p. 11.

24. Castex, *El Escorial de Onganía*, p. 104; Roth, *Los Años de Onganía*, p. 182. On the "Night of the Long Batons" see Selser, *El Onganiato*, vol. I, pp. 127–139. The issue of academic exile during the Argentine Revolution is discussed in vol. I, pp. 273–285 and 289–300, and vol. II, pp. 375–382. On academic exile see also Ernesto Garzón Valdés, "La Emigración Argentina: Acerca de sus Causas Etico-Políticas," in Peter Waldmann and Ernesto Garzón Valdés (eds.), *El Poder Militar en la Argentina (1976–1981)* (Buenos Aires: Editorial Galerna,

1983); and H. J. Maidenberg, "University Teachers Begin Leaving Argentina," *New York Times*, August 19, 1966, p. 13. On the State Department protest and the Argentine response see Richard Eder, "U.S. Aide Rebukes Argentina for Crackdown on Universities," *New York Times*, August 5, 1966, pp. 1, 9; and Richard Eder, "Argentine Issue Dropped By U.S.," *New York Times*, August 12, 1966, p. 12.

25. The Cordobazo derives its name from the famous *Bogotazo* of 1948, which followed the death of Jorge Eliécer Gaitán.

26. On the Cordobazo see Horacio González Trejo, *Argentina: Tiempo de Violencia* (Buenos Aires: Carlos Pérez Editor, 1969); and Laclau, "Argentina," pp. 15–17. For a description of how those in power viewed events in Córdoba see Roth, *Los Años de Onganía*, pp. 317–335; and Alejandro A. Lanusse, *Mi Testimonio* (Buenos Aires: Laserre Editores, 1977), chapter 2.

27. Cavarozzi, *Autoritarismo y Democracia*, p. 46.

28. Several works provide an overview of the Argentine guerrilla movement: *El Terrorismo en la Argentina* (Buenos Aires: Poder Ejecutivo Nacional, 1980); Armando Alonso Piñeiro, *Crónica de la Subversión en la Argentina* (Buenos Aires: Ediciones Depalma, 1980); Pedro A. Barcia, "Las Guerrillas en la Argentina," *Interrogaciones*, 8, 1975, pp. 30–60; Carlos A. Brocato, *La Argentina Que Quisieron* (Buenos Aires: Editorial Sudamericana/Planeta, 1985); Ramón G. Díaz Bessone, *Guerra Revolucionaria en la Argentina (1959–1978)* (Buenos Aires: Editorial Fraterna, 1986); Richard Gillespie, "A critique of the urban guerrilla: Argentina, Uruguay and Brazil," *Conflict Quarterly*, 1:2, 1980, pp. 39–53; "Armed Struggle in Argentina," *New Scholar*, 8:1 & 2, 1982, pp. 387–427; and "Political Violence in Argentina in the 1970s (Guerrillas, Terrorists, State Terrorists and *Carapintadas*)," in Martha Crenshaw (ed.), *Terrorism in Context* (University Park, Pa.: Pennsylvania State University Press, forthcoming); Ignacio González Janzen, *Argentina, 20 años de luchas peronistas* (Mexico: Ediciones de la Patria Grande, 1975); Ernst Halperin, *Terrorism in Latin America* (Beverly Hills, Calif.: Sage Publications, 1976); Claudia Hilb and Daniel Lutzky, *La Nueva Izquierda Argentina: 1960–1980 (Política y Violencia)* (Buenos Aires: Centro Editor de América Latina, 1980); James Kohl and John Litt (eds.), *Urban Guerrilla Warfare in Latin America* (Cambridge, Mass.: MIT Press, 1974); Luis Mercier Vega, *Las Guerrillas en América Latina: La Técnica del Contra-estado* (Buenos Aires: Editorial Paidós, 1969); Jorge Pinedo, *Consignas y Lucha Popular en el Proceso Revolucionario Argentino 1955–73* (Buenos Aires: Editorial Freeland, 1974); Peter Waldmann, "Anomia Social y Violencia," in Alain Rouquié (ed.), *Argentina, Hoy* (Buenos Aires: Siglo Veintiuno Editores, 1982).

29. On the Uturuncos see Emilio Morales, *Uturunco y las Guerrillas en la Argentina* (Montevideo: Editorial Sepe, 1964).

30. The letter is reprinted in Jorge R. Masseti, *Los Que Luchan y Los Que Lloran* (Buenos Aires: Editorial Jorge Alvarez, 1969). On the EGP see also Ricardo Rojo, *My Friend Che* (New York: Dial Press, 1968), chapter 7.

31. Interview with Envar El Kadri in Buenos Aires on June 26, 1987. See also Carlos Aznarez, "Cacho El Kadri: 'No tropezar dos veces con la misma piedra'," *Caras y Caretas*, 85:2209, April 1987, pp. 23–25, 31–35. Verdinelli, Caride, and El Kadri remained in prison until the 1973 amnesty. Caride and El Kadri later formed FAP 17, which under Caride joined the Montoneros. Caride died in combat in 1976. El Kadri went into exile and works as a film producer in Paris.

32. Zabala Rodríguez became a Montonero and was killed in action in 1976.

33. Details on FAP taken from an interview with Envar El Kadri in Buenos Aires on June 26, 1987, and an unpublished guerrilla document, not for citation.

34. The communiqué is reprinted in Mario Firmenich and Norma Arrostito, "Como murió Aramburu," *La Causa Peronista,* 1:9, September 3, 1974, pp. 25–31: 31. Emphasis in the original.

35. On the Montoneros see Miguel Bonasso, *Recuerdo de la Muerte* (Buenos Aires: Editorial Bruguera, 1984); Juan Gasparini, *Montoneros: Final de Cuentas* (Buenos Aires: Puntosur Editores, 1988); Richard Gillespie, *Soldiers of Perón: Argentina's Montoneros* (Oxford: Clarendon Press, 1982); Pablo Giussani, *Montoneros: La Soberbia Armada* (Buenos Aires: Editorial Sudamericana/Planeta, 1984); James, "The Peronist Left"; Eugenio Méndez, *Confesiones de un Montonero* (Buenos Aires: Editorial Sudamericana/Planeta, 1985), and *Aramburu: El Crimen Imperfecto* (Buenos Aires: Editorial Sudamericana/Planeta, 1987).

36. Mendizábal, Habegger, and de Gregorio became prominent Montoneros. Mendizábal died in the 1979 counteroffensive; Habegger and de Gregorio disappeared during the dirty war. Details on the Descamisados taken from an unpublished guerrilla document, not for citation.

37. I interviewed one of the founders of the group in Buenos Aires on September 1, 8, and 18, 1987.

38. See Héctor Víctor Suárez, "FAR: Con el fusil del Che," *Granma,* December 12, 1970, p. 7; and "FAL: El Marxismo en la Cartuchera," *Cristianismo y Revolución,* IV:28, April 1971, pp. 73–77.

39. See "Aporte al proceso de confrontación de posiciones y polémica pública que abordamos con el ERP," *Militancia,* 4, July 5, 1973, pp. 35–49.

40. *Militancia,* 15, September 20, 1973, p. 46.

41. Under Moreno, *La Verdad* fused with the Argentine Socialist Party in 1972 to form the Workers' Socialist Party (Partido Socialista de los Trabajadores or PST). For a glimpse into Mario Santucho's early life and his participation in FRIP see Witold Gombrowicz, *Journal 1957–1960* (Paris: Editions Denoël, 1976).

42. The episode inspired Graham Greene's *Honorary Consul* (Harmondsworth: Penguin Books, 1986). On the ERP see James Petras, "Building a Popular Army in Argentina," *New Left Review,* 71, 1972, pp. 45–55; Julio Santucho, *Los Ultimos Guevaristas: Surgimiento y Eclipse del Ejército Revolucionario del Pueblo* (Buenos Aires: Puntosur Editores, 1988); Mario R. Santuchò, *Poder Burgués y Poder Revolucionario* (Buenos Aires: N.p., 1974); Luis Mattini, *Hombres y Mujeres del PRT-ERP* (Buenos Aires: Editorial Contrapunto, 1990); and María Seoane, *Todo o Nada* (Buenos Aires: Editorial Planeta, 1992).

43. Father Hernán Benítez, cited in "Suplemento: Los sueños de la guerrilla," *El Porteño,* V:52, April 1986, pp. 35–50: 39.

44. Father Erio Vaudagna, cited in "El Calerazo y las Guerrillas," *Confirmado,* VI:264, July 8, 1970, pp. 16–17: 17. Emphasis in the original.

45. O'Donnell, *El Estado Burocrático Autoritario,* pp. 464–465.

46. Cited in Francis Godolphin, "Terrorismo y anticultura," *El Burgués,* III:55, May 23, 1973, pp. 7–8: 8.

47. I should like to thank Drs. Esteban Vergara and Miguel del Pino for an opportunity to discuss various aspects of the Argentine legal system. Dr. Vergara, one of the nine justices in the Federal Penal Chamber, was interviewed in Buenos Aires on December 2 and 4, 1986. Dr. del Pino, a lifelong member of the judiciary and member of the Appellate Criminal Court in 1978–84, was interviewed in Buenos Aires on September 15, 1987. For a description of the Rawson Maximum Security prison, see "Por primera vez, en Rawson, hay mujeres entre los

presos políticos," *La Opinión*, October 7, 1971, p. 9; and *Máxima Peligrosidad* (Buenos Aires: Editorial Candela, 1973).

48. Francisco Urondo, *Trelew* (Havana: Casa de las Américas, 1976), p. 106. The claim that there had been no autopsies was made by the three survivors and by the families of the deceased. The judge in question was Dr. Jorge Quiroga, a member of the Federal Penal Chamber, of the same courtroom as Dr. Esteban Vergara. Dr. Vergara explained to me that although he had not seen the autopsy reports, he was almost certain that these had been performed. In any case, the wounds and lesions sustained by the survivors substantiated the guerrillas' version of the events. Whether or not he ordered autopsies performed, the incident at Trelew cost Judge Quiroga his life. He was killed by ERP 22 in April 1974. On the Trelew massacre see also *La Masacre de Trelew* (Caracas: Ediciones Bárbara, 1972); Tomás Eloy Martínez, *La Pasión según Trelew* (Buenos Aires: Granica Editor, 1973); Humberto Costantini, *Libro de Trelew* (Buenos Aires: Granica Editor, 1973); and "Vasto operativo de terroristas en el Sur," *La Nación*, International Edition, August 21, 1972, pp. 1, 5.

49. There were two additional revenge killings connected with the Trelew massacre, of Judge Jorge Quiroga and of Radical politician Arturo Mor Roig, murdered by Montoneros in July 1974. Mor Roig was Lanusse's Interior Minister.

50. On the Lanusse-Perón confrontation see Wayne S. Smith, "The Return of Peronism," in Frederick C. Turner and José E. Miguens (eds.), *Juan Perón and the Reshaping of Argentina* (Pittsburgh: University of Pittsburgh Press, 1983), pp. 100–112. Only someone as blinded by ambition as Lanusse became could have failed to notice that to try to perpetuate the rule of the armed forces through constitutional means invalidated the very purpose of the elections. See also Mariano N. Castex, *Un Año de Lanusse; del Acuerdo Increíble al Retorno Imposible* (Buenos Aires: Achával Solo, 1973).

51. Liliana de Riz, *Retorno y Derrumbe: El Ultimo Gobierno Peronista* (Buenos Aires: Hyspamérica Ediciones, 1987), p. 45.

52. Lanusse, *Mi Testimonio*, pp. 276–277.

53. Smith, "The Return of Peronism," p. 124.

54. Lester A. Sobel, *Argentina & Perón 1970–75* (New York: Facts on File, 1975), p. 42.

55. McGuire, "Peronism without Perón," appendix 1; di Tella, *Argentina under Perón*, p. 25; Darío Cantón, *Elecciones y Partidos Políticos en la Argentina; Historia, Interpretación y Balance: 1910–1966* (Buenos Aires: Siglo Veintiuno Editores, 1973), p. 71; and James W. Rowe, *The Argentine Elections of 1963* (Washington, D.C.: Institute for the Comparative Study of Political Systems, n.d.), p. 8.

56. Robert J. Alexander, *Juan Domingo Perón: A History* (Boulder, Colo.: Westview Press, 1979), p. 131; and Walter Little, *Peronism: Was It and Is It Populist?* (University of Glasgow: Institute of Latin American Studies, Occasional Papers no. 20, 1975), pp. 10–11. See also Manuel Mora y Araujo and Santiago Llorente (eds.), *El Voto Peronista: Ensayos de Sociología Electoral Argentina* (Buenos Aires: Editorial Sudamericana, 1980).

57. Darío Cantón and Jorge R. Jorrat, "Occupation and Vote in Urban Argentina: The March 1973 Presidential Elections," *Latin American Research Review*, 13:1, 1978, pp. 146–157: 151. See also José Enrique Miguens, "The Presidential Elections of 1973 and the End of an Ideology," in Turner and Miguens, *Juan Perón*, pp. 161–163.

58. The letter is reprinted in Rodolfo Baschetti (ed.), *Documentos de la Resistencia Peronista 1955–1970* (Buenos Aires: Puntosur Editores, 1988), pp. 439–440, capital letters in the original.

59. *Oscar R. Anzorena, Tiempo de Violencia y Utopía (1966–1976)* (Buenos Aires: Edito-

rial Contrapunto, 1988), pp. 194–195, 199. Perón's endorsement of armed struggle (through letters, tapes, and interviews) was constant between 1969 and 1973. For additional examples see the Montoneros' letter to Perón after the murder of Aramburu and his reply, both published in Firmenich and Arrostito, "Como murió Aramburu," pp. 26–29.

60. See Rouquié, "Le Vote Peroniste en 1973"; and Oscar Landi, *La Tercera Presidencia de Perón: Gobierno de Emergencia y Crisis Política* (Buenos Aires: CEDES, Documento CEDES/CLACSO no. 10, 1978).

61. On the 1973–1976 period see Anzorena, *Tiempo de Violencia y Utopía;* Jorge Luis Bernetti, *El Peronismo de la Victoria* (Buenos Aires: Editorial Legasa, 1983); Juan E. Corradi, Eldon Kenworthy and William Wipfler, "Argentina 1973–1976: The Background to Violence," *LASA Newsletter,* 8:3, September 1976, pp. 3–28; de Riz, *Retorno y Derrumbe;* di Tella, *Argentina under Perón;* José Pablo Feinmann, *López Rega, la cara oscura de Perón* (Buenos Aires: Editorial Legasa, 1987); Julio Godio, *El Ultimo Año de Perón* (Bogota: Universidad Simón Bolívar, 1981); Kenneth F. Johnson, *Peronism: The Final Gamble* (London: Institute for the Study of Conflict, 1974); Pablo Kandel and Mario Monteverde, *Entorno y Caída* (Buenos Aires: Editorial Planeta Argentina, 1976); Landi, *La Tercera Presidencia.*

62. Armando Croatto, Santiago Díaz Ortiz, Jorge Glellel, Aníbal Iturrieta, Carlos Kunkel, Diego Muñiz Barreto, Roberto Vidaña, and Rodolfo Vittar resigned in protest at the reintroduction of antiterrorist legislation in January 1974. Muñiz Barreto, scion of a wealthy family, went on to finance the radicalized weekly *Puro Pueblo* (which closed after four issues) and disappeared in 1977. Kunkel was apprehended as a Montonero in 1975 and Croatto went into exile and returned to Argentina as commander of the Montoneros' 1979 counteroffensive, in which he died.

63. In *Soldiers of Perón,* p. 132, Gillespie states that "Montonero nominees also gained some fifty posts in provincial governments, as well as seats in local legislatures and governments," though he does not back this statement with evidence. In any case Bernetti, *El Peronismo,* p. 107, mentions the Montoneros and FAR had sent Perón a list of 300 people they considered worthy of government posts, a fact confirmed by a Montonero interviewed in Buenos Aires on July 23, 1987.

64. For a summary of the Peronist program see the *Buenos Aires Herald,* March 13, 1973, p. 7.

65. The debate over the amnesty was more than adequately covered by one of the leading Buenos Aires dailies, *La Opinión,* between March and May 1973. See "Tres variantes sobre la amnistía analizan los abogados peronistas," March 21, p. 8; "Existen instrucciones de Perón para que se elaboren las pautas de la ley de amnistía," April 4, p. 11; "Anuncian el alcance de la ley de amnistía," April 21, p. 7; minor discussions on May 10, p. 1; May 17, p. 10; "Asumió el gobierno de Héctor José Cámpora y decretó la libertad de todos los presos políticos," May 26, p. 1; and two articles on May 27, "Aprobación unánime de la amnistía y derogación de los mecanismos represivos," p. 1, and "Los proyectos de amnistía y derogación de medidas represivas que trata el parlamento," p. 7. For a list of the 371 names see "Mas de 100 presos liberados en Rawson," *La Razón,* May 26, 1973, p. 10.

66. See *Porqué el ERP no dejará de combatir: Respuesta al Presidente Cámpora* (Buenos Aires: N.p., April 13, 1973), and *Al Pueblo: Porqué y contra qué seguirá combatiendo el ERP* (Buenos Aires: N.p., May 25, 1973). See also "Anunció el ERP que no dejará las armas," *La Opinión,* April 25, 1973, p. 11; and on Kloosterman, *La Opinión,* May 23, 1973, p. 9.

67. I am grateful to Dr. Esteban Righi for his analysis of this and other aspects of his

brief tenure as Interior Minister during a lengthy interview in Buenos Aires on December 25, 1987.

68. This represented 12 percent of the country's population at the time. See "El arribo al país de Perón produjo una movilización popular sin precedentes," *La Opinión,* June 21, 1973, p. 6.

69. The casualty figures provided here result from a scrutiny of all the Buenos Aires dailies for the week following the tragedy. Newspaper coverage included lists of people hospitalized in critical condition at various medical facilities in the Greater Buenos Aires area. The government stuck to its original version of 13 dead and more than 200 wounded. Two years later, and during his most spectacular press conference, Montonero leader Mario Firmenich referred to 182 fatalities. Firmenich, who was at Ezeiza when it happened, never explained how he arrived at such figures. According to the late Pablo Giussani, who attended the press conference, none of the journalists present, foreign or Argentine, asked Firmenich about these figures. Giussani, editor-in-chief of the daily *Noticias* (a newspaper supportive of the Montoneros, in circulation between 1973 and 1974) and author of a book very critical of the Montoneros, was interviewed in Buenos Aires on December 11, 1987. In *Ezeiza* (Buenos Aires: Editorial Contrapunto, 1986), pp. 117–119, Horacio Verbitsky's total is 13 dead and 365 wounded and he categorically denies Firmenich's version of 182 dead. See also "Explicaciones, armas y fuerzas de los dos sectores que se balearon en Ezeiza" and "Dos informes policiales indicarían que los primeros disparos partieron desde el palco," *La Opinión,* June 22, 1973, p. 8.

70. Perón's entire speech is reproduced in Verbitsky, *Ezeiza,* pp. 204–209.

71. de Riz, *Retorno y Derrumbe,* p. 75.

72. Corradi et al., "Argentina 1973–1976," p. 10.

73. di Tella, *Argentina under Perón,* p. 62.

74. On the Social Pact see de Riz, *Retorno y Derrumbe,* chapter 5; di Tella, *Argentina under Perón,* chapter 4; and Godio, *El Ultimo Año de Perón,* chapter 9.

75. Cited in de Riz, *Retorno y Derrumbe,* p. 104.

76. See "Iñíguez: El ERP se atribuyó el crimen," *La Nación,* September 27, 1973, p. 6.

77. "Drásticas instrucciones a los dirigentes del Movimiento para que excluyan todo atisbo de heterodoxia marxista," *La Opinión,* October 2, 1973, p. 1. Gillespie, *Soldiers of Perón,* p. 165 fn. 4, also views Grynberg's death, which was clearly the work of right-wing paramilitaries, as a case of revenge murder and indication that Perón must have suspected the Montoneros.

78. *El Mundo* in September 1973; *El Descamisado* and *Militancia* in April 1974; and *El Peronista* in June 1974. *El Mundo* was owned by the ERP, and the other publications were organs of the Revolutionary Tendency.

79. See "Varios diputados de la Nación, amenazados," *Crónica,* November 28, 1973, p. 2.

80. See "Fijan su posición las FAP: Ampliar el frente nacional," *Crónica,* September 1, 1973, p. 8; and "Se desprendió de la FAP un núcleo y da a conocer sus razones," *La Razón,* August 30, 1973, p. 16.

81. See FAR/Montoneros, "Acta de Unidad," *Militancia,* 19, October 18, 1973, pp. 26–27.

82. Ejército Revolucionario del Pueblo Fracción Roja, "A la clase obrera y al pueblo," *Crónica,* July 25, 1973, p. 15; and Ejército Revolucionario del Pueblo 22 de Agosto, "A las organizaciones revolucionarias y al pueblo," *Crónica,* July 31, 1973, p. 11.

83. "Gorilla," a term originally used to designate supporters of the 1955 coup, has since been applied to anti-Peronists in general.

84. The entire speech is reproduced in "Severa calificación para los infiltrados," *La Prensa*, May 2, 1974, p. 1.

85. *Noticias* in August and *La Causa Peronista* in September 1974.

86. Alberto Martínez Baca, governor of Mendoza, was deposed in July; Jorge Cepernic, governor of Santa Cruz, in October; and Miguel Ragone, governor of Salta, in November 1974. Article 6 of the Argentine constitution allows the federal government to remove all provincial authorities and replace them with federal appointees if the safety of the province in question is at stake, a procedure known also as intervention.

87. See Eduardo J. Paredes, "En un abierto desafío al gobierno constitucional la organización Montoneros optó por marginarse de la ley," *La Opinión*, September 7, 1974, p. 24; and *Buenos Aires Herald*, September 7, 1974, p. 7.

88. "Un muerto cada 19 horas," *La Opinión*, September 17, 1974, p. 32.

89. See, for example, Firmenich and Arrostito, "Como murió Aramburu."

90. For an excellent analysis of the Process of National Reorganization's objectives and the disparity between its objectives and actual achievements, see Arnold Spitta, "El 'Proceso de Reorganización Nacional' de 1976 a 1981: los objetivos básicos y su realización práctica," in Waldmann and Garzón Valdés, *El Poder Militar*. See also Juan E. Corradi, "The Mode of Destruction: Terror in Argentina," *Telos*, 54, Winter 1982–83, pp. 61–76.

91. On illegal repression after 1976 see my "'Dirty War' in Argentina: Was it a war and how dirty was it?" in Peter Waldmann and Hans Werner Tobler (eds.), *Staatliche und parastaatliche Gewalt in Lateinamerika* (Frankfurt: Vervuert Verlag, 1991).

92. This is obvious if one considers guerrilla behavior before the coup. It was also confirmed to me by every other former guerrilla I interviewed in Argentina during 1987.

93. Partido Revolucionario de los Trabajadores, *VI Congreso: Mayo 1979* (N.p., n.d.), p. 32.

94. Gorriarán Merlo commanded the ERP faction that killed Anastasio Somoza in Paraguay and is said to have collaborated in the planning of an attempt to start a new campaign of armed struggle in Argentina ten years after the one described in this book had ended. The first act in this campaign, the attack on the La Tablada army barracks on January 23, 1989, was also the last. Most of the participants died in the attack. See "Más de 30 muertos y 44 heridos en el ataque a una unidad militar," *La Nación*, January 24, 1989, pp. 1, 7; and "Pedido de los Fiscales: Perpetua por La Tablada," *Página 12*, May 5, 1989, p. 9.

95. Edouard Bailby, "Trêve pour la Coupe du Monde," *L'Express*, 1396, 10–16 April 1978, p. 61.

Part I. Patterns of Violence

1. This definition borrows heavily from Ted Robert Gurr's description of "turmoil" in *Why Men Rebel* (Princeton, N.J.: Princeton University Press, 1970), p. 11. For other attempts to distinguish among different types of collective political violence (of which armed struggle and collective violent protest are types) see Harry Eckstein, "Theoretical Approaches to Explaining Collective Political Violence," in Ted Robert Gurr (ed.), *Handbook of Political Conflict* (New York: The Free Press, 1980); Henry Bienen, *Violence and Social Change: A Review of Current Literature* (Chicago: University of Chicago Press, 1968), p. 5; and Wolfgang J. Mommsen, "Non-Legal Violence and Terrorism in Western Industrial Societies: An Historical

Analysis," in Wolfgang J. Mommsen and Gerhard Hirschfeld (eds.), *Social Protest, Violence and Terror in 19th and 20th Century Europe* (London: Macmillan, 1982), pp. 393–396.

2. There are, however, some fragmentary analyses of different types of violence during this period. The Argentine Federal Police compiled a list of victims of guerrilla violence, published in Jorge Muñoz, *Seguidme! Vida de Alberto Villar* (Buenos Aires: Ediciones Informar, 1984), pp. 181–196. María Matilde Ollier, *El Fenómeno Insurreccional y la Cultura Política, 1969–1973* (Buenos Aires: Centro Editor de América Latina, 1986), pp. 83–85 and 117–119, provides figures for the total number of operations that each guerrilla group staged in the 1970–72 period. Guillermo O'Donnell, *1966–1973 El Estado Burocrático Autoritario: Triunfos, Derrotas y Crisis* (Buenos Aires: Editorial de Belgrano, 1982), p. 450, presents a monthly count of all guerrilla violence (excluding bombings) for 1969–72. Charles A. Russell, James A. Miller, and James F. Schenkel, "Urban Guerrillas in Argentina: A Select Bibliography," *Latin American Research Review*, 9:3, 1974, pp. 53–89: 81–89, review the most important guerrilla operations in 1969–74. Juan Carlos Marín discusses collective violent protest in the context of a wider analysis of violence during the 1973–76 Peronist administrations in his *Los hechos armados, un ejercicio posible* (Buenos Aires: CICSO, 1984), p. 114. Graham-Yooll provides a death count for 1975, and Escobar and Velázquez do the same for 1974–75, but in each case there is no attempt to distinguish casualties according to whether they were the result of armed struggle, paramilitary activity, or collective violence. See Andrew Graham-Yooll, *De Perón a Videla* (Buenos Aires: Editorial Legasa, 1989), appendix III; and Justo Escobar and Sebastián Velázquez, *Examen de la Violencia Argentina* (Mexico: Fondo de Cultura Económica, 1975), pp. 165–183. A preliminary list of disappeared persons during the dirty war appeared as Amnesty International, *The "disappeared" of Argentina: List of cases reported to Amnesty International, March 1976–February 1979* (London: Amnesty International, 1979). The most ambitious list of disappearances, reporting 8,961 cases between 1971 and 1983, appeared as Comisión Nacional sobre la Desaparición de Personas, *Anexos del Informe de la Conadep* (Buenos Aires: Eudeba, 1985).

3. Robert Cox, *The Sound of One Hand Clapping: A Preliminary Study of the Argentine Press in a Time of Terror* (Washington, D.C.: The Wilson Center, Latin American Program, Working Paper no. 83, 1980), pp. 9–10. Cox repeatedly highlights the plight of Argentine journalists who, during the Peronist interregnum and beyond, were subject to threats and attacks from the right and the left. However, it should be said that what the left objected to was not the reporting of its deeds (which it welcomed) but the analysis or interpretation of them. Cox's article implicitly supports the view that most of the distortions of the truth occurred in connection with paramilitary violence and not armed struggle.

4. The official list appears in *El Terrorismo en la Argentina* (Buenos Aires: Poder Ejecutivo Nacional, 1980), pp. 250–258. On Holmberg's death see "La conexión Massera-Montoneros," *Testigo*, 1:11, March 14, 1984, pp. 4–10.

5. Interview with a former police officer in Buenos Aires, June 26, 1987. For descriptions of the handful of guerrilla operations not carried out by armed organizations but blamed on them, see Martin Edwin Andersen, *Dossier Secreto: Argentina's Desaparecidos and the Myth of the "Dirty War"* (Boulder, Colo.: Westview Press, 1993), passim.

6. Information supplied by a former Montonero interviewed in Buenos Aires, September 23, 1987.

7. The National Commission on the Disappearance of Persons was appointed by President Raúl Alfonsín in December 1983. Its final report was presented to the president nine months later and provided the basis for the historic Juntas Trial in 1985 in which four junta

members were acquitted. General Jorge R. Videla and Admiral Emilio E. Massera received life sentences, and Brigadier Orlando R. Agosti, Admiral Armando Lambruschini, and General Roberto E. Viola were sentenced to 4, 8, and 17 years' imprisonment, respectively. Agosti served his full sentence, and the others were pardoned by Alfonsín's successor, President Carlos Menem.

8. All statistics in the next four chapters represent mutually exclusive counts. For example, if the seizure of a police precinct resulted in a theft of arms, the operation is recorded in both categories. Statistics for all three types of violence are grouped into three periods: violence during the Argentine Revolution (January 1, 1969–May 24, 1973), the Peronist interregnum (May 25, 1973–March 23, 1976), and the Process of National Reorganization (March 24, 1976–December 31, 1979). Even though the military government known as the Argentine Revolution began on June 28, 1966, and the Process of National Reorganization ended with the inaugural of Raúl Alfonsín in December 1983, the 1969–79 time frame reflects the period during which guerrilla groups were active.

9. Interview with a former Montonero, Buenos Aires, October 1, 1987.

Chapter 3. Armed Struggle

1. Tables 3.1–3.3 show aggregate figures on the total volume of guerrilla violence for each period. For variations on the location of attacks, the size of guerrilla commandos or group responsibility within each type of operation, see María José Moyano, "Armed Struggle in Argentina, 1969–1979," Ph.D. diss., Yale University, 1990, Appendix A.

2. Tierra del Fuego, which at the time was a territory and not a province, is not listed. No attacks took place there.

3. The notion of the Second War of Independence is discussed in chapter 8.

4. Instituto Nacional de Estadísticas y Censos, *Censo Nacional de Población, Familias y Viviendas de 1970: Compendio de sus Resultados Provisionales* (Buenos Aires: INDEC, N.d.), p. 7.

5. "Tucumán," *La Opinión,* November 24, 1976, p. 1. See also Martin Edwin Andersen, *Dossier Secreto: Argentina's Desaparecidos and the Myth of the "Dirty War"* (Boulder, Colo.: Westview Press, 1993), pp. 127–139.

6. Significantly,the ERP has avoided any lengthy analysis of the rural campaign, but some considerations are made in Partido Revolucionario de los Trabajadores, *Documentos del Comité Ejecutivo "Comandante Mario R. Santucho"* (Madrid: Gráficas Halar, 1977), and *VI Congreso: Mayo 1979* (N.p., n.d.).

7. Both Roqué and Urondo were originally members of FAR and were among those amnestied in May 1973. Both died in combat, Urondo in 1976 and Roqué in 1977.

8. See Moyano, "Armed Struggle," Appendix A.

9. See Moyano, "Armed Struggle," Appendix B.

10. A number of scholars of political violence point out that violence flourishes under democratic conditions because participants can count on freedom of expression and freedom of movement. In both the Spanish and Argentine experiences, armed operations increased with the advent of democracy, and there were also incidents of collective protest. But I am trying to explain why certain types of armed operations and not others occurred after 1973 and not before, or at least not so frequently. On the relation between armed struggle and democracy see Paul Wilkinson, *Terrorism & the Liberal State* (New York: New York University Press, 1986), chapter 6; and Walter Laqueur, *The Age of Terrorism* (Boston: Little, Brown, 1987), chapter 4.

On ETA see Francisco J. Llera, José M. Mata, and Cynthia L. Irwin, "ETA: From Secret Army to Social Movement—The Post-Franco Schism of the Basque Nationalist Movement," *Terrorism and Political Violence*, 5:3, 1993, pp. 106–134; and on mass action during the Spanish transition, Ramón Adell Argilés, "La Transición Política en la Calle: Manifestaciones Políticas de Grupos y Masas. Madrid, 1976–1987," Ph.D. diss., Universidad Complutense de Madrid, 1989.

11. And this at the time which, in worldwide terms, represented the heyday of airplane hijacking. For a brief description of the hijacking frenzy in the late sixties and seventies, see George Rosie, *The Directory of International Terrorism* (Edinburgh: Mainstream Publishing, 1986), pp. 43–44, 94–96, 142–144, 181–182.

12. I refer to the crash of Pan Am flight 103 over Lockerbie, Scotland, on December 21, 1988, following the explosion of a bomb set on board the airplane by the Popular Front for the Liberation of Palestine—General Command. See Steve Emerson and Brian Duffy, "Pan Am 103: The German Connection," *New York Times Magazine*, March 18, 1990, pp. 28–33, 72–74, 84–87.

13. Descriptions of similar situations are provided by Eugenio Méndez, *Confesiones de un Montonero* (Buenos Aires: Editorial Sudamericana/Planeta, 1985), pp. 99–101; and Martín Caparrós, *No Velas a Tus Muertos* (Buenos Aires: Ediciones de la Flor, 1986), p. 66.

14. This is not always the case. On occasions guerrilla groups lose some of their own combatants through faulty handling of bombs resulting in premature explosions. This was particularly true of the IRA in the early seventies: between 1970 and 1972 at least 25 Provos died in this fashion. But these accidents hardly ever occurred in Argentina. On the IRA deaths see Jack Holland, *Too Long a Sacrifice: Life and Death in Northern Ireland since 1969* (Harmondsworth: Penguin Books, 1982), p. 129.

15. For the Tupamaros' own account of the seizure see *Actas Tupamaras* (Madrid: Ediciones Revolución, 1982), pp. 141–183.

16. On the Army Medical Corps operation see "Copó un grupo terrorista un comando del Ejército," *La Nación*, September 7, 1973, pp. 1, 6. On Azul see "Sorprende por su audacia el ataque al Regimiento 10 de Caballería de Azul, la guarnición de tanques mas importante del país," *La Opinión*, January 22, 1974, pp. 10–11. On Villa María see "Características similares al copamiento de Azul tuvo el operativo guerrillero contra la fábrica de Villa María," *La Opinión*, August 13, 1974, p. 8. On the 17th Airborne see "Efectivos del Ejército mataron en combate a 15 extremistas en Catamarca," *La Opinión*, August 13, 1974, p. 1; and "Fue diezmada la columna guerrillera en Catamarca," *La Opinión*, August 14, 1974, pp. 1, 24. On Matienzo airport see "Contra un avión de la Fuerza Aérea se atentó en el aeropuerto de Tucumán," *La Nación*, August 29, 1974, pp. 1, 6. On Formosa see "Conmocionaron al país las características y dimensiones del cruento ataque extremista en Formosa," *La Opinión*, October 7, 1975, p. 15. On Monte Chingolo see "Feroz Ataque Subversivo," *La Opinión*, December 26, 1975, p. 20.

17. In spite of Greene's denial, it is generally believed that *The Honorary Consul* (Harmondsworth: Penguin Books, 1986) is based on the kidnapping of Stanley Sylvester, executive in the Swift plant and honorary British consul in Rosario, by the ERP.

18. On the Lockwood kidnappings see "Charles Lockwood, o de como ganar amigos apelando a la flema británica," *La Opinión*, August 16, 1973, p. 11; and "Secuestraron por segunda vez a un empresario," *La Nación*, August 1, 1975, pp. 1, 14. For an eyewitness account of the press conference in which the Montoneros announced they had cashed the ransom and released Jorge Born, see Andrew Graham-Yooll, *A Matter of Fear: Portrait of an Argentinian Exile*

(Westport, Conn.: Lawrence Hill, 1981), chapter 4. On the abduction of Aramburu's coffin see "Los restos de Eva Perón están en la Argentina" and "Devuelven el cadáver de Aramburu," *Gente*, 9:487, November 21, 1974, pp. 4–9, 10–11.

19. On Sallustro see *La Opinión*, March 25, 1972, p. 7, and April 11, 1972, p. 1. On D'Aquila see *La Opinión*, January 14, 1973, p. 11. The D'Aquila interrogation was published as *Máxima Peligrosidad* (Buenos Aires: Editorial Candela, 1973).

20. On Alemán see *La Opinión*, April 15, 1973, p. 1; and on Pita, *La Opinión*, December 8, 1976, p. 1.

21. It would appear that immediately following the Ford incident, other companies like Coca-Cola and Otis Elevators were asked to pay the revolutionary tax, but it is difficult to find out which companies paid the tax and which refused due to the fact that the practice was illegal. Similarly in Spain, ETA makes widespread use of the revolutionary tax, and yet it is impossible to gauge what companies are paying it. See "El método de los raptos logra un record con el pago de mil millones por el rescate de un gerente de Ford," *La Opinión*, May 25, 1973, p. 8; Lewis H. Diuguid, "Campora Fails to End Terror In Argentina," *Washington Post*, June 2, 1973, p. A12; and *Crónica*, August 12, 1973, p. 8.

22. If Walter Laqueur's figures are correct, then the only groups with an annual budget higher than that of Argentine guerrillas are the PLO in the 1970s and 1980s and the Colombian FARC and M-19 in the mid-1980s. See his discussion of terrorist finances in *The Age of Terrorism*, pp. 96–103. The Red Peril thesis was extremely popular in the 1960s and 1970s. For a general formulation see John Barron, *KGB: The Secret Work of Soviet Secret Agents* (New York: Reader's Digest Press, 1974); Brian Crozier, *The Surrogate Forces of the Soviet Union* (London: Institute for the Study of Conflict, 1978); and Brian Crozier (ed.), *We Will Bury You: Studies in Left-Wing Subversion Today* (London: Tom Stacey, 1970); Jacques Kaufmann, *L'Internationale Terroriste* (Paris: Librairie Plon, 1977). For applications to Latin America in general and Argentina in particular see Pierre F. de Villemarest, *Les Stratèges de la Peur: Vingt Ans de Guerre Revolutionnaire en Argentine* (Geneva: Editions Voxmundi, 1981); William E. Ratliff, *Castroism and Communism in Latin America, 1959–1976: The Varieties of Marxist-Leninist Experience* (Washington, D.C.: American Enterprise Institute for Public Policy Research, 1976); and Juan Vivés, *Los Amos de Cuba* (Buenos Aires: Emecé Editores, 1982).

23. On the ERP's retaliation for the events at Catamarca see *La Opinión*, September 18, 1974, p. 12; and *La Prensa*, December 2, 1974, pp. 1, 6. For examples of Montonero attacks against policemen see *La Opinión*, March 25, 1975, p. 16, and June 21, 1975, p. 7; and *Evita Montonera*, 2:12, February-March 1976, pp. 32–35. Union leaders accused of being traitors to the working class and executives and plant managers in companies undergoing labor disputes were also targeted for specific campaigns.

24. On Lambruschini see *El Terrorismo en la Argentina* (Buenos Aires: Poder Ejecutivo Nacional, 1980), pp. 241–248. On Juan and Jorge Born see "Un grupo comando secuestró ayer al gerente y al director de la empresa Bunge y Born," *La Opinión*, September 20, 1974, p. 10.

25. Fuerzas Armadas Peronistas, "Las Fuerzas Armadas Peronistas (FAP) se dirigen a la Policía," *Cristianismo y Revolución*, IV:26, November-December 1970, p. 54. Emphasis in the original.

26. Fuerzas Armadas Revolucionarias, "Comunicado No. 1—Comunicado No. 2," *Cristianismo y Revolución*, IV:25, September 1970, pp. 59–60.

27. Francisco Cerecedo, "Los montoneros se explican," *Cambio 16*, 245, August 16, 1976, p. 41.

Chapter 4. Collective Violent Protest

1. See Guillermo O'Donnell, "Argentina: La Cosecha del Miedo," *Alternativas*, 1, September 1983, pp. 5–14.

2. Cited in Jorge Pinedo, *Consignas y Lucha Popular en el Proceso Revolucionario Argentino 1955–73* (Buenos Aires: Editorial Freeland, 1974), p. 58. *Barrio Norte* is the upper- and upper-middle-class neighborhood in downtown Buenos Aires. This and all subsequent slogans cited were chanted at riots and demonstrations or appeared as graffito.

3. Ibid., pp. 138, 133. Rear Admiral Emilio Berisso was killed in December 1972 in retaliation for the Navy's role in the Trelew massacre.

4. Ibid., pp. 94, 102.

5. Samuel P. Huntington, *Political Order in Changing Societies* (New Haven and London: Yale University Press, 1968), pp. 290–291.

6. Daniel James, *Resistance and Integration: Peronism and the Argentine Working Class, 1946–1976* (Cambridge: Cambridge University Press, 1988), part 5. See also Daniel James, "Rationalization and Working Class Response: The Contexts and Limits of Factory Floor Activity in Argentina," *Journal of Latin American Studies*, 13:26, 1981, pp. 375–402; and Daniel James, "Power and Politics in Peronist Trade Unions," *Journal of Interamerican Studies and World Affairs*, 20:1, 1978, pp. 3–36. The study of the corruption of Argentine union bosses which has become a classic is Jorge Correa, *Los Jerarcas Sindicales* (Buenos Aires: Editorial Obrador, 1974).

7. Cited in Guillermo O'Donnell, *1966–1973 El Estado Burocrático Autoritario. Triunfos, Derrotas y Crisis* (Buenos Aires: Editorial de Belgrano, 1982), p. 456.

8. President Videla quoted in Peter Strafford, "Argentina: Back on the rails, but at what cost?" *Times*, January 4, 1978, p. 12.

9. Since voting is compulsory in Argentina, a blank vote is the equivalent of absenteeism.

10. Throughout this chapter, collective action by prison inmates refers to common criminals. Political prisoners never resorted to violence to protest prison conditions.

11. On the Paris revolt see Philippe Bénéton and Jean Touchard, "Les Intérpretations de la Crise de Mai-Juin 1968," *Revue Française de Science Politique*, 20:3, 1970, pp. 503–544; and Bernard E. Brown, *Protest in Paris: Anatomy of a Revolt* (Morristown, N.J.: General Learning Press, 1974). On protest in West Germany and Italy see Jillian Becker, *Hitler's Children: The Story of the Baader-Meinhof Terrorist Gang* (London: Michael Joseph, 1977), pp. 21–105; and Alessandro Silj, *Mai più senza fucile! alle origini dei NAP e delle BR* (Florence: Vallechi, 1977), part 1. On American students see Todd Gitlin, *The Sixties: Years of Hope, Days of Rage* (New York: Bantam Books, 1989); and Kirkpatrick Sale, *S.D.S.* (New York: Vintage Books, 1974). On Argentine students see Juan Carlos Agulla, *Diagnóstico Social de una Crisis: Córdoba Mayo de 1969* (Buenos Aires: Editel, 1969) passim; Francisco J. Delich, *Crisis y protesta social: Córdoba, mayo de 1969* (Buenos Aires: Ediciones Signos, 1970), especially chapter 4; and François Gèze and Alain Labrousse, *Argentine: Révolution et Contre-révolutions* (Paris: Editions du Seuil, 1975), pp. 121–127.

12. "Balance político del movimiento estudiantil: El avance del reformismo y el apoyo a las elecciones dominaron el año 1972," *La Opinión*, January 2, 1973, p. 15. See also "A

seis años de 'la noche de los bastones largos.' El desarrollo del movimiento estudiantil se vió favorecido por su proscripción," *La Opinión*, July 28, 1972, p. 17.

13. "Finalizó la huelga universitaria en Santa Fe," *La Opinión*, September 24, 1971, p. 13.

14. "Murió un estudiante tucumano y el clima de agitación se extiende por todo el país," *La Opinión*, June 25, 1972, p. 9.

15. "El nuevo decano deberá afrontar la creciente rebelión estudiantil," *La Opinión*, September 24, 1971, p. 12.

16. "Los alumnos rinden con sus propios programas ante docentes auxiliares," *La Opinión*, August 4, 1971, p. 12.

17. "Fueron interrogados los detenidos de Bellas Artes," *La Opinión*, September 28, 1971, p. 15; "La renovación periódica de planes de estudio no se respeta totalmente," *La Opinión*, November 11, 1971, p. 13.

18. James, *Resistance and Integration*, p. 219.

19. Combativo leader Agustín Tosco, cited in Ibid., p. 229.

20. On the labor movement under Onganía see James, *Resistance and Integration*, part 5; and Ronaldo Munck, Ricardo Falcón, and Bernardo Galitelli, *Argentina: From Anarchism to Peronism—Workers, Unions and Politics, 1855–1985* (London: Zed Books, 1987), chapter 13. For examples of labor conflicts erupting into violence see "Hubo un muerto y cinco heridos en un incidente entre gremialistas," *La Prensa*, March 9, 1971, p. 5; "Pese a ser declarado ilegal tuvo eco masivo el paro de la CGT," *La Opinión*, March 2, 1972, p. 24. On combativos and clasistas see "La experiencia gremial de Sitrac-Sitram intenta proyectarse como línea política," *La Opinión*, August 23, 1972, p. 7.

21. Beba Balvé et al., *Lucha de Calles Lucha de Clases: Elementos para su análisis: Córdoba 1971–1969* (Buenos Aires: Ediciones La Rosa Blindada, 1973), p. 184.

22. *Córdoba*, May 29, 1969, cited in Balvé, *Lucha de Calles*, p. 120. Following the popular terminology adopted at the time of the Cordobazo, all these riots became known as "the blow from . . ." On the Cordobazo see "Produjéronse varios muertos en los disturbios de Córdoba," *La Prensa*, May 30, 1969, pp. 1, 10; "Hubo confusión y tiroteos en Córdoba durante todo el día," *La Prensa*, May 31, 1969, pp. 1, 7–8. On the Cipollettazo see "No asumió en Cipolletti el interventor designado," *La Prensa*, September 14, 1969, p. 13. On the Rosariazo see "El paro ferroviario provocó graves desórdenes en Rosario," *La Prensa*, September 17, 1969, pp. 1, 12. On the Tucumanazo see "Hubo nuevos incidentes estudiantiles en Tucumán," *La Prensa*, November 26, 1970, p. 13. On the Viborazo see "Desórdenes y un muerto causó el paro en Córdoba," *La Prensa*, March 13, 1971, pp. 1, 6–7; "Se cumplirá hoy el paro activo dispuesto por la CGT de Córdoba," *La Prensa*, March 15, 1971, p. 11. On the Mendozazo see "Estalló en Mendoza un pronunciamiento popular que provocó un muerto y la ocupación militar de la ciudad," *La Opinión*, April 5, 1972, pp. 1, 24; "Continúan los disturbios en Mendoza y la ciudad está totalmente paralizada," *La Opinión*, April 7, 1972, pp. 1, 9; "Aún rige el toque de queda," *La Opinión*, April 8, 1972, p. 1. On the Rocazo see "Es grave la situación en General Roca donde ayer se produjeron nuevos choques," *La Opinión*, July 7, 1972, p. 8; "Disturbios y hechos de violencia se repiten constantemente en General Roca," *La Opinión*, July 8, 1972, p. 10; "Adoptan severas medidas militares en General Roca," *La Opinión*, July 12, 1972, p. 1.

23. Guerrilla perceptions at the time are discussed in chapters 7 and 8. On the reading of the situation made by the military and the bourgeoisie see O'Donnell, *El Estado Burocrático Autoritario*, pp. 454ff.

24. James William McGuire, "Peronism without Perón: Unions in Argentine politics, 1955–1966," Ph.D. diss., University of California, Berkeley, 1989, pp. 279, 281.

25. Santiago Luis Guevara, "Desató violentos incidentes populares un conflicto gremial en San Francisco," *La Opinión*, July 31, 1973, p. 8. See also Jonathan Kandell, "Leftists in Key Argentine City Chafe at Peronist Conservatives," *New York Times*, July 8, 1973, p. 9; and Munck, Falcón, and Galitelli, *Argentina,* chapter 14.

26. Ricardo Frascara, "Paro en los ingenios y enérgico repudio de Atilio Santillán a la intervención de FOTIA," *La Opinión*, September 15, 1974, p. 14.

27. On the Villa Constitución episode see "Denuncian que fue desbaratado un complot destinado a paralizar la industria pesada," *La Opinión*, March 21, 1975, p. 24. On the July days see "La Presidente responde hoy a la CGT sobre los convenios paritarios," *La Opinión*, June 28, 1975, pp. 1, 6–11, 20; "Paro General Desde El Lunes," *La Opinión*, July 5, 1975, pp. 1, 6–8; "La CGT dispuso levantar el paro al haber obtenido la homologación de los convenios," *La Opinión*, July 9, 1975, p. 13; "López Rega Se Fue Del País," *La Opinión*, July 20, 1975, p. 1.

28. "Fueron ocupadas por peronistas todas las facultades de Buenos Aires y La Plata," *La Opinión*, May 29, 1973, p. 17; "Fue ocupada durante tres horas una radio cordobesa," *La Opinión*, May 30, 1973, p. 10.

29. "Lema: ocupar para destituir," *Crónica*, June 13, 1973, p. 5. See also "La búsqueda de canales orgánicos para la participación popular," *La Opinión*, June 18, 1973, p. 8.

30. "Ocupan los obreros un astillero en Tigre," *La Opinión*, May 31, 1973, p. 4; "Lucha de tendencias en las ocupaciones de centros laborales," *La Opinión*, June 13, 1973, p. 8; "La rebelión de los presos comunes desnudó fallas en el sistema penal y carcelario," *La Opinión*, July 8, 1973, p. 7; Jonathan Kandell, "Prison Mutinies Sweep Argentina," *New York Times*, July 6, 1973, p. 4. Prison inmates obtained all their objectives: prison conditions improved, and the government passed a law expediting the administration of justice. Newspapers do not report whether the other seizures achieved the reforms and resignations originally demanded.

31. Interview with Dr. Esteban Righi, Interior Minister at the time, in Buenos Aires, December 25, 1987. See "Venció el plazo para cesar las ocupaciones: actitudes confusas," *Crónica*, June 28, 1973, p. 5; "El gobierno precisó ayer las órdenes impartidas a las fuerzas de seguridad," *La Opinión*, June 30, 1973, p. 6.

32. *La Opinión*, July 22, 1973, p. 20.

33. Redundancy Law, cited in Arnold Spitta, "El 'Proceso de Reorganización Nacional' de 1976 a 1981: Los Objetivos Básicos y su Realización Práctica," in Peter Waldmann and Ernesto Garzón Valdés (eds.), *El Poder Militar en la Argentina (1976–1981)* (Buenos Aires: Editorial Galerna, 1983), p. 81.

34. "Fue puesta en vigencia una ley de Seguridad Industrial," *La Opinión*, September 9, 1976, p. 1.

35. Marcos Cristal, "Desde enero los ingresos cayeron un 43%," *La Opinión*, September 2, 1976, p. 13. See also Francisco Delich, "Después del Diluvio, la Clase Obrera," in Alain Rouquié (ed.), *Argentina, Hoy* (Buenos Aires: Siglo Veintiuno Editores, 1982).

36. "Despidos en SEGBA," *La Opinión*, October 5, 1976, p. 13; "Siguen los paros en Segba e Italo," *La Opinión*, October 9, 1976, p. 1. Luz y Fuerza is the union grouping all electrical power workers. Among those dismissed was Oscar Smith, general secretary of Luz y Fuerza. According to Guillermo Calisto ("Conjeturas acerca del conflicto," *La Opinión*, October 8, 1976, p. 1), the SEGBA conflict became so virulent because, unlike previous appli-

cations of the Redundancy Law, those declared redundant at the power companies were union leaders. Oscar Smith disappeared in February 1977.

37. On the unfolding of the SEGBA conflict see "Advertencia del Comando Militar," *La Opinión*, October 7, 1976, p. 13; "Se recupera paulatinamente el ritmo de las tareas en Segba," *La Opinión*, October 12, 1976, p. 13; "Condena de Segba por tres secuestros," *La Opinión*, October 13, 1976, p. 1; "El conflicto suscitado con el sindicato de Luz y Fuerza alcanzó ayer nivel crítico," *La Opinión*, October 14, 1976, p. 28; "La situación en Segba e Italo se regulariza," "Una nueva sustracción de cables," and "Episodios en el sector de los bancos," *La Opinión*, October 19, 1976, p. 15.

38. Comisión Nacional sobre la Desaparición de Personas, *Nunca Mas* (Buenos Aires: Eudeba, 1985), p. 296.

Chapter 5. Right-Wing Violence

1. That death squad activity between 1969 and 1973 should be regarded as a case of vigilantism was confirmed by the interviews with former police officers mentioned in notes below.

2. Interview with a former police officer in Buenos Aires, June 26, 1987. See also the lists of "Repressors" at the end of each chapter in Alipio E. Paoletti, *Como los Nazis, Como en Vietnam* (Buenos Aires: Editorial Contrapunto, 1987); and Alberto Ottalagano, *Soy Fascista: Y Qué?* (Buenos Aires: Ro. Ca. Producciones, 1983), pp. 14–17.

3. On the synarchy see Ignacio González Janzen, *La Triple-A* (Buenos Aires: Editorial Contrapunto, 1986), pp. 87–92.

4. Quoted in Jacobo Timerman, *Prisoner Without a Name, Cell Without a Number* (New York: Vintage Books, 1982), p. 130.

5. On anti-Semitism in the armed forces and the Andinia Plan see John Simpson and Jana Bennett, *The Disappeared: Voices From a Secret War* (London: Robson Books, 1985), pp. 54–55, 210–212, 225, 263–264; and Timerman, *Prisoner Without a Name*, particularly pp. 72–78. See also Iain Guest, *Behind the Disappearances: Argentina's Dirty War Against Human Rights and the United Nations* (Philadelphia: University of Pennsylvania Press, 1990), pp. 287–290.

6. Quoted in Eric A. Nordlinger, *Soldiers in Politics: Military Coups and Governments* (Englewood Cliffs, N.J.: Prentice-Hall, 1977), pp. 19–20. It is because of this speech that Argentines refer to the "Ideological Frontiers" as the "Onganía Doctrine" or the "West Point Doctrine."

7. Timerman, *Prisoner Without a Name*, p. 102. See also Miguel Angel Scenna, *Los Militares* (Buenos Aires: Editorial de Belgrano, 1980), pp. 247–353; Eduardo L. Duhalde, *El Estado Terrorista Argentino* (Buenos Aires: Ediciones El Caballito, 1983), pp. 32–44, 73–75; Alain Rouquié, "El poder militar en la Argentina de hoy: cambio y continuidad," in Peter Waldmann and Ernesto Garzón Valdés (eds.), *El Poder Militar en la Argentina (1976–1981)* (Buenos Aires: Editorial Galerna, 1983). At the same time that the Latin American military were developing the Doctrine of Ideological Frontiers, the United States abandoned the idea of hemispheric defense in favor of the notion of internal security. Through military aid and training for Latin American officers, the U.S. helped promote this "new professionalism." See Alfred Stepan, "The New Professionalism of Internal Warfare and Military Role Expansion," in Alfred Stepan (ed.), *Authoritarian Brazil: Origins, Policies, and Future* (New Haven and London: Yale University Press, 1973); and Maria Helena Moreira Alves, *State and Opposition in Military Brazil* (Austin: University of Texas Press, 1985), part 1. See also Michael T. Klare

and Peter Kornbluh (eds.), *Low Intensity Warfare* (New York: Pantheon Books, 1988); and for a discussion of the British and French contributions see Roger Faligot, *Guerre Spéciale en Europe: Le Laboratoire Irlandais* (Paris: Textes/Flammarion, 1980). The presence of two military missions in Buenos Aires in the 1960s and well into the 1970s, one American and one made up of former Organisation de l'Armée Secrète officers, was confirmed to me by a source connected to the top echelons of the 1976–83 administration interviewed (not for attribution) in Buenos Aires, April 1987.

8. This fact was confirmed by a former police officer interviewed in Buenos Aires, June 26, 1987. When asked whether the Triple A had been partly staffed by police officers, he responded, "Of course. Such organizations always are." See also "Se teme que actúen organismos fuera del control del poder político," *La Opinión,* July 19, 1971, p. 12, and "Denuncian en Córdoba la existencia de una campaña de terrorismo blanco," *La Opinión,* August 24, 1971, p. 13.

9. On the early Tacuara see Rogelio García Lupo, *La Rebelión de los Generales* (Buenos Aires: Editorial Jamcana, 1963), ch. 9; and González Janzen, *La Triple-A,* pp. 28–32. Members of a left-wing splinter of Tacuara, the Tacuara Revolutionary National Movement, went on to stage the first urban guerrilla operation in Argentina, the 1963 payroll theft at the Bank Employees Union Clinic, known as Operation Rosaura. Most of the participants were captured. One of them, José Luis Nell, escaped from the law court, joined the Uruguayan Tupamaros, returned to Argentina and became a Montonero. Paralyzed from the waist down after the Ezeiza massacre, Nell shot himself in 1974. Another Rosaura participant, Jorge Caffatti, became one of the founders of FAP. Yet another, Joe Baxter, joined the Tupamaros, fought in Vietnam, returned to Argentina to join the ERP, and led the splinter ERP FR. Baxter was killed in an airplane crash at Orly, Paris, in 1973. Montonero founding members Carlos Gustavo Ramus and Fernando Abal Medina were also tacuaristas even though they abandoned the group before the Tacuara Revolutionary National Movement was created. Ramus and Abal Medina went on to participate in the kidnapping of Aramburu and were ambushed by the police on September 7, 1970, which became known as the Day of the Montonero. On Operation Rosaura see *La Razón,* March 25, 1964, p. 1. See also *Militancia,* 6, July 19, 1973, p. 35; and *La Opinión,* October 6, 1971, p. 11, March 17, 1972, p. 12, and March 18, 1973, p. 12.

10. Interview with Envar El Kadri, founder of the Peronist Youth, in Buenos Aires, June 26, 1987. On orthodox Peronist organizations see Horacio Verbitsky, *Ezeiza* (Buenos Aires: Editorial Contrapunto, 1984), passim.

11. It is for these reasons that the Peronist left referred to right-wing Peronist organizations as "rubber stamps." For an excellent analysis of the different groups within the Peronist movement circa 1973 see "Una compleja estructura partidaria que se unifica en el liderazgo de Perón," *La Opinión,* June 27, 1973, p. 8.

12. Richard Gillespie, *Soldiers of Perón: Argentina's Montoneros* (Oxford: Clarendon Press, 1982), p. 185 n64; Oscar R. Anzorena, *Tiempo de Violencia y Utopía (1966–1976)* (Buenos Aires: Editorial Contrapunto, 1988), p. 322; González Janzen, *La Triple-A,* p. 20.

13. The description of the Triple A death squad is taken from my " 'Dirty War' in Argentina: Was it a war and how dirty was it?" in Peter Waldmann and Hans Werner Tobler (eds.), *Staatliche und parastaatliche Gewalt in Lateinamerika* (Frankfurt: Vervuert Verlag, 1991). On the life of López Rega see Tomás Eloy Martínez, "El ascenso, triunfo, decadencia y derrota de José López Rega," *La Opinión,* October 22, 1975, pp. 1, 24; and Gente, *25 de Mayo de 1973–24 de Marzo de 1976: Fotos, hechos, testimonios de 1035 dramáticos días* (Buenos Aires:

Editorial Abril, 1976), pp. 131–151. One of Villar's subordinates, incidentally also a member of the Triple A, wrote his biography: Jorge Muñoz, *Seguidme! Vida de Alberto Villar* (Buenos Aires: Ediciones Informar, 1984).

14. Former police inspector Rodolfo Peregrino Fernández testified before the Argentine Commission on Human Rights at Geneva in March 1983. Salvador Horacio Paino, formerly one of López Rega's bodyguards, testified in February 1976 before the Special Congressional Committee on the Ministry of Social Welfare's misuse of public funds.

15. Rodolfo Peregrino Fernández, *Autocrítica Policial* (Buenos Aires: El Cid Editor, 1983), pp. 10, 59; Verbitsky, *Ezeiza*, p. 54; "Las revelaciones de Paino," *La Opinión*, February 12, 1976, second section, pp. 1–4: 1–2; and González Janzen, *La Triple-A*, p. 15.

16. The "links" have been identified as two of López Rega's most trusted aides, Jorge Conti and Carlos Villone. See "Diéronse detalles sobre la conducción de la Triple A," *La Nación*, February 2, 1976, p. 12.

17. "Las revelaciones de Paino," p. 2; and "A Rucci lo mató la Triple A," *Gente*, 18:946, September 8, 1983, pp. 54–63: 60; González Janzen, *La Triple-A*, pp. 15–16.

18. "Varios diputados de la nación, amenazados," *Crónica*, November 28, 1973, p. 2. On September 11, 1973, prior to its official launching, the Triple A provoked a fire at the newspaper *Clarín*, which had been forced to publish a paid denunciation of López Rega when guerrillas of the ERP kidnapped a member of *Clarín*'s editorial staff. On the *Clarín* episode see "Las revelaciones de Paino," p. 2, and "A Rucci lo mató la Triple A," p. 60. For a list of the Triple A's victims see Justo Escobar and Sebastián Velázquez, *Examen de la Violencia Argentina* (Mexico: Fondo de Cultura Económica, 1975), pp. 164–183.

19. The list includes all the names of those identified by the following sources: Fernández, *Autocrítica Policial;* González Janzen, *La Triple-A;* Verbitsky, *Ezeiza;* Heriberto Kahn, *Doy Fe* (Buenos Aires: Editorial Losada, 1979); Paoletti,*Como los Nazis;* "Las revelaciones de Paino"; "Diéronse detalles sobre la conducción de la Triple A"; "A Rucci lo mató la Triple A."

20. "Las revelaciones de Paino," p. 4; Fernández, *Autocrítica Policial*, p. 16; Paoletti, *Como los Nazis*, p. 339; Kahn, *Doy Fe*, pp. 62–64 and 89–94.

21. On the responsibility shared by the governments of Perón and his wife see José Pablo Feinmann, *López Rega, la cara oscura de Perón* (Buenos Aires: Editorial Legasa, 1987), part 2; and Juan E. Corradi, Eldon Kenworthy, and William Wipfler, "Argentina 1973–1976: The Background to Violence," *LASA Newsletter*, 8:3, September 1976, pp. 3–28.

22. Dr. Esteban Righi, Interior Minister during the Cámpora administration (when the seizure frenzy was in full swing), provided a different interpretation. His view is that one ought to distinguish between seizures which expressed reasonable sectoral demands, such as those analyzed in chapter 4, and seizures by the Peronist right which intended to provoke the government into adopting a more severe security policy. Righi was interviewed in Buenos Aires, December 25, 1987. For an analysis that implicitly agrees with Righi see "Crea un falso clima de vacío de poder la ola de ocupaciones en todo el país," *La Opinión*, June 15, 1973, p. 1.

23. On the methodology of disappearances see Amnesty International, *"Disappearances": A Workbook* (New York: Amnesty International USA, 1981).

24. The National Commission on the Disappearance of Persons does not refer to "deaths" but to "detained-disappeared" persons. The commission's report, *Nunca Mas* (Buenos Aires: Eudeba, 1985), refers to a total of 8,961 disappearances. This is the figure usually quoted in the literature, which overlooks the fact that a number of those disappearances occurred before the 1976 coup. The percentages provided here refer to disappearances occurring on or after March 24, 1976.

25. Journalist Mariano Grondona, an apologist for the regime, was briefly kidnapped along with his wife. The kidnappers told him that they wished to discuss the motivations behind their actions. Because he was a popular television personality, the kidnappers expected Grondona to publicize their views on the air. See two articles in *La Opinión:* "El secuestro de Mariano Grondona," August 13, 1976, p. 11; and "Citaría el juez al periodista Grondona," September 13, 1976, p. 13.

26. Consejo de Defensa, *Directiva del Consejo de Defensa Nro 1/75 (Lucha contra la subversión)* (Buenos Aires: N.p., 1975); Comando General de Ejército, *Directiva del Comandante General del Ejército Nro 404/75 (Lucha contra la subversión)* (Buenos Aires: N.p, 1975); Comando General de Ejército, *Directiva del Comandante en Jefe del Ejército Nro 504/77 (Continuación de la ofensiva contra la subversión en el período 1977–78)* (Buenos Aires: N.p, 1978); Comando General de Ejército, *Directiva del Comandante en Jefe del Ejército Nro 604/79 (Continuación de la ofensiva contra la subversión)* (Buenos Aires: N.p, 1979). See also Simpson and Bennett, *The Disappeared*, p. 88; Fernández, *Autocrítica Policial*, pp. 22–24; Comisión Nacional sobre la Desaparición de Personas, *Nunca Mas*, pp. 256–259. The description of the organization of the dirty war in this section is an abridged version of that appearing in Moyano, "The 'Dirty War.' "

27. At the time the jurisdictions of the Army Corps were the following: First Corps: Buenos Aires city and parts of the provinces of Buenos Aires and La Pampa; Second Corps: Santa Fe, Chaco, Formosa, and eastern Argentina; Third Corps: Córdoba, Mendoza, Tucumán and northwestern Argentina; Fifth Corps: southern Buenos Aires and Patagonia. The Fourth Army Corps, which has no territorial jurisdiction, is in charge of logistics.

28. Comando General de Ejército, *Orden Parcial Nro 405/76 (Reestructuración de jurisdicciones y adecuación orgánica para intensificar las operaciones contra la subversión)* (Buenos Aires: N.p, 1976), pp. 3–4.

29. Comando Zona 1, *Anexo 4 (Ejecución de blancos) a la Orden de Operaciones Nro 9/77 (Continuación de la ofensiva contra la subversión durante el período 1977)* (Buenos Aires: N.p, 1977), pp. 1–2.

30. Fernández, *Autocrítica Policial*, pp. 35–36.

31. On the CCDs see Comisión Nacional sobre la Desaparición de Personas, *Nunca Mas*, pp. 54–59, 80–128; and *Anexos al Informe de la Conadep* (Buenos Aires: Eudeba, 1985), *"Listado de Centros Clandestinos de Detención."* This section is based on information provided by Paoletti, *Como los Nazis;* Simpson and Bennett, *The Disappeared;* Guest, *Behind the Disappearances;* Comisión Nacional sobre la Desaparición de Personas, *Nunca Mas;* Horacio Verbitsky (ed.), *Rodolfo Walsh y la Prensa Clandestina, 1976–1978* (Buenos Aires: Ediciones De La Urraca, 1985); *El Libro del Juicio* (Buenos Aires: Editorial Testigo, 1985); Miguel Bonasso, *Recuerdo de la Muerte* (Buenos Aires: Editorial Bruguera, 1984); Eugenio Méndez, *Confesiones de un Montonero* (Buenos Aires: Editorial Sudamericana/Planeta, 1985). I interviewed a former member of the GT 4 in Buenos Aires, July 1, 1987.

32. See Verbitsky, *Rodolfo Walsh y la Prensa Clandestina*, pp. 27–28; Guest, *Behind the Disappearances*, p. 40. Other torture methods were the airplane, the burial and the corkscrew. The airplane involved tying the prisoner's hands and feet together behind his or her back, and sometimes the prisoner was then suspended from a metal bar. Descriptions of the airplane are not very clear but the method seems very similar to the parrot's perch used in Brazil. See Paoletti, *Como los Nazis*, p. 31; *El Libro del Juicio*, p. 194; and *"Pau de Arara" La Violencia Militar en el Brasil* (Mexico: Siglo Veintiuno Editores, 1972). Victims were "buried" up to their neck in the ground in a vertical position. In the case of the "corkscrew" the victim

was eviscerated through the anus. For a description of the "corkscrew" and other more abhorrent methods see Bonasso, *Recuerdo de la Muerte*, p. 121; Paoletti, *Como los Nazis*, p. 73; Verbitsky, *Rodolfo Walsh y la Prensa Clandestina*, p. 28; Méndez, *Confesiones*, pp. 148–149.

33. Comisión Nacional sobre la Desaparición de Personas, *Nunca Mas*, pp. 408–416.

34. The application of the "escape law" was widespread. For a few examples see Verbitsky, *Rodolfo Walsh y la Prensa Clandestina*, pp. 41, 48, 55–56, 81.

35. Paoletti, *Como los Nazis*, p. 96; Comisión Nacional sobre la Desaparición de Personas, *Nunca Mas*, pp. 69, 235–246.

36. On the rehabilitation process at the ESMA see Bonasso, *Recuerdo de la Muerte*, pp. 94–97, 287–289, 298–300; Méndez, *Confesiones*, ch. 10; Simpson and Bennett, *The Disappeared*, pp. 290–297; Comisión Nacional sobre la Desaparición de Personas, *Nunca Mas*, pp. 134–135. The work of the 20 or so members of the Staff could best be described as slave labor. Staff members were even responsible for the drafting of a monograph on the history of the Peruvian army which enabled Captain Acosta's brother, an Army major, to pass his War College exam. See Paoletti, *Como los Nazis*, p. 175; and Bonasso, *Recuerdo de la Muerte*, p. 353.

37. On the Quinta de Funes and Operation Mexico see Bonasso, *Recuerdo de la Muerte*, pp. 123–129, 177–210.

Chapter 6. Patterns of Violence Compared

1. This is a variation on the old leninist idea that the working class cannot transcend a "trade-union consciousness." See V. I. Lenin, *What is to be Done? Burning Questions of our Movement* (New York: International Publishers, 1981), especially chapter III.

2. María Seoane, *Todo o Nada* (Buenos Aires: Editorial Planeta, 1992), p. 144.

3. Alváro Abós, *El Posperonismo* (Buenos Aires: Editorial Legasa, 1986), pp. 27–29, 34–35.

4. On the Red Brigades see Donatella della Porta, "Terrorism in Italy," in Martha Crenshaw (ed.), *Terrorism in Context* (University Park, Pa.: Pennsylvania State University Press, forthcoming); Donatella della Porta and Sidney Tarrow, "Unwanted children: Political violence and the cycle of protest in Italy, 1966–1973," *European Journal of Political Research*, 14, 1986, pp. 607–632; and Alessandro Silj, *Mai più senza fucile! alle origini dei NAP e delle BR* (Florence: Vallechi, 1977). On the Baader-Meinhof Gang see Klaus Wasmund, "The Political Socialization of West German Terrorists," in Peter H. Merkl (ed.), *Political Violence and Terror: Motifs and Motivations* (Berkeley and Los Angeles: University of California Press, 1986); and Jillian Becker, *Hitler's Children: The Story of the Baader-Meinhof Terrorist Gang* (London: Michael Joseph, 1977).

5. See Pablo Giussani, *Los Días de Alfonsín* (Buenos Aires: Editorial Legasa, 1986), pp. 98–100.

6. These were Mario Firmenich, Fernando Vaca Narvaja, Roberto Perdía, Rodolfo Galimberti, Héctor Pardo, and Ricardo Obregón Cano from Montoneros, and Enrique Gorriarán Merlo from the ERP.

7. Alfonsín's Due Obedience Law of 1987 exempted most of these men from prosecution for human rights violations on the grounds that they were merely carrying out orders. On Alfonsín's human rights policy see Iain Guest, *Behind the Disappearances: Argentina's Dirty*

War Against Human Rights and the United Nations (Philadelphia: University of Pennsylvania Press, 1990), chapter 29.

8. Comisión Nacional sobre la Desaparición de Personas, *Nunca Mas* (Buenos Aires: Eudeba, 1985), p. 7. I should like to thank Drs. Luis Moreno Ocampo and Eduardo Rabossi for the opportunity to discuss different aspects of Alfonsín's human rights policy with them. Dr. Moreno Ocampo was one of the two prosecutors in the Juntas Trial and Dr. Rabossi was a member of the National Commission on the Disappearance of Persons. These conversations, not formally structured as interviews, took place during visits to Yale University by Dr. Moreno Ocampo (March 1988) and Dr. Rabossi (March 1990).

9. The only guerrilla exempted from the pardon was Mario Firmenich, top leader of the Montoneros. In an episode that was never fully clarified, Firmenich gave himself up at the Argentine consulate in Rio de Janeiro, Brazil. The Alfonsín administration immediately started extradition procedures, following which Firmenich was tried in 1987 and given a thirty-year sentence. Once more applying the two terrorisms logic, in December 1990 President Menem pardoned Firmenich and the nine junta members. See Shirley Christian, "Pardoned Argentine officers out of jail," *New York Times,* October 10, 1989, p. A3; James Neilson, "Maniobras militares," *Noticias,* 14:701, June 3, 1990, p. 37; and "Argentine Defends Release of 'Dirty War' Leaders," *New York Times,* December 31, 1990, p. 4. Over the years, there has been speculation on whether Mario Firmenich was an intelligence informer. Authors who defend this thesis point to inconsistencies in the Montoneros' own account of Aramburu's "execution" (Mario Firmenich and Norma Arrostito, "Como murió Aramburu," *La Causa Peronista,* 1:9, September 3, 1974, pp. 25–31), notably the fact that in that account, after Aramburu had been gagged and told the Montoneros were about to kill him, he responded "Proceed, then." Authors who believe Firmenich was an intelligence officer also point to the frequent visits that the Montonero leader made to General Francisco Imaz, Interior Minister under Onganía, in the two months prior to the abduction of Aramburu. The assumption is that Aramburu was killed by the Montoneros but that the crime was instigated by officials in the Onganía regime because Aramburu was willing to take over the government and find an accomodation with Peronists that he had been unwilling to contemplate when he ruled the country in 1955–58. These conspiracy theories are discussed in Próspero G. Fernández Alvariño, *Z: Argentina, el Crimen del Siglo* (Buenos Aires: Edición del Autor, 1973), and Eugenio Méndez, *Aramburu: El Crimen Imperfecto* (Buenos Aires: Editorial Sudamericana/Planeta, 1987). Fernández Alvariño was a personal friend of Aramburu's, and Méndez, a journalist, has been rumored to be an intelligence informer also. Journalist Martin Edwin Andersen expanded on this theory based on information he obtained through U.S. diplomats and intelligence officers stationed in Buenos Aires at the time, who state that Firmenich provided army intelligence with information throughout the 1969–79 period. See his *Dossier Secreto: Argentina's Desaparecidos and the Myth of the "Dirty War"* (Boulder, Colo.: Westview Press, 1993).

10. See Roger Gutiérrez, *Gorriarán: Democracia y Liberación* (Buenos Aires: Ediciones Reencuentro, 1985), pp. 62–66; Juan Gasparini, *Montoneros: Final de cuentas* (Buenos Aires: Puntosur Editores, 1988), pp. 200–214; and a document written by ERP members serving sentences at Villa Devoto prison in 1984, reproduced in Pedro Cazes Camarero (ed.), *Hubo dos Terrorismos?* (Buenos Aires: Ediciones Reencuentro, 1986), pp. 71–79.

11. The decree is reproduced in *El Terrorismo en la Argentina* (Buenos Aires: Poder Ejecutivo Nacional, 1980), pp. 139–140. See also "Documento final de la Junta sobre la lucha antisubversiva," *La Prensa,* April 29, 1983, p. 1.

12. See chapter 8. A good discussion of this issue appears in Giussani, *Los Días de Alfonsín*, pp. 77–79.

13. Mario Firmenich interviewed by Gabriel García Márquez. The interview, which appeared in *L'Espresso* on April 17, 1977, is cited in "Suplemento: Los sueños de la guerrilla," *El Porteño*, V:52, April 1986, pp. 35–50: 50.

14. See Rodolfo Walsh, *Los Papeles de Walsh*, reprinted in *Unidos*, 3:5, April 1985, pp. 151–159, and 3:6, August 1985, pp. 178–193; Alain Rouquié, "El poder militar en la Argentina de hoy: cambio y continuidad," in Peter Waldmann and Ernesto Garzón Valdés (eds.), *El Poder Militar en la Argentina (1976–1981)* (Buenos Aires: Editorial Galerna, 1983), p. 73; Gutiérrez, *Gorriarán*, pp. 26–27; Cazes Camarero, *Hubo dos Terrorismos?*, pp. 30–31, 38; Donald C. Hodges, *Argentina's "Dirty War": An Intellectual Biography* (Austin: University of Texas Press, 1991), p. 123; Daniel Frontalini and María Cristina Caiati, *El Mito de la Guerra Sucia* (Buenos Aires: Centro de Estudios Legales y Sociales, 1984), pp. 65–67; Richard Gillespie, "Armed Struggle in Argentina," *New Scholar*, 8:1 & 2, 1982, pp. 387–427: 387; Julio Santucho, *Los Ultimos Guevaristas: Surgimiento y Eclipse del Ejército Revolucionario del Pueblo* (Buenos Aires: Puntosur Editores, 1988), pp. 216–217.

15. See for example "Llambí: El terrorismo disminuyó en un 80%," *Crónica*, November 13, 1973, p. 3; "Existe una respuesta ideológica del Justicialismo a la guerrilla?" *La Opinión*, July 1, 1973, p. 8; "Importantes detenciones de elementos extremistas," *La Nación*, January 13, 1971, p. 4.

16. "Documento final de la Junta sobre la lucha antisubversiva"; "Palabra por palabra todo lo que dijo Camps," *Siete Días*, XV:816, February 2, 1983, pp. 8–11: 10.

17. One analysis supporting my estimate of guerrilla capabilities in early 1976 is Peter Waldmann, "Anomia Social y Violencia," in Alain Rouquié (ed.), *Argentina, Hoy* (Buenos Aires: Siglo Veintiuno Editores, 1982), pp. 211–213.

18. Comisión Nacional sobre la Desaparición de Personas, *Nunca Mas*, p. 298.

19. This is an impressionistic observation derived from interviews with members of the security forces who used this argument in order to justify torture. See also Guest, *Behind the Disappearances*, pp. 57–58; Miguel Bonasso, *Recuerdo de la Muerte* (Buenos Aires: Editorial Bruguera, 1984), p. 57; "Palabra por palabra todo lo que dijo Camps"; Eugenio Méndez, *Confesiones de un Montonero* (Buenos Aires: Editorial Sudamericana/Planeta, 1985), chapters 9–10.

20. Comisión Nacional sobre la Desaparición de Personas, *Nunca Mas*, p. 17.

21. Bonasso, *Recuerdo de la Muerte*, p. 148.

22. The terms "agitational terror" and "enforcement terror" appear in Thomas Perry Thornton, "Terror as a Weapon of Political Agitation," in Harry Eckstein (ed.), *Internal War: Problems and Approaches* (New York: Free Press of Glencoe, 1964). I am borrowing them for want of a more adequate terminology. It would be incorrect to speak of state and antistate violence in Argentina because violence by the Peronist right was not state violence. It would be equally incorrect to speak of revolutionary and counter-revolutionary violence. Collective violence was not necessarily revolutionary, and the prefix "counter-" indicates a specific temporal sequence.

23. The military staged three rebellions since April 1987 in an attempt to end the trials of officers implicated in illegal repression and to obtain an official vindication of the dirty war. The fact that these rebels were mostly junior officers who were cadets while the war was being waged testifies to the power of the world view imparted at the service academies. For an analy-

sis that supports the idea that the military considered the root of the problem lay in society and not simply within guerrilla groups see Guillermo O'Donnell, *Y a mí qué me importa? Notas sobre sociabilidad y política en Argentina y Brasil* (Buenos Aires: Estudio CEDES, 1984).

24. That a significant number of Argentine academics and intellectuals identify with Peronism probably explains why this issue has been so consistently avoided.

25. Perón's Ezeiza speech is reproduced in Horacio Verbitsky, *Ezeiza* (Buenos Aires: Editorial Contrapunto, 1986), pp. 204–209.

26. "Texto del 'Documento Reservado,' " *La Opinión*, October 2, 1973, p. 1. See also Clive Petersen, "Dealing with Terrorism," *Buenos Aires Herald*, January 25, 1974, p. 6; and Daniel Prieto, "Las Divergencias de un Partido," *Visión*, March 9, 1974, pp. 18–21.

27. Roberto Mero, *Conversaciones con Juan Gelman: Contraderrota—Montoneros y la revolución perdida* (Buenos Aires: Editorial Contrapunto, 1987), p. 79.

28. The six RUC killings have been described by the Manchester policeman appointed to investigate them, John Stalker. See his *Stalker Affair* (New York: Viking Press, 1988); and Martin Dillon, *The Dirty War* (London: Arrow Books, 1990). The GAL have been the subject of an investigation by *Cambio 16*, journalists Manuel Cerdán and Antonio Rubio. See their articles "Toda La Verdad Sobre El Watergal Español," *Cambio 16*, 939, November 27, 1989, pp. 116–122; "Los periodistas descubren un zulo del GAL en la frontera con Francia," *Cambio 16*, 940, December 4, 1989, pp. 120–128; "Agentes de la Ertzantza investigaron a Amedo antes de que los GAL mataran," *Cambio 16*, 941, December 11, 1989, pp. 128–134.

29. By "party" the interviewee meant "armed struggle." Interview with a former Descamisado in Buenos Aires on September 1, 1987. It is important to note that authors who are highly critical of the guerrilla movement still remember with affection friends involved in the struggle, as if condemnation of the guerrillas stopped short of their friends. See references to Francisco Urondo in Pablo Giussani, *Montoneros: La Soberbia Armada* (Buenos Aires: Editorial Sudamericana/Planeta, 1984), pp. 47–48, 71–77, and in José Pablo Feinmann, *López Rega, la cara oscura de Perón* (Buenos Aires: Editorial Legasa, 1987), p. 51; and references to Diego Muñiz Barreto in Roberto Roth, *Los Años de Onganía: Relato de un Testigo* (Buenos Aires: Ediciones La Campana, 1981), pp. 82–84, and in Andrew Graham-Yooll, *A Matter of Fear: Portrait of an Argentinian Exile* (Westport, Conn.: Lawrence Hill, 1981), pp. 58–67.

30. See W. Phillips Davison and Leon Gordenker (eds.), *Resolving Nationality Conflicts: The Role of Public Opinion Research* (New York: Praeger, 1980), passim; Christopher Hewitt, "Terrorism and Public Opinion: A Five Country Comparison," *Terrorism and Political Violence*, 2:2, 1990, pp. 145–170; Juan José Linz, *Conflicto en Euzkadi* (Madrid: Espasa-Calpe, 1986), part 11; and Peter Waldmann, "From the vindication of honor to blackmail: the impact of the changing role of ETA on society and politics in the Basque region of Spain," in Noemi Gal-Or (ed.), *Tolerating terrorism in the west: An international survey* (London and New York: Routledge, 1991).

31. Guillermo O'Donnell, *1966–1973 El Estado Burocrático Autoritario: Triunfos, Derrotas y Crisis* (Buenos Aires: Editorial de Belgrano, 1982), pp. 463–465. On page 463 O'Donnell states societal support for armed struggle in 1971–72 was "remarkable."

32. See for example "Unánime repudio de los métodos terroristas de todo signo," *La Opinión*, October 10, 1974, p. 13.

33. Dr. Righi was interviewed in Buenos Aires, December 25, 1987. The number of people present at rallies organized by the guerrillas also provides an indicator of public support: 40,000 persons in Córdoba in May 1973 for the fourth anniversary of the Cordobazo, and

55,000 in Buenos Aires in August 1973 for the first anniversary of the Trelew massacre. These two events were sponsored by all guerrilla groups. The Montoneros alone mobilized 80,000 in July and 150,000 in August 1973.

34. On the radicalization of Argentine society which resulted in a positive view of the guerrillas and their activity see O'Donnell, *El Estado Burocrático Autoritario*, pp. 459–491, especially 459–466; Giussani, *Montoneros*, pp. 219–227, 251–254; V. S. Naipaul, *The Return of Eva Perón* (New York: Vintage Books, 1981), pp. 105, 117–120, 175–177; and José Antonio Díaz and Alfredo Leuco, *Los Herederos de Alfonsín* (Buenos Aires: Editorial Sudamericana/ Planeta, 1987), chapter 3. The latter provides an account of the process of radicalization within the Radical party youth wing, and its relationship with the Revolutionary Tendency. O'Donnell and Giussani include in their discussion a mea culpa on their role as intellectuals and disseminators of this "culture of violence." In *The Age of Terrorism* (Boston: Little, Brown, 1987), Walter Laqueur devotes an entire chapter to the analysis of terrorism in fiction. Particularly in the last decade, novelists have produced works based partly or wholly on some of the events described in this book. These works of political fiction provide thoughtful insights into the behavior of Argentine guerrillas and the societal reaction to armed struggle. Graham Greene's *Honorary Consul* (Harmondsworth: Penguin Books, 1986) and Silvina Bullrich's *Mal Don* (Buenos Aires: Emecé Editores, 1973) are based on kidnappings by the guerrillas; and Miguel Bonasso's *Recuerdo de la Muerte* is based on the abduction of a guerrilla officer by paramilitaries. Life within guerrilla groups is described in Martín Caparrós, *No Velas a Tus Muertos* (Buenos Aires: Ediciones de la Flor, 1986); Julio Cortázar, *Libro de Manuel* (Barcelona: Editorial Bruguera, 1981); and Tomás Eloy Martínez, *La Novela de Perón* (Buenos Aires: Editorial Legasa, 1986). The 1966–73 military government provides the background for Manuel Puig's *Buenos Aires Affair* (Mexico: Editorial Joaquín Mortíz, 1973); Osvaldo Soriano's *No Habrá Mas Penas Ni Olvido* (Buenos Aires: Editorial Bruguera, 1983) takes place during the restoration of Peronism; and Humberto Costantini's *De Dioses, Hombrecitos y Policías* (Havana: Casa de las Américas, 1979) describes life during the dirty war. The transition to democracy is chronicled in Dalmiro Sáenz and Sergio Joselovsky, *El Día que Mataron a Alfonsín* (Buenos Aires: Ediciones Tarso, 1986).

35. Interview with a former Montonero in Buenos Aires, January 5, 1988.

36. Interview with a former Descamisado in Buenos Aires, September 18, 1987.

37. Transcript of a television appearance by Dr. Eugenio Aramburu on the talk show *Tiempo Nuevo*, October 1989.

38. Guillermo O'Donnell, "Argentina: La Cosecha del Miedo," *Alternativas*, 1, September 1983, pp. 5–14: 6–7. See also Jonathan Kandell, "An Argentine Hopes for Peace," *New York Times*, March 26, 1976, p. 8; and Brian Glanville, "World Cup Soccer Madness in Argentina," *Washington Post*, June 12, 1978, pp. B1, B5.

39. Robert Cox, *The Sound Of One Hand Clapping: A Preliminary Study of the Argentine Press in a Time of Terror* (Washington, D.C.: The Wilson Center, Latin American Program, Working Paper no. 83, 1980), p. 10. Argentines only learnt about the scope and intensity of the dirty war when the report by the National Commission on the Disappearance of Persons was made public. But they cannot claim ignorance of what was going on. The Buenos Aires dailies made periodic references in 1976–77 to relatives of disappeared persons filing writs of habeas corpus, and to individuals being taken from public places by plainclothes members of the security forces. In April 1977 lawyer Emilio Mignone filed a writ of habeas corpus on behalf of 1,221 relatives of 1,541 disappeared persons. It was a Supreme Court case which became famous under the name "Pérez de Smith et al." By early 1977 the government had

opened a special office within the Interior Ministry which would deal with the relatives' inquiries on disappeared persons. See *La Opinión* and the *Buenos Aires Herald,* 1976, passim; and Guest, *Behind the Disappearances,* pp. 51–52.

40. Giussani, *Los Días de Alfonsín,* p. 118. See also pp. 13–14, 154–156, 159–161.

Chapter 7. Guerrilla Lives

1. For a discussion of some of these methodological issues, see Peter H. Merkl's prologue to his edited volume, *Political Violence and Terror: Motifs and Motivations* (Berkeley and Los Angeles: University of California Press, 1986); and George Moyser, "Non-Standardized Interviewing in Elite Research," in Robert Burgess (ed.), *Studies in Qualitative Methodology* (Greenwich, Conn., and London: JAI Press, 1988).

2. Daniel Frontalini and María Cristina Caiati, *El Mito de la Guerra Sucia* (Buenos Aires: Centro de Estudios Legales y Sociales, 1984), chapter 3.

3. Ramón Genaro Díaz Bessone, *Guerra Revolucionaria en la Argentina (1959–1978)* (Buenos Aires: Editorial Fraterna, 1986), p. 25 n17; Frontalini and Caiati, *El Mito de la Guerra Sucia,* p. 72, and Peter Waldmann, "Anomia Social y Violencia," in Alain Rouquié (ed.), *Argentina, Hoy* (Buenos Aires: Siglo Veintiuno Editores, 1982), pp. 211–212.

4. Accurate estimates presented here of Montonero and Descamisado membership for 1969–72 derive from two guerrilla documents, not for citation.

5. This impression was corroborated by a former guerrilla who belonged to FAP's urban contingent, interviewed in Buenos Aires, September 23, 1987.

6. Héctor Víctor Suárez, "FAR: con el fusil del Che," *Granma,* December 12, 1970, p. 7.

7. "FAR: Los de Garín," *Cristianismo y Revolución,* IV:28, April 1971, pp. 56–70: 59. This interview was an expanded version of the Suárez interview. On FAL see "FAL: el marxismo en la cartuchera," *Cristianismo y Revolución,* IV:28, April 1971, pp. 73–77.

8. For early statements about the ERP's strength see for example *La Opinión,* passim, 1971–72; "Argentina: games theory," *Latin America,* VI:12, March 31, 1972, pp. 100–101; "Argentina: armed struggle," *Latin America,* VIII:30, August 2, 1974, pp. 234–236; "Trotskyite Guerrillas Playing Robin Hood to Argentine Poor," *Washington Post,* June 20, 1973, p. A20; and Lewis H. Diuguid, "Argentina Guerrilla Chief Says He Will Defy Cámpora," *Washington Post,* June 29, 1973, p. A28.

9. For a complete list see María José Moyano, "Armed Struggle in Argentina, 1969–1979," Ph.D. diss., Yale University, 1990, Appendix B.

10. "FAR: Los de Garín," p. 59.

11. Interview with a former FAP combatant in Buenos Aires, December 12, 1986.

12. Christopher Roper, "Don't cry for us, say the Montoneros," *Guardian,* March 2, 1977, p. 4. Descamisado estimates taken from guerrilla document, not for citation.

13. According to my guerrilla interviewees, only a handful of amnestied combatants abandoned armed struggle in favor of more conventional political action. Interviewees also said that the massive recruitment drive within both Montoneros and ERP did not start until the electoral campaign was launched in early 1973.

14. Frontalini and Caiati, *El Mito de la Guerra Sucia,* chapter 3. In the case of the ERP the authors cite General Ramón Camps who said that four guerrilla companies operated in Tucumán in 1975. Given that in a regular army a company consists of 120 men, Frontalini and Caiati conclude that ERP membership was 500 in 1975.

15. See table 7.1, below. After scanning the ERP's periodical *Estrella Roja* for the 1974–76 period, I concluded that the ERP's strength in Tucumán oscillated wildly and repeatedly between 20 and 120 combatants.

16. This estimate appears to be corroborated by occasional references to the PRT's and ERP's internal organization made by Luis Mattini, *Hombres y Mujeres del PRT-ERP* (Buenos Aires: Editorial Contrapunto, 1990). Mattini became head of the PRT-ERP after the death of Santucho in July 1976.

17. Interviews with former combatants support this view.

18. Edouard Bailby, "Trêve pour la coupe du monde," *L'Express*, 1396, April 10, 1978, p. 61.

19. Interviews with former Montoneros in Buenos Aires on November 18, 1986, October 1, 1987, and March 3, 1987. In 1979 the ERP stated that 80 percent of the Córdoba regional was destroyed within ten days in 1976. Regionals were to the ERP what columns were to Montoneros. See Partido Revolucionario de los Trabajadores, *VI Congreso: Mayo 1979* (N.p., n.d.), pp. 30–31. On p. 3 the balance sheet for 1976–77 is described as "the disappearance of, practically, the totality of cadres in leadership positions." In this context, disappearance should be taken to mean death.

20. A former police officer who was involved in illegal repression explained that the security forces operated on a column-by-column or regional-by-regional basis. A Montonero column or an ERP regional would be targeted; once it had been crushed, the security forces targeted a new one. One of the methods employed was the address book system—after an individual disappeared, so did everyone listed in that individual's daily planner. If the daily planner was not available, the individual was tortured. The former policeman interviewed in Buenos Aires on July 1, 1987, estimated that a total of 1,500 guerrillas had survived the dirty war. Estimates other than those already cited can be found in "La Guerrilla: La Resistencia Peronista. El Estilo Cubano. Cinco Organizaciones Importantes," *Clarín*, February 26, 1973, p. 14; "Argentina: revolutions within the revolution," *Latin America*, V:43, October 22, 1971, pp. 337–338: 338; Michael Frenchman, "The twilight years of a reign of terror," *The Times*, May 5, 1978, p. 8; Christopher Roper, "Argentina's rebels become restive," *Guardian*, March 26, 1979, p. 6; and Christopher Roper, "The revolutionary retreat from British imperialism," *Guardian*, February 2, 1976, p. 9; Richard Gillespie, *Soldiers of Perón: Argentina's Montoneros* (Oxford: Clarendon Press, 1982), chapter 2, and pp. 178, 252.

21. Ten out of the forty-three former combatants I talked to made a point of telling me how thorough they thought repression had been. My interviews with persons connected with human rights groups were not for attribution. Among former combatants and human rights activists it is considered politically inadvisable to admit that guerrilla groups were wiped out by the dirty war since it is believed that this weakens the condemnation of illegal repression between 1976 and 1983.

22. This is why the Montoneros' logistical plan for 1976 involved the production of 2,000 cyanide capsules, which were distributed to combatants so that they could kill themselves if caught.

23. On Arrostito's sojourn at the Navy Mechanics School see Miguel Bonasso, *Recuerdo de la Muerte* (Buenos Aires: Editorial Bruguera, 1984), pp. 43–44, 269–270.

24. On the events at Sierra Chica see Horacio Verbitsky (ed.), *Rodolfo Walsh y la Prensa Clandestina, 1976–1978* (Buenos Aires: Ediciones de la Urraca, 1985), pp. 41, 55–56, 81–82. Two of my interviewees were present when the five were removed from their cells. On August 14, 1976, p. 10, *La Opinión* reports another case which has since become notorious,

the "escape attempt" by Miguel Vaca Narvaja, Gustavo Brenuil, and Higinio Toranzo. The three were being driven from Penitentiary Unit 1 in Córdoba to their trial for subversive activities by a War Council. The car was in an accident, the three attempted to hide in the bushes, were asked to surrender, refused, and were shot. The same page reports the suicide of another prisoner at a different Córdoba prison, who strangled himself with a cord made with threads from his mattress. This type of newspaper reporting says a lot about a military organization peddling these lies but also about a civilian readership so willing to believe them.

25. I have probably overestimated casualties in Buenos Aires province and underestimated casualties in Buenos Aires city. Greater Buenos Aires is part of Buenos Aires province and sometimes newspapers do not make it clear if they are speaking about the federal capital or the Greater Buenos Aires area.

26. Instituto Nacional de Estadísticas y Censos, *Censo Nacional de Población, Familias y Viviendas de 1970: Compendio de sus Resultados Provisionales* (Buenos Aires: INDEC, N.d.), p. 7.

27. "Seis argentinos implicados en el secuestro de Revelli," *La Prensa,* July 27, 1977, p. 1.

28. "Desmantelan en Uruguay un grupo subversivo argentino," *La Prensa,* December 24, 1977, p. 1.

29. The statement about "the proletariat in arms" was made by ERP member Rubén Pedro Bonet, one of the Trelew victims. He is quoted in Francisco Urondo, *Trelew* (Havana: Casa de las Américas, 1976), pp. 162–163.

30. Pedro A. Barcia, "Las Guerrillas en la Argentina," *Interrogaciones,* 8, 1975, pp. 30–60: 43–45. The author lists other cities which he considers of marginal importance: Mar del Plata and Bahía Blanca (both in Buenos Aires province), Rosario (Santa Fe province), and Mendoza.

31. Richard Gillespie, "Armed Struggle in Argentina," *New Scholar,* 8:1 & 2, 1982, pp. 387–427: Appendix, "The Social Composition of Argentine Guerrilla Organizations."

32. Charles A. Russell and Bowman H. Miller, "Profile of a Terrorist," *Terrorism,* 1:1, 1977, pp. 17–34: 18.

33. Ibid., passim. The figures provided are: less than 16 percent female membership, 75–80 percent single, 90 percent inhabitants of Greater Buenos Aires, 70 percent students, and more than two-thirds middle and upper class.

34. Eugenio Méndez, *Confesiones de un Montonero* (Buenos Aires: Editorial Sudamericana/Planeta, 1985), passim, provides several examples of high school recruits after 1973. For a lively account of the recruitment of high school students into the Italian underground with some parallels to the Argentine situation, see Giorgio Bocca, "6 garantito, viva la squola," in Enzo Forcella (ed.), *Trent'anni di terrorismo* (Rome: Editoriale L'Espresso, 1985).

35. However, the available data on the guerrillas' occupation does not allow us to distinguish between upper- and lower-middle-class membership. It would be wrong to assume, as Richard Gillespie does, that the high number of employees points to the petty-bourgeois origin of combatants. At a time when the state provided free university education and individuals lived with their parents until they got married, part-time employment frequently financed the university student's social life. Francisco J. Delich discusses the issue in *Crisis y protesta social: Córdoba, mayo de 1969* (Buenos Aires: Ediciones Signos, 1969), especially IV.

36. An earlier, shorter version of this section appeared as María José Moyano, "Going Underground in Argentina: A Look at the Founders of a Guerrilla Movement," in Donatella della Porta (ed.), *Social Movements and Violence: Participation in Underground Orga-*

nizations (Greenwich, Conn., and London: JAI Press, 1992). See also María José Moyano, "Argentinien: Die 'unehelichen' Kinder Peróns," in Peter Waldmann (ed.), *Beruf: Terrorist. Lebensläufe im Untergrund* (Munich: C. H. Beck, 1993).

37. See Hannah Arendt, *Eichmann in Jerusalem: A Report on the Banality of Evil* (Harmondsworth: Penguin Books, 1984); and Albert Bandura, "Psychological mechanisms of aggression," in M. von Cranach, K. Froppa, W. Lepenies, and D. Ploog (eds.), *Human Ethology: Claims and Limits of a New Discipline* (Cambridge: Cambridge University Press, 1979). For a good summary of the "terrorist personality" thesis see Walter Laqueur, *The Age of Terrorism* (Boston: Little, Brown, 1987), pp. 76–93, 157–162.

38. Robert P. Clark, "Patterns in the Lives of ETA Members," in Merkl, *Political Violence and Terror,* p. 283. On the lives of *etarras* see also Angel Amigo, *Pertur ETA 71–76* (Donostia: Hordago, 1978). On the lives of *brigattisti* see Alessandro Silj, *Mai più senza fucile! alle origini dei NAP e delle BR* (Florence: Vallechi, 1977); and the writings of Donatella della Porta: "I Militanti delle Organizzazioni Terroriste di Sinistra in Italia," *Rivista Italiana di Scienza Politica,* 17:1, April 1987, pp. 23–55; *Il Terrorismo di Sinistra* (Bologna: Il Mulino, 1990), especially parts 2–4; and "Political Socialization in Left-Wing Underground Organizations: Biographies of Italian and German Militants," in della Porta, *Social Movements and Violence.* On the lives of IRA members see J. Bowyer Bell, *The Gun in Politics: An Analysis of Irish Political Conflict, 1916–1986* (New Brunswick, N.J.: Transaction Books, 1987), chapter 7; and Padraig O'Malley, *Biting at the Grave: The Irish Hunger Strikes and the Politics of Despair* (Boston: Beacon Press, 1990), pp. 36–49, 65–71, 102–112, 128–132. For a comparative analysis that brings several of these groups together see Peter Waldmann, "Ethnic and Socio-revolutionary Terrorism: A Comparison of Structures," in della Porta, *Social Movements and Violence.*

39. See Henry V. Dicks, *Licensed Mass Murder: A Socio-Psychological Study of Some SS Killers* (New York: Basic Books, 1972); Klaus Wasmund, "The Political Socialization of West German Terrorists," in Merkl, *Political Violence and Terror;* and Daniel Goleman, "The Roots of Terrorism are Found in Brutality of Shattered Childhood," *New York Times,* September 2, 1986, pp. C1, C8.

40. Juana and Irene described their families as upper middle class, and Antonio, Héctor, Diego, and Fernando described theirs as lower middle class.

41. Pedro Ibarra Guell, *La Evolución Estratégica de ETA* (San Sebastián: Kriselu, 1989), p. 17.

42. Gillo Pontecorvo's 1965 film about the Algerian National Liberation Front.

43. I am borrowing the term from Wasmund, "Political Socialization of West German Terrorists."

44. Guerrilla dynasties were a frequent phenomenon. Among the original Montoneros, for example, Ignacio Vélez joined with his wife, Carlos Ramus with two sisters, and Mario Firmenich was followed by his wife and brother-in-law. Among the original ERP members, Luis Pujals and Domingo Menna joined with their wives, Mario Delfino was followed by a sister, and Mario Santucho was followed by his wife, two brothers, and a niece. Vélez and his wife were amnestied in 1973, abandoned armed struggle, and went into exile in 1976. Firmenich and his wife went into exile in late 1976 and returned to Argentina in 1986 when Firmenich was extradited from Brazil in order to face trial. He received a presidential pardon in 1990. All the others died in combat or disappeared.

45. "No quiero entregarme viva," *Evita Montonera,* 2:13, April-May 1976, p. 36.

46. The rate of accidents was high throughout the 1969–79 period. However, deaths only

became an important component of the total volume of guerrilla violence after 1973, which may partly explain why the public had such a favorable view of armed organizations up to that date. On accidental deaths see chapter 3 and Moyano, "Armed Struggle in Argentina, 1969–1979," pp. 203–205.

47. Envar El Kadri and Jorge Rulli, *Diálogos en el Exilio* (Buenos Aires: Editorial Foro Sur, 1984), especially chapter 9. See also Méndez, *Confesiones*, and Bonasso, *Recuerdo de la Muerte*.

Chapter 8. Ideological and Organizational Somersaults

1. This chapter relies on a wealth of radicalized periodicals and internal documents from five of the six major groups. The only two "political documents" the Descamisados produced are no longer available. Accounts of the contents of those documents were provided by former members.

2. John Gerassi, *The Great Fear in Latin America* (New York: Collier Books, 1973), p. 405.

3. Rural guerrilla warfare was attempted in Argentina in 1959, Colombia in 1960–61, Ecuador in 1962, Venezuela and Peru in 1962–65, Argentina in 1963–64, Guatemala and Colombia 1964-present, Bolivia in 1965–67, and Argentina in 1968. On this revolutionary decade and the influence of Cuba, see Luis Mercier Vega, *Las Guerrillas en América Latina; La Técnica del Contra-estado* (Buenos Aires: Editorial Paidós, 1969); Luis E. Aguilar, "Fragmentation of the Marxist Left," *Problems of Communism*, 19:4, 1970, pp. 112; and Richard Gott, *Guerrilla Movements in Latin America* (Garden City, N.Y.: Doubleday, 1971).

4. *Foco* is the guerrilla group and *foquismo* its activity. (The latter is sometimes, though rarely, translated as "focoism"). The original formulations of the foco theory are Ernesto Guevara, *Obras Completas* (Buenos Aires: Ediciones Cepe, 1973), vol. III; and Régis Debray, *Revolution in the Revolution? Armed Struggle and Political Struggle in Latin America* (New York: Monthly Review Press, 1967). Critiques are provided by Gérard Chaliand, *Revolution in the Third World* (Harmondsworth: Penguin Books, 1979); Malcolm Deas, "Guerrillas in Latin America," *The World Today*, 24:2, 1968, pp. 72–78; Leo Huberman and Paul M. Sweezy, *Régis Debray and the Latin American Revolution* (New York: Monthly Review Press, 1968); Francisco Mieres, "Lessons of October and Contemporary Revolutionary Movements in Latin America," *World Marxist Review*, 10:11, 1967, pp. 77–81; and João Quartim, "Régis Debray and the Brazilian Revolution," *New Left Review*, 59, 1970, pp. 61–82.

5. Richard Gillespie, "Armed Struggle in Argentina," *New Scholar*, 8:1 & 2, 1982, pp. 387–427: 396. On the second revolutionary decade (1969–79) of urban struggle see Richard Gillespie, "A Critique of the Urban Guerrilla: Argentina, Uruguay and Brazil," *Conflict Quarterly*, 1:2, 1980, pp. 39–53.

6. William E. Ratliff, *Castroism and Communism in Latin America, 1959–1976: The Varieties of Marxist-Leninist Experience* (Washington, D.C.: American Enterprise Institute for Public Policy Research, 1976), pp. 206–208. On Cuban involvement in Latin American insurrections see also Juan Vivés, *Los Amos de Cuba* (Buenos Aires: Emecé Editores, 1982).

7. References to Guevara and discussions of the continental struggle by the guerrilla groups can be found in "Reportaje al ERP," *Cristianismo y Revolución*, IV:27, January-February 1971, pp. 15–16; "FAR: Los de Garín," *Cristianismo y Revolución*, IV:28, April 1971, pp. 56–70; "FAL: El marxismo en la cartuchera," *Cristianismo y Revolución*, IV:28, April 1971, pp. 73–76; Héctor Víctor Suárez, "Montoneros: El llanto para el enemigo,"

Granma, December 5, 1970, p. 7; "Reportaje a las FAP," *Cristianismo y Revolución,* IV:25, September 1970, pp. 17–20.

8. Fermín Muñoz (ed.), *Las Encíclicas del Mundo Moderno* (Barcelona: Editorial Bruguera, 1969), p. 588. On the radicalization of the Catholic church see Antonio O. Donini, "Religion and Social Conflict in the Perón Era," in Frederick C. Turner and José Enrique Miguens (eds.), *Juan Perón and the Reshaping of Argentina* (Pittsburgh: University of Pittsburgh Press, 1983).

9. "La justa violencia de los oprimidos para su liberación: Apelación de sacerdotes al Celam," *Cristianismo y Revolución,* II:9, September 1968, pp. 16–17. Emphasis in the original. See also "Monseñor Pironio elogió el tercermundismo," *La Opinión,* February 22, 1973, p. 9; and Paul E. Sigmund, *Liberation Theology at the Crossroads: Democracy or Revolution?* (New York and Oxford: Oxford University Press, 1990).

10. On the Movement of Third World Priests see Rolando Concatti, "Nuestra Opción por el Peronismo," *Cristianismo y Revolución,* IV:30, September 1971, pp. 27–36; and Lucio Gera and Guillermo Rodríguez Melgarejo, "Apuntes para una Interpretación de la Iglesia Argentina," *Cristianismo y Revolución,* IV:25, September 1970, pp. 61–79. See also Carlos María Gutiérrez, "Des militants chrétiens demandent au pape de renoncer à son voyage en Amérique Latine," *Le Monde,* March 16, 1968, p. 3; and Peter Strafford, "The Church of change," *Times,* December 2, 1977, p. 16.

11. "Entrevista a la Dirección del PRT: Partido Revolucionario de los Trabajadores de Argentina," *Combate,* 116–117, January-February 1985, pp. 6–17: 6. See also "FAR: Los de Garín," pp. 63–64.

12. Fuerzas Armadas de Liberación 22 de Agosto, "Que algo cambie para que todo siga como está," *Militancia,* 1:12, August 30, 1973, pp. 22–23: 23.

13. Suárez, "Montoneros."

14. ERP member Rubén Pedro Bonet at a press conference at Trelew airport on August 15, 1972, quoted in Francisco Urondo, *Trelew* (Havana: Casa de las Américas, 1976), p. 160. Bonet was one of the sixteen guerrillas killed a week after this press conference, at the Almirante Zar naval base.

15. "Hablan los Montoneros," *Cristianismo y Revolución,* IV:26, November-December 1970, pp. 11–14: 11, emphasis and capital letters in the original.

16. Urondo, *Trelew,* pp. 157–158. For other explicit references to the Second War of Independence see "Reportaje al ERP," p. 16; "Reportaje a las FAP," p. 17; "FAR: Los de Garín," p. 68.

17. "FAL: El marxismo en la cartuchera," p. 74; "FAR: Los de Garín," p. 62.

18. Suárez, "Montoneros."

19. On the relationship between armed struggle and mass struggle see Ibid.; "Reportaje a las FAP," pp. 18–19; "FAR: Los de Garín," pp. 62, 69; "FAL: El marxismo en la cartuchera," p. 76; "Resoluciones sobre dinámica y relaciones de nuestra guerra revolucionaria," in Partido Revolucionario de los Trabajadores, *Resoluciones del V Congreso y de los Comité Central y Comité Ejecutivo Posteriores* (Buenos Aires: Ediciones El Combatiente, 1973).

20. The debate between Marxist and Peronist guerrillas is adequately covered in Fuerzas Armadas Revolucionarias, "Aporte al proceso de confrontación de posiciones y polémica pública que abordamos con el ERP," *Militancia,* 4, July 5, 1973, pp. 35–49. See also "Reportaje al FAL," *Cristianismo y Revolución,* IV:24, June 1970, pp. 59–60.

21. Interviews with former combatants and guerrilla documents, not for citation. See also

"El grupo peronista FAR y el trotskista ERP manifestaron la vocación de unirse," *La Opinión,* August 20, 1972, p. 9.

22. Martha Crenshaw, "An Organizational Approach to the Analysis of Political Terrorism," *Orbis,* 29:3, 1985, pp. 465–489: 469–470.

23. Guerrilla groups never provided diagrams of their internal structure. These and subsequent figures result from my reading of internal documents and my conversations with former combatants.

24. FAR and FAP did not have fronts.

25. Quieto broke the organization's security regulations in order to meet with his wife and child for Christmas in 1975 and was captured and supposedly killed by the security forces. Montoneros staged a trial in absentia and condemned him to death. Luis Mattini lived in exile during the dirty war and returned to Argentina with the advent of democracy.

26. See "Resolución sobre la relación partido-éjercito" and "Estatutos del Partido Revolucionario de los Trabajadores," in Partido Revolucionario de los Trabajadores, *Resoluciones;* and Horacio Cabral, "Entre Trotski et Robin des Bois," *L'Express,* 1082, April 3, 1972, p. 64.

27. Ejército Revolucionario del Pueblo, *Porqué el ERP no dejará de combatir: Respuesta al Presidente Cámpora* (Buenos Aires: N.p., April 13, 1973). See also "Guerrilla Groups in Argentina Explain Their Goals," *New York Times,* June 9, 1973, p. 8.

28. Mario R. Santucho, *Poder Burgués y Poder Revolucionario* (Buenos Aires: N.p., 1974). See also "Porqué estamos en un proceso de guerra?" *El Combatiente,* VII:145, November 27, 1974, pp. 11–12.

29. Santucho, *Poder Burgués y Poder Revolucionario,* p. 4.

30. Ibid., pp. 5, 18, 39.

31. The resolutions adopted by the PRT's September 1974 Central Committee are printed in Ibid., pp. 50–62.

32. *La Opinión,* April 18, 1973, p. 11.

33. "Aportes para una Autocrítica de la Tendencia," *Militancia,* 1:9, August 9, 1973, pp. 12–14: 12.

34. Quoted in Silvia Sigal and Eliseo Verón, *Perón o Muerte: Los fundamentos discursivos del fenómeno peronista* (Buenos Aires: Editorial Legasa, 1986), p. 162. In "A Romper el Cerco con la Organización Popular," *Militancia,* 1:5, July 12, 1973, pp. 4–6: 4, the June 1973 situation was compared to that of September 1955. The argument was that another hedge had provoked the downfall of Perón twenty years earlier.

35. *El Descamisado,* 1:10, July 24, 1973. See also "Marcha sobre Olivos: termina el retroceso," *Militancia,* 1:7, July 26, 1973, pp. 4–6.

36. See for example Fuerzas Armadas Peronistas, "A la clase obrera y al pueblo peronista," *Militancia,* 1:22, November 8, 1973, pp. 44–45.

37. Interview with Envar El Kadri in Buenos Aires on June 26, 1987. The polemic split FAP in two, the "obscure" (movementist) and the "enlightened" (alternativist). The enlightened argued that FAP should stop staging operations against the military regime and engage in a process of serious ideological debate, which they called "process of compulsive political homogenization." The obscure left FAP and alternativism became the group's official policy.

38. "FAR y Montoneros: conferencia de prensa," *Militancia,* 1:1, June 14, 1973, pp. 9–10: 9. See also "Roberto Quieto," *El Descamisado,* 1:23, October 23, 1973, p. 20.

39. Rubén R. Dri, "La alternativa y la lucha de clases," *Militancia,* 2:33, January 31, 1974, pp. 20–22: 20–21.

40. Ibid., p. 22, emphasis in the original. See also "Aportes para una Autocrítica de la Tendencia"; Fuerzas Armadas Peronistas, "Aporte para el análisis de la situación actual," *Militancia*, 1:10, August 16, 1973, pp. 19–21.

41. For alternativist declarations by the Marxist splinters see Fuerzas Armadas de Liberación 22 de Agosto, "Que algo cambie"; Ejército Revolucionario del Pueblo 22 de Agosto, "El ERP 22 de Agosto al pueblo," *Militancia*, 1:3, June 28, 1973, p. 12; and *Militancia*, 1:27, December 13, 1973, pp. 46–47. After adopting alternativism FAP split once more. Both wings, FAP CN and FAP 17, believed that the union bureaucracy should be fought with rank-and-file organization. But FAP CN found a shortcut to union democracy, namely the assassination of corrupt union bosses. The split occurred because FAP 17 opposed this policy. See "FAP '17 de Octubre,'" *El Descamisado*, 1:16, September 4, 1973, p. 29; and "Se desprendió de la FAP un núcleo y da a conocer sus razones," *La Razón*, August 30, 1973, p. 16.

42. "Hablemos Claro," *Militancia*, 1:23, November 15, 1973, p. 3. At times alternativists accepted Perón's class alliance as long as the working class became "hegemonic" within it. No further elaboration was offered. See Dri, "La alternativa y la lucha de clases"; and two communiqués by FAP in *La Opinión*, on March 18, 1972, p. 11, and March 21, 1972, p. 12. The first accepts and the second rejects the class alliance nature of Peronism.

43. Editorial in *El Descamisado*, quoted in Sigal and Verón, *Perón o Muerte*, p. 201. See also "Palabras de Firmenich," *Militancia*, 2:37, March 14, 1974, pp. 38–42: 41.

44. "Combativos o Vandoristas?" *El Descamisado*, 1:16, September 4, 1973, p. 27.

45. The lecture was summarized by former officers who attended, since no written records have survived. The movementism/alternativism polemic produced two splinters within the Montoneros in 1973: the José Sabino Navarro Column, which believed in alternativism, and the Loyalty group, which believed in movementism. Navarro was not the name of an official Montonero column, only the name adopted by the splinter group. In numerical terms, both splinters were marginal and disappeared within the year.

46. "Reportaje a Mario Firmenich: El Valor Político del Fusil," *El Descamisado*, 1:17, September 11, 1973, p. 3. See also "Palabras de Firmenich," p. 38.

47. The only written discussions of socialismo nacional appear in *Militancia*. In 1973 the periodical transcribed what was stated at a series of round tables on that topic. The discussion that follows is based on these articles. See in particular "Patria Peronista Patria Socialista," *Militancia*, 1:6, July 19, 1973, p. 7; "El Socialismo Nacional," *Militancia*, 1:20, October 25, 1973, pp. 36–39; "El Socialismo Nacional," *Militancia*, 1:24, November 22, 1973, pp. 38–40.

48. Three of my interviewees stated that socialismo nacional did not entail the complete abolition of private property but the establishment of a mixed economy. There is no mention of this in the *Militancia* articles. Another interviewee stated that "Combatants fought for socialism. Period." Yet another said that the difference between Marxism and socialismo nacional was "the desire to be different from the ERP. And nationalists."

49. Luis Mattini, *Hombres y Mujeres del PRT-ERP* (Buenos Aires: Editorial Contrapunto, 1990), p. 295. Emphasis in the original. In spite of the fact that official ERP documents record the introduction of ranks in 1974, former ERP combatants stated that ranks were introduced in some units in 1973. Three different interviewees estimated that by the end of that year 60 combatants had been awarded a military rank. The ERP combatants were interviewed in Buenos Aires on December 28, 1987, January 4, 1988, and January 6, 1988.

50. A source close to the highest echelons of General Videla's administration (1976–81) explained to me that the ERP copied the Argentine Army's ternary division: three squadrons

formed a platoon, three platoons a company, and three companies a battalion. The interview was not for attribution. See also Ibid., p. 293.

51. Ibid., p. 248.

52. Partido Revolucionario de los Trabajadores, *VI Congreso: Mayo 1979* (N. p., n. d.), p. 22.

53. Ibid., p. 19.

54. See Ibid., p. 41; "Entrevista a la Dirección del PRT," p. 9; and Julio Santucho, *Los Ultimos Guevaristas: Surgimiento y Eclipse del Ejército Revolucionario del Pueblo* (Buenos Aires: Puntosur Editores, 1988), p. 150.

55. Mattini, *Hombres y Mujeres,* p. 255.

56. See "Sobre la construcción del Frente Revolucionario," *El Compañero,* 3, January–February 1974, pp. 3–10; and Organización Comunista Poder Obrero, *Lucha Democrática y Hegemonía Proletaria* (Buenos Aires: N.p., 1977). The latter is a lengthy critique of the ERP's ambivalence toward mass action by a 1975 splinter faction.

57. Montoneros were also notoriously absent from the Jornadas.

58. Montonero documents date the full development of professional forces in 1976. However, several of my interviewees mentioned the existence of professionals, in addition to those in the GECs, by 1974.

59. Guerrilla document, not for citation. Hobert was killed resisting arrest in 1976.

60. "La JP explicó su plan comunitario," *La Opinión,* October 2, 1973, p. 8; "Campaña comunitaria de la JP en el Gran Buenos Aires," *La Opinión,* January 19, 1974, p. 8.

61. "Mugica murió entre dos fuegos," *Movimiento,* 2, May 1974, pp. 15–17: 16.

62. Cited in Julio Santucho, *Los Ultimos Guevaristas,* pp. 143–144.

63. "La CGT en la Resistencia," *Evita Montonera,* 2:13, April-May 1976, pp. 14–16: 14.

64. In his study of the Montoneros Pablo Giussani describes a chance meeting with Joe Baxter, future ERP leader, shortly after the Night of the Long Batons in 1966. Baxter was ecstatic at what he considered one big step forward toward revolution. Giussani then uses the expression "jubilant conscience of emergent fascism" to refer to the Latin American left's belief that the system must be made to drop appearances and show its truly repressive nature (*Montoneros: La Soberbia Armada* [Buenos Aires: Editorial Sudamericana/Planeta, 1984], pp. 23–24, 31–32). There might have been an element of truth in this. In 1979 the PRT admitted that "deep down we thought that the coup represented one step forward in the process . . . the idealist conception that the coup would signify a qualitative leap in the process of revolutionary war is what explains Commandant Santucho's editorial 'Argentinians, to Arms' " (*VI Congreso,* pp. 28–29). On the day of the coup Montoneros Daniel and Fernando Vaca Narvaja "celebrated in a street corner of Buenos Aires: 'we brought them to our terrain; we will vanquish them' said Fernando to Daniel" (Juan Gasparini, *Montoneros: Final de Cuentas* [Buenos Aires: Puntosur Editores, 1988], pp. 198–199).

65. *VI Congreso,* pp. 30–31.

66. *VI Congreso,* pp. 31–32.

67. On Santucho's death see "Con las botas puestas," *Cambio 16,* 244, August 9, 1976, p. 44.

68. See Partido Revolucionario de los Trabajadores, *Documentos del Comité Ejecutivo "Comandante Mario R. Santucho"* (Madrid: Gráficas Halar, 1977), especially chapters 3–5.

69. Partido Revolucionario de los Trabajadores, *VII Congreso: Informe al Congreso* (Buenos Aires: N. p., 1987), p. 23.

70. "Editorial," *Evita Montonera,* 2:13, April-May 1976, pp. 2–3: 2.

71. "Llenar el vacío de conducción," *Evita Montonera*, 2:13, April-May 1976, pp. 4-8: 6.

72. Figure 8.6 provides a simplified version of Montonero organization during this period. Regionals and columns replicated the national structure in that they also had four secretaryships devoted to services known as "Areas"; and they also had Political, Military, Press, and Organization secretaryships, known collectively as Regional Secretariat or Column Secretariat. There have been other attempts to portray Montonero organizational structures after 1976, which provide variations on figure 8.6. See Richard Gillespie, *Soldiers of Perón: Argentina's Montoneros* (Oxford: Clarendon Press, 1982), pp. 278-279; Daniel Frontalini and María Cristina Caiati, *El Mito de la Guerra Sucia* (Buenos Aires: Centro de Estudios Legales y Sociales, 1984), pp. 67-69; and Gasparini, *Montoneros*, pp. 263-264. That these authors and I have all provided different graphs testifies to the unreadable prose in the Montonero documents on which we base them.

73. Regulations on the use of uniforms are reproduced in Gasparini, *Montoneros*, pp. 257-262.

74. Partido Montonero, "Crítica y Autocrítica," *Vencer*, 2/3, 1979, pp. III-XXXII: X. See also "Entrevista al Comandante Firmenich: Poder Sindical o Destrucción Nacional," *Vencer*, 1, 1979, pp. 4-10: 7.

75. Partido Montonero, "Crítica y Autocrítica," p. XIV.

76. "Entrevista al Comandante Firmenich," p. 7.

77. Partido Montonero, "Crítica y Autocrítica," p. XIII.

78. Giussani, *Montoneros*, p. 68.

79. Partido Montonero, "Crítica y Autocrítica," pp. XXVI-XXVII.

80. Reviewing the leadership's decision to go abroad, a former Montonero told me that "Wellington directed Waterloo from the top of a hill" (interview in Buenos Aires, July 23, 1987).

81. For example, the decision that made it compulsory for ambushed combatants to swallow the cyanide capsule issued by the EM to avoid being captured alive. The decision was adopted in 1976 and rescinded in 1978.

82. On the 1978 counteroffensive see Julio Scherer García, "La Junta Militar, en la vereda de la derrota," *Proceso*, June 5, 1978, pp. 6-12; and Xavier Domingo, "Bazookas contra Videla," *Cambio 16*, 344, July 9, 1978, pp. 50-52. On the 1979 offensive see Ejército Montonero, *Argentina: En Marcha la Contraofensiva Popular* (N.p., n.d.). This offensive provoked two splits within Montoneros. The first, led by Rodolfo Galimberti and Juan Gelman, occurred before the counteroffensive. The organization condemned the dissidents to death but the sentence was never carried out. The second splinter, led by Miguel Bonasso and Jaime Dri, emerged after the military disaster. Gelman, Bonasso, and Dri live in exile. Galimberti reconciled himself with the Montoneros, became a member of the executive board of Revolutionary Peronism, the name by which Firmenich and his associates went after 1983, and returned to Argentina in October 1989 after President Carlos Menem granted an amnesty for guerrillas and members of the armed forces prosecuted for human rights violations. He now works for the Born brothers, in whose kidnapping he participated. On the 1978 and 1979 splits see "Deux résponsables peronistes Montoneros quittent l'organisation," *Le Monde*, February 25, 1979, p. 15; German Sopeña, "Rodolfo Galimberti: La Violencia, Nunca Mas," *Siete Días*, 15:825, April 6, 1983, pp. 3-13; Roberto Mero, *Conversaciones con Juan Gelman: Contraderrota. Montoneros y la revolución perdida* (Buenos Aires: Editorial Contrapunto, 1987); and Miguel Bonasso, *Recuerdo de la Muerte* (Buenos Aires: Editorial Bruguera, 1984).

Chapter 9. The Lost Patrol Revisited

1. Barbara W. Tuchman, *The Guns of August* (New York: Bantam Books, 1980), pp. 96–100.

2. See Samuel P. Huntington, *The Soldier and the State* (Cambridge, Mass., and London: The Belknap Press, 1985), chapter 3.

3. On Balbín's relationship with the Peróns and the armed forces see Heriberto Kahn, *Doy Fe* (Buenos Aires: Editorial Losada, 1979).

4. Alfred Vagts, *A History of Militarism Civilian and Military* (New York: The Free Press, 1959), p. 13.

5. The expression appears in decree S 261 which launched Operation Independence against the ERP in Tucumán. The decree is reproduced in *El Terrorismo en la Argentina* (Buenos Aires: Poder Ejecutivo Nacional, 1980), pp. 139–140.

6. Rodolfo Walsh, *Los Papeles de Walsh*. Published as "Escritos Póstumos: Rodolfo Walsh y los Montoneros." Part 1, *Unidos*, 3:5, April 1985, pp. 151–159. Part 2, *Unidos*, 3:6, August 1985, pp. 178–193.

7. Donatella della Porta and Sidney Tarrow, "Unwanted Children: Political Violence and the Cycle of Protest in Italy, 1966–1972," *European Journal of Political Research*, 14, 1986, pp. 607–632. For discussions of the intrinsic and extrinsic determinants of the strategic choices of armed organizations see the works of Martha Crenshaw: "An Organizational Approach to the Analysis of Political Terrorism," *Orbis*, 29:3, 1985, pp. 465–489; "How Terrorism Declines," *Terrorism and Political Violence*, 3:1, 1991, pp. 69–87; and "The logic of terrorism: Terrorist behavior as a product of strategic choice," in Walter Reich (ed.), *Origins of terrorism: Psychologies, ideologies, theologies, states of mind* (Cambridge and New York: Cambridge University Press, 1990).

8. See Helena Cobban, *The Palestinian Liberation Organization: People, Power and Politics* (New York: Cambridge University Press, 1984); David Th. Schiller, "A Battlegroup Divided: The Palestinian Fedayeen," in David C. Rapoport (ed.), *Inside Terrorist Organizations* (New York: Columbia University Press, 1988); and, on the IRA-INLA rivalry, Christopher Dobson and Ronald Payne, *The Never-Ending War: Terrorism in the 80s* (New York and Oxford: Facts on File, 1987), chapter 14.

9. Richard Gillespie, "Political Violence in Argentina in the 1970s (Guerrillas, Terrorists, State Terrorists and *Carapintadas*)," in Martha Crenshaw (ed.), *Terrorism in Context* (University Park, Pa.: Pennsylvania State University Press, forthcoming); Juan Gasparini, *Montoneros: Final de Cuentas* (Buenos Aires: Puntosur Editores, 1988); Envar El Kadri and Jorge Rulli, *Diálogos en el Exilio* (Buenos Aires: Editorial Foro Sur, 1984); Miguel Bonasso, *Recuerdo de la Muerte* (Buenos Aires: Editorial Bruguera, 1984).

10. See Frances Fox Piven and Richard Cloward, *Poor People's Movements: Why They Succeed, How They Fail* (New York: Vintage Books, 1979); and Robert Michels, *Political Parties* (New York: The Free Press, 1968).

11. Mario Firmenich, cited in Gasparini, *Montoneros*, p. 129.

12. For an analysis of the IRA that implicitly demonstrates that compartmentalization does not always operate as smoothly as the literature on armed organizations suggests, see Padraig O'Malley, *Biting at the Grave: The Irish Hunger Strikes and the Politics of Despair* (Boston: Beacon Press, 1990), part 1.

13. Cited in "Suplemento: Los Sueños de la Guerrilla," *El Porteño*, V:52, April 1986, pp. 35–50: 41, emphasis in the original.

14. My remarks on ETA, the Baader-Meinhof Gang, the IRA, and the Red Brigades are based on the following works: Francisco J. Llera, José M. Mata, and Cynthia L. Irwin, "ETA: From Secret Army to Social Movement—The Post-Franco Schism of the Basque Nationalist Movement," *Terrorism and Political Violence,* 5:3, 1993, pp. 106–134; Pedro Ibarra Guell, *La Evolución Estratégica de ETA* (San Sebastián: Kriselu, 1989); Jillian Becker, *Hitler's Children: The Story of the Baader-Meinhof Terrorist Gang* (London: Michael Joseph, 1977); Peter H. Merkl, "West German Left Wing Terrorism," in Crenshaw, *Terrorism in Context;* Klaus Wasmund, "The Political Socialization of West German Terrorists," in Peter H. Merkl (ed.), *Political Violence and Terror: Motifs and Motivations* (Berkeley and Los Angeles: University of California Press, 1986); O'Malley, *Biting at the Grave;* Jack Holland, *Too Long a Sacrifice: Life and Death in Northern Ireland Since 1969* (Harmondsworth: Penguin Books, 1982); Donatella della Porta, "I Militanti delle Organizzazioni Terroriste di Sinistra in Italia," *Rivista Italiana di Scienza Politica,* 17:1, April 1987, pp. 23–55; "Terrorism in Italy," in Crenshaw, *Terrorism in Context;* "Political Socialization in Left-Wing Underground Organizations," in Donatella della Porta (ed.), *Social Movements and Violence: Participation in Underground Organizations* (Greenwich, Conn., and London: JAI Press, 1992); and "Social Movements and Terrorism in Italy and West Germany: Strategic Choices and Escalation Dynamics in Underground Organizations," paper presented at the XII World Congress of Sociology, Madrid, July 9–13, 1990.

15. della Porta, "Social Movements and Terrorism," p. 15.

16. Merkl, "West German Left Wing Terrorism," p. 30.

17. Llera, Mata, and Irwin, "ETA," pp. 108–109, 121.

18. O'Malley, *Biting at the Grave,* p. 44.

19. Wasmund, "Political Socialization of West German Terrorists," p. 204; and O'Malley, *Biting at the Grave,* p. 108.

20. della Porta, "Political Socialization," pp. 263–266.

21. Ibarra Guell, *La Evolución Estratégica de ETA,* p. 165.

22. della Porta, "Political Socialization," p. 279. Emphasis in the original.

23. Walsh's "Letter to my friends" on the death of his daughter is reprinted in Horacio Verbitsky (ed.), *Rodolfo Walsh y la Prensa Clandestina 1976–1978* (Buenos Aires: Ediciones de la Urraca, 1985), pp. 119–120. On the cult of the hero in Italy see della Porta, "Terrorism in Italy," pp. 31, 46; "Social Movements and Terrorism," p. 17; "Political Socialization," pp. 270–284. On IRA funerals see Holland, *Too Long a Sacrifice,* pp. 57–58, 121.

24. Ibarra Guell, *La Evolución Estratégica de ETA,* pp. 155–156, emphasis in the original.

25. On comparative legal and military responses to armed struggle see Christopher Hewitt, *The Effectiveness of Anti-Terrorist Policies* (Lanham, Md., New York, and London: University Press of America, 1984).

Bibliography

The first section of this bibliography lists all newspapers and periodicals I consulted on a regular basis—either because, as is the case with radicalized Argentine periodicals, I read entire collections; or because, as in the case of European newspapers, I consulted them extensively for the eleven-year period covered by this study. The second section lists all books, articles and documents cited throughout the book. Included here are authored newspaper and periodical articles but not unauthored ones. The latter are adequately cited in the different chapters. Since this study makes such extensive use of this type of primary source, including unauthored articles in this bibliography would have turned it into an unmanageable proposition.

Newspapers and Periodicals

A) Argentine

Ambito Financiero
América Latina
Aquí y Ahora
Las Bases
Boletín Peronista de Información y Reflexión
Buenos Aires Herald
El Burgués
Caras y Caretas
El Caudillo
La Causa Peronista
Clarín
El Combatiente
Confirmado
Cristianismo y Revolución
Crónica
Cuestionario
De Frente
El Descamisado
Los Descamisados
Estrella Roja
Evita Montonera

Fin de Siglo
Gente
Libre
Militancia
Movimiento
La Nación
La Opinión
Página 12
Panorama
El Periodista
El Peronista
El Porteño
La Prensa
Primera Plana
Puro Pueblo
La Razón
La Semana
Siete Días
Somos
Testigo
Unidas
Unidos

B) Foreign

Abc (Madrid)
Cambio 16 (Madrid)
Christian Science Monitor (Boston)
Economist (London)
L'Express (Paris)
Granma (Havana)
Guardian (London)
Latin America (London)
Le Monde (Paris)
New York Times
Proceso (Mexico)
The Times (London)
Visión (Mexico)
Washington Post

Books, Articles, and Documents

Abós, Alvaro, *El Posperonismo* (Buenos Aires: Editorial Legasa, 1986).

Adell Argilés, Ramón, "La Transición Política en la Calle: Manifestaciones Políticas de Grupos y Masas. Madrid, 1976–1987," Ph.D. diss., Universidad Complutense de Madrid, 1989.

Aguilar, Luis E., "Fragmentation of the Marxist Left," *Problems of Communism*, 19:4, 1970, pp. 1–12.

Agulla, Juan Carlos, *Diagnóstico Social de una Crisis: Córdoba Mayo de 1969* (Buenos Aires: Editel, 1969).

Alexander, Robert J., *Juan Domingo Perón: A History* (Boulder, Colo.: Westview Press, 1979).

Alonso Piñeiro, Armando, *Crónica de la Subversión en la Argentina* (Buenos Aires: Ediciones Depalma, 1980).

Amigo, Angel, *Pertur ETA 71–76* (Donostia: Hordago, 1978).

Amnesty International, *"Disappearances": A Handbook* (New York: Amnesty International USA, 1981).

——— , *The "disappeared" of Argentina: List of cases reported to Amnesty International, March 1976–February 1979* (London: Amnesty International, 1979).

Andersen, Martin Edwin, *Dossier Secreto: Argentina's Desaparecidos and the Myth of the "Dirty War"* (Boulder, Colo.: Westview Press, 1993).

Anzorena, Oscar R., *Tiempo de Violencia y Utopía (1966–1976)* (Buenos Aires: Editorial Contrapunto, 1988).

Arendt, Hannah, *Eichmann in Jerusalem. A Report on the Banality of Evil* (Harmondsworth: Penguin Books, 1984).

Aust, Stefan, *The Baader-Meinhof Group: The Inside Story of a Phenomenon* (London: The Bodley Head, 1987).

Aznarez, Carlos, "Cacho El Kadri: 'No tropezar dos veces con la misma piedra,' " *Caras y Caretas*, 85:2209, April 1987, pp. 23–25, 31–35.

Bailby, Edouard, "Trêve pour la coupe du monde," *L'Express*, 1396, April 10, 1978, p. 61.

Balvé, Beba, et al., *Lucha de Calles, Lucha de Clases: Elementos para su Análisis: Córdoba 1971–1969* (Buenos Aires: Ediciones La Rosa Blindada, 1973).

Bandura, Albert, "Psychological mechanisms of aggression," in M. von Cranach, K. Froppa, W. Lepenies, and D. Ploog (eds.), *Human Ethology: Claims and Limits of a New Discipline* (Cambridge: Cambridge University Press, 1979).

Barcia, Pedro A., "Las Guerrillas en la Argentina," *Interrogaciones*, 8, 1975, pp. 30–60.

Barron, John, *KGB: The Secret Work of Soviet Secret Agents* (New York: Reader's Digest Press, 1974).

Baschetti, Rodolfo (ed.), *Documentos de la Resistencia Peronista 1955–1970* (Buenos Aires: Puntosur Editores, 1988).

Becker, Jillian, *Hitler's Children: The Story of the Baader-Meinhof Terrorist Gang* (London: Michael Joseph, 1977).

Bell, J. Bowyer, *The Gun in Politics: An Analysis of Irish Political Conflict, 1916–1986* (New Brunswick, N.J., and Oxford: Transaction Books, 1987).

Bénéton, Philippe, and Touchard, Jean, "Les Intérpretations de la Crise de Mai-Juin 1968," *Revue Française de Science Politique*, 20:3, 1970, pp. 503–544.

Bernetti, Jorge Luis, *El Peronismo de la Victoria* (Buenos Aires: Editorial Legasa, 1983).

Bienen, Henry, *Violence and Social Change: A Review of Current Literature* (Chicago: University of Chicago Press, 1968).

Bocca, Giorgio, "6 garantito, viva la squola," in Enzo Forcella (ed.), *Trent'anni di terrorismo* (Rome: Editoriale L'Espresso, 1985).

Bonasso, Miguel, *Recuerdo de la Muerte* (Buenos Aires: Editorial Bruguera, 1984).

Botana, Natalio R., Braun, Rafael, and Floria, Carlos A., *El Régimen Militar 1966–1973* (Buenos Aires: Ediciones La Bastilla, 1973).

Brocato, Carlos A., *La Argentina que Quisieron* (Buenos Aires: Editorial Sudamericana/Planeta, 1985).

Brown, Bernard E., *Protest in Paris: Anatomy of a Revolt* (Morristown, N.J.: General Learning Press, 1974).

Bullrich, Silvina, *Mal Don* (Buenos Aires: Emecé Editores, 1973).

Cabral, Horacio, "Entre Trotski et Robin des Bois," *L'Express*, 1082, April 3, 1972, p. 64.

Calisto, Guillermo, "Conjeturas acerca del conflicto," *La Opinión*, October 8, 1976, p. 1.

Cantón, Darío, *Elecciones y Partidos Políticos en la Argentina; Historia, Interpretación y Balance: 1910–1966* (Buenos Aires: Siglo Veintiuno Editores, 1973).

Cantón, Darío, and Jorrat, Jorge R., "Occupation and Vote in Urban Argentina: The March 1973 Presidential Elections," *Latin American Research Review*, 13:1, 1978, pp. 146–157.

Caparrós, Martín, *No Velas a tus Muertos* (Buenos Aires: Ediciones de la Flor, 1986).

Castex, Mariano N., *El Escorial de Onganía* (Buenos Aires: Ediciones Hespérides, 1981).

———. *Un Año de Lanusse; Del Acuerdo Increíble al Retorno Imposible* (Buenos Aires: Achával Solo, 1973).

Cavarozzi, Marcelo, *Autoritarismo y Democracia, 1955–1983* (Buenos Aires: Centro Editor de América Latina, 1983).

Cazes Camarero, Pedro (ed.), *Hubo Dos Terrorismos?* (Buenos Aires: Ediciones Re-encuentro, 1986).

Cerdán, Manuel, and Rubio, Antonio, "Agentes de la Ertzantza investigaron a Amedo antes de que los GAL mataran," *Cambio 16*, 941, December 11, 1989, pp. 128–134.

———. "Los periodistas descubren un zulo del GAL en la frontera con Francia," *Cambio 16*, 940, December 4, 1989, pp. 120–126.

———, "Toda La Verdad Sobre El Watergal Español," *Cambio 16*, 939, November 27, 1989, pp. 115–122.

Cerecedo, Francisco, "Los montoneros se explican," *Cambio 16*, 245, August 16, 1976, pp. 40–43.

Chaliand, Gérard, *Revolution in the Third World* (Harmondsworth: Penguin Books, 1979).

Christian, Shirley, "Pardoned Argentine officers out of jail," *New York Times*, October 10, 1989, p. A3.

Clark, Robert P., "Patterns in the Lives of ETA Members" in Peter H. Merkl (ed.), *Political Violence and Terror: Motifs and Motivations* (Berkeley and Los Angeles: University of California Press, 1986).

———, *The Basque Insurgents: ETA, 1952–80* (Madison: University of Wisconsin Press, 1984).

Cobban, Helena, *The Palestinian Liberation Organization: People, Power and Politics* (New York: Cambridge University Press, 1984).

Comando General de Ejército, *Directiva del Comandante en Jefe del Ejército Nro 604/79 (Continuación de la ofensiva contra la subversión)* (Buenos Aires: N.p., 1979).

———, *Directiva del Comandante en Jefe del Ejército Nro 504/77 (Continuación de la ofensiva contra la subversión en el período 1977–78)* (Buenos Aires: N.p., 1978).

———, *Orden Parcial Nro 405/76 (Reestructuración de jurisdicciones y adecuación orgánica para intensificar las operaciones contra la subversión)* (Buenos Aires: N.p., 1976).

———, *Directiva del Comandante General del Ejército Nro 404/75 (Lucha contra la subversión)* (Buenos Aires: N.p., 1975).

Comando Zona 1, *Orden de Operaciones Nro 9/77 (Continuación de la ofensiva contra la subversión durante el período 1977)* (Buenos Aires: N.p., 1977).

Comisión Nacional sobre la Desaparición de Personas, *Nunca Mas* (Buenos Aires: Eudeba, 1985).

———, *Anexos del Informe de la Conadep* (Buenos Aires: Eudeba, 1985).

Concatti, Rolando, "Nuestra Opción por el Peronismo," *Cristianismo y Revolución,* IV:30, September 1971, pp. 27–36.

Consejo de Defensa, *Directiva del Consejo de Defensa Nro 1/75 (Lucha contra la subversión)* (Buenos Aires: N.p., 1975).

Coogan, Tim Pat, *The I.R.A.* (London: Fontana Paperbacks, 1982).

Corradi, Juan E., "The Mode of Destruction: Terror in Argentina," *Telos,* 54, Winter 1982–83, pp. 61–76.

Corradi, Juan E., Kenworthy, Eldon, and Wipfler, William, "Argentina 1973–1976: The Background to Violence," *LASA Newsletter,* 8:3, September 1976, pp. 3–28.

Correa, Jorge, *Los Jerarcas Sindicales* (Buenos Aires: Editorial Obrador, 1974).

Cortázar, Julio, *Libro de Manuel* (Barcelona: Editorial Bruguera, 1981).

Costantini, Humberto, *De Dioses, Hombrecitos y Policías* (Havana: Casa de las Américas, 1979).

———, *Libro de Trelew* (Buenos Aires: Granica Editor, 1973).

Cox, Robert, *The Sound Of One Hand Clapping: A Preliminary Study of the Argentine Press in a Time of Terror* (Washington, D.C.: The Wilson Center, Latin American Program, Working Paper no. 83, 1980).

Crelinsten, Ronald D., "The Internal Dynamics of the FLQ During the October Crisis of 1970," in David C. Rapoport (ed.), *Inside Terrorist Organizations* (New York: Columbia University Press, 1988).

Crenshaw, Martha, "How Terrorism Declines," *Terrorism and Political Violence,* 3:1, 1991, pp. 69–87.

———, "The logic of terrorism: Terrorist behavior as a product of strategic choice," in Walter Reich (ed.), *Origins of terrorism: Psychologies, ideologies, theologies, states of mind* (Cambridge and New York: Cambridge University Press, 1990).

———, *Terrorism and International Cooperation* (New York: Institute for East-West Security Studies, 1989).

———, "An Organizational Approach to the Analysis of Political Terrorism," *Orbis,* 29:3, 1985, pp. 465–489.

———, "Reflections on the Effects of Terrorism," in Martha Crenshaw (ed.), *Terrorism, Legitimacy, and Power* (Middletown, Conn.: Wesleyan University Press, 1983).

Cristal, Marcos, "Desde enero los ingresos cayeron un 43%," *La Opinión,* September 2, 1976, p. 13.

Crozier, Brian, *The Surrogate Forces of the Soviet Union* (London: Institute for the Study of Conflict, 1978).

——— (ed.), *We Will Bury You: Studies in Left-Wing Subversion Today* (London: Tom Stacey, 1970).

Davison, W. Phillips, and Gordenker, Leon (eds.), *Resolving Nationality Conflicts: The Role of Public Opinion Research* (New York: Praeger Publishers, 1980).

Deas, Malcolm, "Guerrillas in Latin America," *The World Today,* 24:2, 1968, pp. 72–78.

Debray, Régis, *Revolution in the Revolution? Armed Struggle and Political Struggle in Latin America* (New York: Monthly Review Press, 1967).

Delich, Francisco J., "Después del Diluvio, la Clase Obrera," in Alain Rouquié (ed.), *Argentina, Hoy* (Buenos Aires: Siglo Veintiuno Editores, 1982).

————, *Crisis y protesta social: Córdoba, mayo de 1969* (Buenos Aires: Ediciones Signos, 1970).

della Porta, Donatella, "Terrorism in Italy," in Martha Crenshaw (ed.), *Terrorism in Context* (University Park, Pa.: Pennsylvania State University Press, forthcoming).

————, "Political Socialization in Left-Wing Underground Organizations: Biographies of Italian and German Militants," in Donatella della Porta (ed.), *Social Movements and Violence: Participation in Underground Organizations* (Greenwich, Conn., and London: JAI Press, 1992).

————, *Il Terrorismo di Sinistra* (Bologna: Il Mulino, 1990).

————, "Social Movements and Terrorism in Italy and West Germany: Strategic Choices and Escalation Dynamics in Underground Organizations," paper presented at the XII World Congress of Sociology, Madrid, July 9–13, 1990.

————, "I Militanti delle Organizzazioni Terroriste di Sinistra in Italia," *Rivista Italiana di Scienza Politica,* XVII:1, April 1987, pp. 23–55.

della Porta, Donatella, and Tarrow, Sidney, "Unwanted children: Political violence and the cycle of protest in Italy, 1966–1973," *European Journal of Political Research,* 14, 1986, pp. 607–632.

de Riz, Liliana, *Retorno y Derrumbe: El Ultimo Gobierno Peronista* (Buenos Aires: Hyspamérica Ediciones, 1987).

de Villemarest, Pierre F., *Les Stratèges de la Peur: Vingt Ans de Guerre Révolutionnaire en Argentine* (Geneva: Editions Voxmundi, 1981).

Díaz, José Antonio, and Leuco, Alfredo, *Los Herederos de Alfonsín* (Buenos Aires: Editorial Sudamericana/Planeta, 1987).

Díaz Alejandro, Carlos F., *Ensayos sobre la Historia Económica Argentina* (Buenos Aires: Amorrortu Editores, 1983).

Díaz Bessone, Ramón Genaro, *Guerra Revolucionaria en la Argentina (1959–1978)* (Buenos Aires: Editorial Fraterna, 1986).

Dicks, Henry V., *Licensed Mass Murder: A Socio-Psychological Study of Some SS Killers* (New York: Basic Books, 1972).

Dillon, Martin, *The Dirty War* (London: Arrow Books, 1990).

di Tella, Guido, *Argentina under Perón, 1973–1976: The Nation's Experience with a Labor-Based Government* (New York: St. Martin's Press, 1983).

Diuguid, Lewis H., "Argentina Guerrilla Chief Says He Will Defy Cámpora," *Washington Post,* June 29, 1973, p. A28.

————, "Campora Fails To End Terror In Argentina," *Washington Post,* June 2, 1973, p. A12.

Dobson, Christopher, and Payne, Ronald, *The Never-Ending War: Terrorism in the 80s* (New York and Oxford: Facts on File, 1987).

Domingo, Xavier, "Bazookas contra Videla," *Cambio 16,* 344, July 9, 1978, pp. 50–52.

Donini, Antonio O., "Religion and Social Conflict in the Perón Era," in Frederick C. Turner and José Enrique Miguens (eds.), *Juan Perón and the Reshaping of Argentina* (Pittsburgh: University of Pittsburgh Press, 1983).

Dri, Rubén R., "La alternativa y la lucha de clases," *Militancia,* 2:33, January 31, 1974, pp. 20–22.

Duhalde, Eduardo L., *El Estado Terrorista Argentino* (Buenos Aires: Ediciones El Caballito, 1983).

Eckstein, Harry, "Theoretical Approaches to Explaining Collective Political Violence," in Ted Robert Gurr (ed.), *Handbook of Political Conflict* (New York: The Free Press, 1980).

Eder, Richard, "Argentine Issue Dropped By U.S.," *New York Times,* August 12, 1966, p. 12.

———, "U.S. Aide Rebukes Argentina For Crackdown on Universities," *New York Times,* August 5, 1966, pp. 1, 9.

Ejército Montonero, *Argentina: En Marcha la Contraofensiva Popular* (N.p., n.d.).

Ejército Revolucionario del Pueblo, *Al pueblo: Porqué y contra qué seguirá combatiendo el ERP* (Buenos Aires: N.p., May 25, 1973).

———, *Porqué el ERP no dejará de combatir: Respuesta al Presidente Cámpora* (Buenos Aires: N.p., April 13, 1973).

Ejército Revolucionario del Pueblo Fracción Roja, "A la clase obrera y al pueblo," *Crónica,* July 25, 1973, p. 15.

Ejército Revolucionario del Pueblo 22 de Agosto, "A las organizaciones revolucionarias y al pueblo," *Crónica,* July 31, 1973, p. 11.

———, "El ERP 22 de Agosto al pueblo," *Militancia,* 1:3, June 28, 1973, p. 12.

El Kadri, Envar, and Rulli, Jorge, *Diálogos en el Exilio* (Buenos Aires: Editorial Foro Sur, 1984).

El Libro del Juicio (Buenos Aires: Editorial Testigo, 1985).

El Terrorismo en la Argentina (Buenos Aires: Poder Ejecutivo Nacional, 1980).

Emerson, Steven, and Duffy, Brian, "Pan Am 103: The German Connection," *New York Times Magazine,* March 18, 1990, pp. 28–33, 72–74, 84–87.

Escobar, Justo, and Velázquez, Sebastián, *Examen de la Violencia Argentina* (Mexico: Fondo de Cultura Económica, 1975).

Faligot, Roger, *Nous Avons Tué Mountbatten: L'IRA Parle* (Paris: Editions Jean Picollec, 1981).

———, *Guerre Spéciale en Europe: Le Laboratoire Irlandais* (Paris: Textes/Flammarion, 1980).

Fayt, Carlos S., *El Político Armado: Dinámica del Proceso Político Argentino, 1960–1971* (Buenos Aires: Ediciones Pannedile, 1971).

Feinmann, José Pablo, *López Rega, la cara oscura de Perón* (Buenos Aires: Editorial Legasa, 1987).

Fernández, Rodolfo Peregrino, *Autocrítica Policial* (Buenos Aires: El Cid Editor, 1983).

Fernández Alvariño, Próspero G., Z. *Argentina, el Crimen del Siglo* (Buenos Aires: Edición del Autor, 1973).

Ferns, H. S., *La Argentina* (Buenos Aires: Editorial Sudamericana, 1973).

Firmenich, Mario, and Arrostito, Norma, "Como murió Aramburu," *La Causa Peronista,* 1:9, September 3, 1974, pp. 25–31.

Frascara, Ricardo, "Paro en los ingenios y enérgico repudio de Atilio Santillán a la intervención de FOTIA," *La Opinión,* September 15, 1974, p. 14.

Frenchman, Michael, "The twilight years of a reign of terror," *Times,* May 5, 1978, p. 8.

Frontalini, Daniel, and Caiati, María Cristina, *El Mito de la Guerra Sucia* (Buenos Aires: Centro de Estudios Legales y Sociales, 1984).

Fuerzas Armadas de Liberación 22 de Agosto, "Que algo cambie para que todo siga como está," *Militancia,* 1:12, August 30, 1973, pp. 22–23.

Fuerzas Armadas Peronistas, "A la clase obrera y al pueblo peronista," *Militancia,* 1:22, November 8, 1973, pp. 44–45.

———, "Aporte para el análisis de la situación actual," *Militancia,* 1:10, August 16, 1973, pp. 19–21.

———, "Las Fuerzas Armadas Peronistas (FAP) se dirigen a la Policía," *Cristianismo y Revolución,* IV:26, November-December 1970, p. 54.

Fuerzas Armadas Revolucionarias, "Aporte al proceso de confrontación de posiciones y polémica pública que abordamos con el ERP," *Militancia*, 4, July 5, 1973, pp. 35–49.

———, "Comunicado No. 1—Comunicado No. 2," *Cristianismo y Revolución*, IV:25, September 1970, pp. 59–60.

Fuerzas Armadas Revolucionarias/Montoneros, "Acta de Unidad," *Militancia*, 19, October 18, 1973, pp. 26–27.

Gabetta, Carlos, *Todos Somos Subversivos* (Buenos Aires: Editorial Bruguera, 1984).

García Lupo, Rogelio, *La Rebelión de los Generales* (Buenos Aires: Editorial Jamcana, 1963).

Garzón Valdés, Ernesto, "La Emigración Argentina: Acerca de sus Causas Etico-Políticas," in Peter Waldmann and Ernesto Garzón Valdés (eds.), *El Poder Militar en la Argentina (1976–1981)* (Buenos Aires: Editorial Galerna, 1983).

Gasparini, Juan, *Montoneros: Final de Cuentas* (Buenos Aires: Puntosur Editores, 1988).

Gearty, Conor, "What is Terror?," *Times Saturday Review*, March 9, 1991, pp. 10–12.

Gente, *25 de Mayo de 1973—24 de Marzo de 1976: Fotos, Hechos, Testimonios de 1035 Dramáticos Días* (Buenos Aires: Editorial Abril, 1976).

Gera, Lucio, and Rodríguez Melgarejo, Guillermo, "Apuntes para una Interpretación de la Iglesia Argentina," *Cristianismo y Revolución*, IV:25, September 1970, pp. 61–79.

Gerassi, John, *The Great Fear in Latin America* (New York: Collier Books, 1973).

Gèze, François, and Labrousse, Alain, *Argentine: Révolution et Contre-révolutions* (Paris: Editions du Seuil, 1975).

Gillespie, Richard, "Political Violence in Argentina in the 1970s (Guerrillas, Terrorists, State Terrorists and *Carapintadas*)," in Martha Crenshaw (ed.), *Terrorism in Context* (University Park, Pa.: Pennsylvania State University Press, forthcoming).

———, "Armed Struggle in Argentina," *New Scholar*, 8:1 & 2, 1982, pp. 387–427.

———, *Soldiers of Perón: Argentina's Montoneros* (Oxford: Clarendon Press, 1982).

———, "A Critique of the Urban Guerrilla: Argentina, Uruguay and Brazil," *Conflict Quarterly*, 1:2, 1980, pp. 39–53.

Gitlin, Todd, *The Sixties: Years of Hope, Days of Rage* (New York: Bantam Books, 1989).

Giussani, Pablo, *Los Días de Alfonsín* (Buenos Aires: Editorial Legasa, 1986).

———, *Montoneros: La Soberbia Armada* (Buenos Aires: Editorial Sudamericana/Planeta, 1984).

Glanville, Brian, "World Cup Soccer Madness in Argentina," *Washington Post*, June 12, 1978, pp. B1, B5.

Godio, Julio, *El Ultimo Año de Perón* (Bogota: Universidad Simón Bolívar, 1981).

Godolphin, Francis, "Terrorismo y anticultura," *El Burgués*, III:55, May 23, 1973, pp. 7–8.

Goleman, Daniel, "The Roots of Terrorism are Found in Brutality of Shattered Childhood," *New York Times*, September 2, 1986, pp. C1, C8.

Gombrowicz, Witold, *Journal 1957–1960* (Paris: Editions Denoël, 1976).

González Janzen, Ignacio, *La Triple-A* (Buenos Aires: Editorial Contrapunto, 1986).

———, *Argentina: 20 Años de Luchas Peronistas* (Mexico: Ediciones de la Patria Grande, 1975).

González Trejo, Horacio, *Argentina: Tiempo de Violencia* (Buenos Aires: Carlos Pérez Editor, 1969).

Goshko, John M., "Onganía Given Dictator Power," *Washington Post*, June 30, 1966, p. A21.

Gott, Richard, *Guerrilla Movements in Latin America* (Garden City, N.Y.: Doubleday, 1971).

Graham-Yooll, Andrew, *De Perón a Videla* (Buenos Aires: Editorial Legasa, 1989).

————, *A Matter of Fear: Portrait of an Argentinian Exile* (Westport, Conn.: Lawrence Hill, 1981).

————, *Tiempo de Violencia: Cronología del "Gran Acuerdo Nacional"* (Buenos Aires: Granica Editor, 1973).

————, *Tiempo de Tragedia (Cronología de la "Revolución Argentina")* (Buenos Aires: Ediciones de la Flor, 1972).

Greene, Graham, *The Honorary Consul* (Harmondsworth: Penguin Books, 1986).

Guest, Iain, *Behind the Disappearances: Argentina's Dirty War Against Human Rights and the United Nations* (Philadelphia: University of Pennsylvania Press, 1990).

Guevara, Ernesto, *Obras Completas* (Buenos Aires: Ediciones Cepe, 1973).

Guevara, Santiago Luis, "Desató violentos incidentes populares un conflicto gremial en San Francisco," *La Opinión,* July 31, 1973, p. 8.

Gurr, Ted Robert, "Some Characteristics of Political Terrorism in the 1960s," in Michael Stohl (ed.), *The Politics of Terrorism* (New York: Marcel Dekker, 1988).

————, *Why Men Rebel* (Princeton, N.J.: Princeton University Press, 1970).

Gutiérrez, Carlos María, "Des militants chrétiens demandent au pape de renoncer à son voyage en Amérique Latine," *Le Monde,* March 16, 1968, p. 3.

Gutiérrez, Roger, *Gorriarán: Democracia y Liberación* (Buenos Aires: Ediciones Reencuentro, 1985).

Halperin, Ernst, *Terrorism in Latin America* (Beverly Hills, Calif.: Sage Publications, 1976).

Hewitt, Christopher, "Terrorism and Public Opinion: A Five Country Comparison," *Terrorism and Political Violence,* 2:2, 1990, pp. 145–170.

————, *The Effectiveness of Anti-Terrorist Policies* (Lanham, Md., New York, and London: University Press of America, 1984).

Hilb, Claudia, and Lutzky, Daniel, *La Nueva Izquierda Argentina: 1960–1980 (Política y Violencia)* (Buenos Aires: Centro Editor de América Latina, 1980).

Hirschman, Albert O., *Exit, Voice and Loyalty: Responses to Decline in Firms, Organizations, and States* (Cambridge, Mass., and London: Harvard University Press, 1970).

Hodges, Donald C., *Argentina's "Dirty War": An Intellectual Biography* (Austin: University of Texas Press, 1991).

Hodges, Donald C. (ed.), *Philosophy of the Urban Guerrilla: The Revolutionary Writings of Abraham Guillén* (New York: William Morrow, 1973).

Holland, Jack, *Too Long a Sacrifice: Life and Death in Northern Ireland since 1969* (Harmondsworth: Penguin Books, 1982).

Huberman, Leo, and Sweezy, Paul M., *Régis Debray and the Latin American Revolution* (New York: Monthly Review Press, 1968).

Huntington, Samuel P., *The Soldier and the State* (Cambridge, Mass., and London: The Belknap Press, 1985).

————, *Political Order in Changing Societies* (New Haven and London: Yale University Press, 1968).

Hyams, Edward S., *Terrorists and Terrorism* (London: J. M. Dent, 1975).

Ibarra Guell, Pedro, *La Evolución Estratégica de ETA* (San Sebastián: Kriselu, 1989).

Instituto Nacional de Estadísticas y Censos, *Censo Nacional de Población, Familias y Viviendas de 1970: Compendio de sus Resultados Provisionales* (Buenos Aires: INDEC, N.d.).

Jackson, Sir Geoffrey, *Secuestrado por el Pueblo* (Barcelona: Editorial Pomaire, 1974).

James, Daniel, *Resistance and Integration: Peronism and the Argentine Working Class, 1946–1976* (Cambridge: Cambridge University Press, 1988).

———, "Rationalization and Working Class Response: The Contexts and Limits of Factory Floor Activity in Argentina," *Journal of Latin American Studies*, 13:26, 1981, pp. 375–402.

———, "Power and Politics in Peronist Trade Unions," *Journal of Interamerican Studies and World Affairs*, 20:1, 1978, pp. 3–36.

———, "The Peronist Left, 1955–1975," *Journal of Latin American Studies*, 8:2, 1976, pp. 273–296.

Johnson, Chalmers, *Revolutionary Change* (Stanford, Calif.: Stanford University Press, 1982).

Johnson, Kenneth F., *Peronism: The Final Gamble* (London: Institute for the Study of Conflict, 1974).

———, *Argentina's Mosaic of Discord 1966–68* (Washington, D.C.: Institute for the Comparative Study of Political Systems, 1969).

Kahn, Heriberto, *Doy Fe* (Buenos Aires: Editorial Losada, 1979).

Kandel, Pablo, and Monteverde, Mario, *Entorno y Caída* (Buenos Aires: Editorial Planeta Argentina, 1976).

Kandell, Jonathan, "An Argentine Hopes for Peace," *New York Times*, March 26, 1976, p. 8.

———, "Leftists in Key Argentine City Chafe at Peronist Conservatives," *New York Times*, July 8, 1973, p. 9.

———, "Prison Mutinies Sweep Argentina," *New York Times*, July 6, 1973, p. 4.

Kaplan, Marcos, "50 Años de Historia Argentina (1925–1975): El Laberinto de la Frustración," in Pablo González Casanova (ed.), *América Latina: Historia de Medio Siglo* (Mexico: Siglo Veintiuno Editores, 2 vols., 1982).

Kaufmann, Jacques, *L'Internationale Terroriste* (Paris: Librairie Plon, 1977).

Klare, Michael T., and Kornbluh, Peter (eds.), *Low Intensity Warfare* (New York: Pantheon Books, 1988).

Kohl, James, and Litt, John (eds.), *Urban Guerrilla Warfare in Latin America* (Cambridge, Mass.: Massachusetts Institute of Technology Press, 1974).

Laclau, Ernesto, "Argentina—Imperialist Strategy and the May Crisis," *New Left Review*, 62, 1970, pp. 3–21.

La Masacre de Trelew (Caracas: Ediciones Bárbara, 1972).

Landi, Oscar, *La Tercera Presidencia de Perón: Gobierno de Emergencia y Crisis Política* (Buenos Aires: Documento CEDES/CLACSO no. 10, 1978).

Lanusse, Alejandro A., *Mi Testimonio* (Buenos Aires: Laserre Editores, 1977).

Laqueur, Walter, *The Age of Terrorism* (Boston: Little, Brown, 1987).

———, *Terrorism* (Boston: Little, Brown, 1977).

———, *Guerrilla: A Historical and Critical Study* (Boston: Little, Brown, 1976).

Lenin, V. I., *What is to be Done? Burning Questions of our Movement* (New York: International Publishers, 1981).

———, *Collected Works* (Moscow: Progress Publishers, 1964).

Linz, Juan J., *Conflicto en Euzkadi* (Madrid: Espasa-Calpe, 1986).

———, *The Breakdown of Democratic Regimes: Crisis, Breakdown, and Reequilibration* (Baltimore and London: Johns Hopkins University Press, 1978).

Little, Walter, *Peronism: Was it and is it Populist?* (University of Glasgow: Institute of Latin American Studies, Occasional Papers no. 20, 1975).

Llera, Francisco J., Mata, José M., and Irwin, Cynthia L., "ETA: From Secret Army to Social Movement—The Post-Franco Schism of the Basque Nationalist Movement," *Terrorism and Political Violence,* 5:3, 1993, pp. 106–134.

Luna, Félix, *Argentina, de Perón a Lanusse, 1943–1973* (Barcelona: Editorial Planeta, 1972).

Maidenberg, H. J., "University Teachers Begin Leaving Argentina," *New York Times,* August 19, 1966, p. 13.

——— , "4 of 8 Rectors Quit Posts," *New York Times,* August 1, 1966, p. 11.

Marín, Juan Carlos, *Los hechos armados, un ejercicio posible* (Buenos Aires: CICSO, 1984).

Martínez, Tomás Eloy, *La Novela de Perón* (Buenos Aires: Editorial Legasa, 1986).

——— , "El ascenso, triunfo, decadencia y derrota de José López Rega," *La Opinión,* October 22, 1975, pp. 1, 24.

——— , *La Pasión Según Trelew* (Buenos Aires: Granica Editor, 1973).

Masetti, Jorge R., *Los que Luchan y Los que Lloran* (Buenos Aires: Editorial Jorge Alvarez, 1969).

Mattini, Luis, *Hombres y Mujeres del PRT-ERP* (Buenos Aires: Editorial Contrapunto, 1990).

Máxima Peligrosidad (Buenos Aires: Editorial Candela, 1973).

McGuire, James William, "Peronism without Perón: Unions in Argentine politics, 1955–1966." Ph.D. diss., University of California, Berkeley, 1989.

Méndez, Eugenio, *Aramburu: El Crimen Imperfecto* (Buenos Aires: Editorial Sudamericana/Planeta, 1987).

——— , *Confesiones de un Montonero* (Buenos Aires: Editorial Sudamericana/Planeta, 1985).

Mercier Vega, Luis, *Las Guerrillas en América Latina; La Técnica del Contra-estado* (Buenos Aires: Editorial Paidós, 1969).

Merkl, Peter H., "West German Left Wing Terrorism," in Martha Crenshaw (ed.), *Terrorism in Context* (University Park, Pa.: Pennsylvania State University Press, forthcoming).

——— (ed.), *Political Violence and Terror: Motifs and Motivations* (Berkeley and Los Angeles: University of California Press, 1986).

Mero, Roberto, *Conversaciones con Juan Gelman. Contraderrota. Montoneros y la revolución perdida* (Buenos Aires: Editorial Contrapunto, 1987).

Michels, Robert, *Political Parties* (New York: The Free Press, 1968).

Mieres, Francisco, "Lessons of October and Contemporary Revolutionary Movements in Latin America," *World Marxist Review,* 10:11, 1967, pp. 77–81.

Miguens, José Enrique, "El Militarismo como Patología en la Milicia y en la Política," paper presented at the conference "Armed Forces, State, Defense and Society," Buenos Aires, October 26–28, 1988.

——— , "The Presidential Elections of 1973 and the End of an Ideology," in Frederick C. Turner and José Enrique Miguens (eds.), *Juan Perón and the Reshaping of Argentina* (Pittsburgh: University of Pittsburgh Press, 1983).

Mommsen, Wolfgang J., "Non-Legal Violence and Terrorism in Western Industrial Societies: An Historical Analysis," in Wolfgang J. Mommsen and Gerhard Hirschfeld (eds.), *Social Protest, Violence and Terror in 19th and 20th Century Europe* (London: Macmillan, 1982).

Morales, Emilio, *Uturunco y las Guerrillas en la Argentina* (Montevideo: Editorial Sepe, 1964).

Mora y Araujo, Manuel, and Llorente, Santiago (eds.), *El Voto Peronista: Ensayos de Sociología Electoral Argentina* (Buenos Aires: Editorial Sudamericana, 1980).

Moreira Alves, Maria Helena, *State and Opposition in Military Brazil* (Austin: University of Texas Press, 1985).

Moyano, María José, "Argentinien: Die 'unehelichen' Kinder Peróns," in Peter Waldmann (ed.), *Beruf: Terrorist. Lebensläufe im Untergrund* (Munich: C. H. Beck, 1993).

———, "Going Underground in Argentina: A Look at the Founders of a Guerrilla Movement," in Donatella della Porta (ed.), *Social Movements and Violence: Participation in Underground Organizations* (Greenwich, Conn., and London: JAI Press, 1992).

———, "The 'Dirty War' in Argentina: Was it a war and how dirty was it?," in Peter Waldmann and Hans Werner Tobler (eds.), *Staatliche und parastaatliche Gewalt in Lateinamerika* (Frankfurt: Vervuert Verlag, 1991).

———, "Armed Struggle in Argentina, 1969–1979." Ph.D. diss., Yale University, 1990.

Moyser, George, "Non-Standardized Interviewing in Élite Research," in Robert Burgess (ed.), *Studies in Qualitative Methodology* (Greenwich, Conn., and London: JAI Press, 1988).

Munck, Ronaldo, Falcón, Ricardo, and Galitelli, Bernardo, *Argentina: From Anarchism to Peronism. Workers, Unions and Politics, 1855–1985* (London: Zed Books, 1987).

Muñoz, Fermín (ed.), *Las Encíclicas del Mundo Moderno* (Barcelona: Editorial Bruguera, 1969).

Muñoz, Jorge, *Seguidme! Vida de Alberto Villar* (Buenos Aires: Ediciones Informar, 1984).

Naipaul, V. S., *The Return of Eva Perón* (New York: Vintage Books, 1981).

Neilson, James, "Maniobras militares," *Noticias,* XIV:701, June 3, 1990, p. 37.

Nordlinger, Eric A., *Soldiers in Politics: Military Coups and Governments* (Englewood Cliffs, N.J.: Prentice-Hall, 1977).

O'Brien, Conor Cruise, "Terrorism under Democratic Conditions: The Case of the IRA," in Martha Crenshaw (ed.), *Terrorism, Legitimacy, and Power* (Middletown, Conn.: Wesleyan University Press, 1983).

O'Donnell, Guillermo, *Y a mí qué me importa? Notas sobre sociabilidad y política en Argentina y Brasil* (Buenos Aires: Estudio CEDES, 1984).

———, "Argentina: La Cosecha del Miedo," *Alternativas,* 1, September 1983, pp. 5–14.

———, *1966–1973 El Estado Burocrático Autoritario. Triunfos, Derrotas y Crisis* (Buenos Aires: Editorial de Belgrano, 1982).

———, "Permanent Crisis and the Failure to Create a Democratic Regime: Argentina, 1955–66," in Juan J. Linz and Alfred Stepan (eds.), *The Breakdown of Democratic Regimes* (Baltimore: Johns Hopkins University Press, 1980).

———, "State and Alliances in Argentina, 1956–1976," *Journal of Development Studies,* 15:1, 1978, pp. 3–32.

Ollier, María Matilde, *El Fenómeno Insurreccional y la Cultura Política, 1969–1973* (Buenos Aires: Centro Editor de América Latina, 1986).

O'Malley, Padraig, *Biting at the Grave: The Irish Hunger Strikes and the Politics of Despair* (Boston: Beacon Press, 1990).

Organización Comunista Poder Obrero, *Lucha Democrática y Hegemonía Proletaria* (Buenos Aires: N.p., 1977).

Ottalagano, Alberto, *Soy Fascista. Y Qué?* (Buenos Aires: Ro. Ca. Producciones, 1983).

Page, Joseph A., *Perón, A Biography* (New York: Random House, 1983).

Paoletti, Alipio E., *Como los Nazis, Como en Vietnam* (Buenos Aires: Editorial Contrapunto, 1987).

Paredes, Eduardo J., "En un abierto desafío al gobierno constitucional la organización Montoneros optó por marginarse de la ley," *La Opinión*, September 7, 1974, p. 24.

Partido Montonero, "Crítica y Autocrítica," *Vencer*, 2/3, 1979, pp. III–XXXII.

Partido Revolucionario de los Trabajadores, *VII Congreso: Informe al Congreso* (Buenos Aires: N.p., 1987).

———, *VI Congreso: Mayo 1979* (N.p., n.d.).

———, *Documentos del Comité Ejecutivo "Comandante Mario R. Santucho"* (Madrid: Gráficas Halar, 1977).

———, *Resoluciones del V Congreso y de los Comité Central y Comité Ejecutivo Posteriores* (Buenos Aires: Ediciones El Combatiente, 1973).

"Pau de Arara" La Violencia Militar en el Brasil (Mexico: Siglo Veintiuno Editores, 1972).

Petersen, Clive, "Dealing with Terrorism," *Buenos Aires Herald*, January 25, 1974, p. 6.

Petras, James, "Building a Popular Army in Argentina," *New Left Review*, 71, 1972, pp. 45–55.

Pinedo, Jorge, *Consignas y Lucha Popular en el Proceso Revolucionario Argentino 1955–73* (Buenos Aires: Editorial Freeland, 1974).

Piven, Frances Fox, and Cloward, Richard A., *Poor People's Movements: Why They Succeed, How They Fail* (New York: Vintage Books, 1979).

Portantiero, Juan Carlos, "Economía y Política en la Crisis Argentina: 1958–1973," *Revista Mexicana de Sociología*, 77:2, 1977, pp. 531–565.

Potash, Robert A., *The Army and Politics in Argentina 1945–1962: Perón to Frondizi* (Stanford, Calif.: Stanford University Press, 1980).

Prieto, Daniel, "Las Divergencias de un Partido," *Visión*, March 9, 1974, pp. 18–21.

Puig, Manuel, *The Buenos Aires Affair* (Mexico: Editorial Joaquín Mortíz, 1973).

Quartim, João, "Régis Debray and the Brazilian Revolution," *New Left Review*, 59, 1970, pp. 61–82.

Ratliff, William E., *Castroism and Communism in Latin America, 1959–1976: The Varieties of Marxist-Leninist Experience* (Washington, D.C.: American Enterprise Institute for Public Policy Research, 1976).

Raufer, Xavier, *Terrorisme: Maintenant la France? La Guerre des Partis Communistes Combattants* (Paris: Garnier, 1982).

Rayment, Tim, Davison, John, and Darlymple, James, "IRA devastates heart of the City," *The Sunday Times*, April 25, 1993, pp. 1, 24.

Reinares, Fernando, "La violencia política civil y organizada en un contexto de democratización: consideraciones para una interpretación del caso vasco," paper presented at the III Congress of Sociology, Donostia-San Sebastián, September 1989.

Rock, David, *Argentina 1516–1987: From Spanish Colonization to Alfonsín* (Berkeley and Los Angeles: University of California Press, 1987).

———, *Politics in Argentina 1890–1930: The Rise and Fall of Radicalism* (Cambridge: Cambridge University Press, 1975).

——— (ed.), *Argentina in the Twentieth Century* (Pittsburgh: University of Pittsburgh Press, 1975).

Rojo, Ricardo, *My Friend Che* (New York: Dial Press, 1968).

Roper, Christopher, "Argentina's rebels become restive," *Guardian*, March 26, 1979, p. 6.

———, "Don't cry for us, say the Montoneros," *Guardian*, March 2, 1977, p. 4.

————, "The revolutionary retreat from British imperialism," *Guardian*, February 2, 1976, p. 9.

Rosie, George, *The Directory of International Terrorism* (Edinburgh: Mainstream Publishing, 1986).

Roth, Roberto, *Los Años de Onganía: Relato de un Testigo* (Buenos Aires: Ediciones La Campana, 1981).

Rouquié, Alain, *Poder Militar y Sociedad Política en la Argentina* (Buenos Aires: Emecé Editores, 2 vols., 1983).

————, "El Poder Militar en la Argentina de Hoy: Cambio y Continuidad," in Peter Waldmann and Ernesto Garzón Valdés (eds.), *El Poder Militar en la Argentina (1976–1981)* (Buenos Aires: Editorial Galerna, 1983).

————, *Radicales y Desarrollistas en la Argentina* (Buenos Aires: Schapire Editor, 1975).

————, "Le Vote Peroniste en 1973," *Revue Française de Science Politique*, 24:3, 1974, pp. 469–499.

Rowe, James W., *The Argentine Elections of 1963* (Washington, D.C.: Institute for the Comparative Study of Political Systems, N.d.).

Russell, Charles A., and Miller, Bowman H., "Profile of a Terrorist," *Terrorism*, 1:1, 1977, pp. 17–34.

Russell, Charles A., Miller, James A., and Schenkel, James F., "Urban Guerrillas in Argentina: A Select Bibliography," *Latin American Research Review*, 9:3, 1974, pp. 53–89.

Sáenz, Dalmiro, and Joselovsky, Sergio, *El Día que Mataron a Alfonsín* (Buenos Aires: Ediciones Tarso, 1986).

Sale, Kirkpatrick, *S.D.S.* (New York: Vintage Books, 1974).

Santucho, Julio, *Los Ultimos Guevaristas: Surgimiento y Eclipse del Ejército Revolucionario del Pueblo* (Buenos Aires: Puntosur Editores, 1988).

Santucho, Mario R., *Poder Burgués y Poder Revolucionario* (Buenos Aires: N.p., 1974).

Scenna, Miguel Angel, *Los Militares* (Buenos Aires: Editorial de Belgrano, 1980).

Scherer García, Julio, "La Junta Militar, en la vereda de la derrota," *Proceso*, June 5, 1978, pp. 6–12.

Schiller, David Th., "A Battlegroup Divided: The Palestinian Fedayeen," in David C. Rapoport (ed.), *Inside Terrorist Organizations* (New York: Columbia University Press, 1988).

Schmidt, William E., "Bombed Again by I.R.A., London Goes to Work Undaunted," *New York Times*, April 27, 1993, p. A3.

Schmitt, Carl, *The Concept of the Political* (New Brunswick, N.J.: Rutgers University Press, 1976).

Selser, Gregorio, *El Onganiato* (Buenos Aires: Hyspamérica Ediciones, 2 vols., 1986).

Seoane, María, *Todo o Nada* (Buenos Aires: Editorial Planeta, 1992).

Sigal, Silvia, and Verón, Eliseo, *Perón o Muerte: Los fundamentos discursivos del fenómeno peronista* (Buenos Aires: Editorial Legasa, 1986).

Sigmund, Paul E., *Liberation Theology at the Crossroads: Democracy or Revolution?* (New York and Oxford: Oxford University Press, 1990).

Silj, Alessandro, *Mai più senza fucile! alle origini dei NAP e delle BR* (Florence: Vallechi, 1977).

Simpson, John, and Bennett, Jana, *The Disappeared: Voices from a Secret War* (London: Robson Books, 1985).

Skjelsbaek, Kjell, "Militarism, its Dimensions and Corollaries: An Attempt at Conceptual Clarification," in Asbjorn Eide and Marek Thee (eds.), *Problems of Contemporary Militarism* (London: Croom Helm, 1980).

Smith, Peter H., *Argentina and the Failure of Democracy: Conflict Among Political Elites, 1904–1955* (Madison: University of Wisconsin Press, 1974).

Smith, Wayne S., "The Return of Peronism," in Frederick C. Turner and José Enrique Miguens (eds.), *Juan Perón and the Reshaping of Argentina* (Pittsburgh: University of Pittsburgh Press, 1983).

Snow, Peter G., *Political Forces in Argentina* (New York: Praeger Publishers, 1979).

Sobel, Lester A., *Argentina & Perón 1970–75* (New York: Facts on File, 1975).

Sopeña, Germán, "Rodolfo Galimberti: La Violencia, Nunca Mas," *Siete Días*, XV:825, April 6, 1983, pp. 3–13.

Soriano, Osvaldo, *No Habrá Mas Penas Ni Olvido* (Buenos Aires: Editorial Bruguera, 1983).

Spitta, Arnold, "El 'Proceso de Reorganización Nacional' de 1976 a 1981: Los Objetivos Básicos y su Realización Práctica," in Peter Waldmann and Ernesto Garzón Valdés (eds.), *El Poder Militar en la Argentina (1976–1981)* (Buenos Aires: Editorial Galerna, 1983).

Stalker, John, *The Stalker Affair* (New York: Viking Press, 1988).

Stepan, Alfred, *Brasil: Los Militares y la Política* (Buenos Aires: Amorrortu Editores, 1974).

———, "The New Professionalism of Internal Warfare and Military Role Expansion," in Alfred Stepan (ed.), *Authoritarian Brazil: Origins, Policies and Future* (New Haven and London: Yale University Press, 1973).

Strafford, Peter, "Argentina: back on the rails, but at what cost?," *Times*, January 4, 1978, p. 12.

———, "The Church of change," *Times*, December 2, 1977, p. 16.

Suárez, Héctor Víctor, "FAR: Con el fusil del Che," *Granma*, December 12, 1970, p. 7.

———, "Montoneros: El llanto para el enemigo," *Granma*, December 5, 1970, p. 7.

Thornton, Thomas Perry, "Terror as a Weapon of Political Agitation," in Harry Eckstein (ed.), *Internal War: Problems and Approaches* (New York: Free Press of Glencoe, 1964).

Timerman, Jacobo, *Prisoner Without a Name, Cell Without a Number* (New York: Vintage Books, 1982).

Tuchman, Barbara W., *The Guns of August* (New York: Bantam Books, 1980).

Tupamaros, *Actas Tupamaras* (Madrid: Ediciones Revolución, 1982).

Turner, Frederick C., "The Study of Argentine Politics through Survey Research," *Latin American Research Review*, 10:2, 1975, pp. 73–116.

Urondo, Francisco, *Trelew* (Havana: Casa de las Américas, 1976).

Vagts, Alfred, *A History of Militarism Civilian and Military* (New York: The Free Press, 1959).

Verbitsky, Horacio, *Ezeiza* (Buenos Aires: Editorial Contrapunto, 1986).

——— (ed.), *Rodolfo Walsh y la Prensa Clandestina, 1976–1978* (Buenos Aires: Ediciones de la Urraca, 1985).

Vivés, Juan, *Los Amos de Cuba* (Buenos Aires: Emecé Editores, 1982).

Waisman, Carlos H., *Reversal of Development in Argentina: Postwar Counterrevolutionary Policies and Their Structural Consequences* (Princeton, N.J.: Princeton University Press, 1987).

Waldmann, Peter, "Ethnic and Sociorevolutionary Terrorism: A Comparison of Structures," in Donatella della Porta (ed.), *Social Movements and Violence: Participation in Underground Organizations* (Greenwich, Conn., and London: JAI Press, 1992).

———, "From the vindication of honor to blackmail: the impact of the changing role of ETA on society and politics in the Basque region of Spain," in Noemi Gal-Or (ed.), *Tolerating terrorism in the west. An international survey* (London and New York: Routledge, 1991).

———, "Anomia Social y Violencia," in Alain Rouquié (ed.), *Argentina, Hoy* (Buenos Aires: Siglo Veintiuno Editores, 1982).

———, *El Peronismo, 1943–1955* (Buenos Aires: Editorial Sudamericana, 1981).

Walsh, Rodolfo, *Quién Mató a Rosendo?* (Buenos Aires: Ediciones de la Flor, 1986).

———, *Los Papeles de Walsh*. Published as "Escritos Póstumos: Rodolfo Walsh y los Montoneros." Part I, *Unidos,* 3:5, April 1985, pp. 151–159. Part II, *Unidos,* 3:6, August 1985, pp. 178–193.

———, *Operación Masacre* (Buenos Aires: Ediciones de la Flor, 1984).

Walter, Eugene V., *Terror and Resistance: A Study of Political Violence with Case Studies of Some Primitive African Communities* (New York: Oxford University Press, 1969).

Wasmund, Klaus, "The Political Socialization of West German Terrorists," in Peter H. Merkl (ed.), *Political Violence and Terror: Motifs and Motivations* (Berkeley and Los Angeles: University of California Press, 1986).

Weinberg, Leonard, and Eubank, William Lee, *The Rise and Fall of Italian Terrorism* (Boulder, Colo.: Westview Press, 1987).

Wilkinson, Paul, *Terrorism & the Liberal State* (New York: New York University Press, 1986).

———, *Political Terrorism* (London: Macmillan, 1974).

Index

Abal Medina, Fernando, 134, 136, 140, 187n9
Agosti, Brigadier Orlando R., 180n7
Alemán, Francisco, 58
Alfonsín, Raúl, 16, 74, 91, 179n7, 180n8, 190n7
Algeria, 4, 118, 198n42
Allende, Salvador, 64
Alsogaray, Juan Carlos, 134
Alsogaray, General Julio, 134, 164
alternativism, 40, 143–145, 150, 202n42
anti-Semitism: 76, 186n5. *See also* Tacuara
Aramburu, General Pedro Eugenio: 14;
    kidnapping and execution by Montoneros, 25,
    29, 58, 62, 97–98, 149, 176n59, 187n9,
    191n9
Argentine Anti-Communist Alliance (AAA): 40,
    41, 46, 71, 76, 84, 188n18; organization of,
    38, 75, 82–83, 187n8
Argentine Revolution: 16, 71, 82, 180n8;
    support for, 16–17, 33; radicalization under,
    17–21, 65. *See also* Cordobazo; Onganiato;
    Night of the Long Batons; Trelew massacre;
    universities; Viborazo
armed struggle in Argentina: definition, 178n1;
    rural attempts, 21–22, 46; urban campaign
    launched, 22–27; joint operations, 55, 58;
    membership levels, 102–105; social origin of
    combatants, 105–113; individual motivation
    of participants, 113–130; internal organization
    of groups, 138–140; and collective violent
    protest, 88–90, 138; and right-wing violence,
    91–92; popular reaction to, 27–28, 41, 96–
    98, 152, 193n33, 199n46. *See also under*
    individual groups; Second War of
    Independence
Arrostito, Norma, 108, 134, 196n23

Baader-Meinhof Gang, 4, 90, 161–163
Balbín, Ricardo, 157
Basque Homeland and Freedom (ETA), 4, 7, 8,
    89, 95, 112, 115, 116, 161–163, 169n16,
    170n18, 182n21

Baxter, Joe, 134, 187n9, 203n64
Berisso, Rear Admiral Emilio, 29, 30, 64, 183n3
Bidegain, Oscar, 38, 57
Bonasso, Miguel, 204n82
Born, Jorge, 41, 42, 57, 61, 181n18, 204n82
Born, Juan, 41, 42, 57, 61, 181n18, 204n82
Bosch, Alberto, 61
Brenuil, Gustavo, 197n24

Cabo, Dardo, 108
Caffatti, Jorge, 187n9
Cámpora, Héctor J., 31, 34, 35, 36, 69, 164
Cardozo, María Graciela, 62
Caride, Carlos, 22, 173n31
Castro, Fidel, 21, 133
Cepernic, Jorge, 178n86
CGT. *See* General Labor Confederation
Chejolán, Alberto, 151
Clausewitz, Carl von, 6
Cordobazo: 25, 26, 28, 65, 88, 89, 117, 173n25,
    184n22; as expression of societal
    radicalization, 17, 27, 67; events during,
    20–21, 68
Cox, Robert, 47
CPL. *See* Liberation Popular Commandos
Crea, Horacio
Croatto, Armando, 176n62

D'Aquila, Hugo, 58, 182n19
de Gregorio, Oscar, 25, 174n36
Debray, Regis, 133. *See also foco* theory
Delfino, Mario, 198n44
del Pino, Miguel, 174n47
Descamisados: 22, 25–26, 53, 136, 138. *See also*
    alternativism; armed struggle in Argentina;
    movementism
Díaz Ortiz, Santiago, 176n62
Direct Action, 4, 119
dirty war: 1, 3, 5, 42, 46, 84, 167n5, 174n36,
    192n23; defined as a war, 92–94; organization
    of, 85–86; aimed against armed

dirty war (*continued*)
  organizations, 86–87, 127–129, 196*n21–22*, 204*n81*. *See also* National Commission on the Disappearance of Persons; Navy Mechanics School; Process of National Reorganization; torture
Doctrine of Ideological Frontiers, 76–77, 186*n6–7*
Dri, Jaime, 204*n82*

El Kadri, Envar, 22, 173*n31*, 174*n33*, 187*n10*, 201*n37*
ERP. *See* People's Revolutionary Army
ESMA. *See* Navy Mechanics School
ETA. *See* Basque Homeland and Freedom
Evita Group of the Feminine Branch (AE), 150
Ezeiza massacre, 35–36, 38, 177*n69*, 187*n9*

FAL. *See* Liberation Armed Forces
FAP. *See* Peronist Armed Forces
FAR. *See* Revolutionary Armed Forces
Federal Penal Chamber of the Nation, 67, 164, 174*n47*, 175*n48*
Fernández, Antonio del Carmen, 134
Firmenich, Mario Eduardo, 37, 92, 95, 136, 140, 145, 177*n69*, 190*n6*, 191*n9*, 198*n44*, 204*n82*
foco theory, 21, 32, 133–134, 199*n4*
Frondizi, Arturo, 21, 45
Front for the Liberation of Quebec (FLQ), 4

Galimberti, Rodolfo, 105, 190*n6*, 204*n82*
Galtieri, General Leopoldo, 87
García Elorrio, Juan, 135
Gay, Colonel Camilo, 56
Gelín, Raquel Liliana, 26
Gelman, Juan, 204*n82*
General Labor Confederation (CGT): 14, 25, 29, 59, 73; *combativos*, 14, 67, 71, 89, 93; *clasistas*, 64, 67, 71, 93; Struggle Plans, 14, 15; Law of Professional Associations, 69. *See also* July Days; Peronist Resistance; Rucci, José Ignacio
Georgeades, Jorge, 108
Giussani, Pablo, 177*n69*, 203*n64*
Glellel, Jorge, 176*n62*
González, Ana María, 62
González, Daniel, 56
Gorriarán Merlo, Enrique, 42, 178*n94*, 190*n6*
Great National Agreement (GAN), 30
Greene, Graham, 57, 174*n42*, 181*n17*
Grynberg, Enrique, 38, 177*n17*
guerrilla warfare: *See* under individual groups; armed struggle in Argentina; terrorism
Guevara, Ernesto (Che): 26, 133, 134, 135. *See also foco* theory

Habegger, Norberto, 25, 174*n36*
hedge theory, 125, 126, 143
Hobert, Carlos, 149, 150, 203*n59*
Holmberg, Elena, 47

Ibarzábal, Lieutenant Colonel Jorge, 56
Illia, Arturo, 17, 22
Invernizzi, Hernán, 160
Iribarren, Colonel Héctor, 29, 30
Irish Republican Army (IRA), 3, 4, 5, 112, 158, 168*n9*, 181*n14*, 205*n12*
Iturrieta, Aníbal, 176*n62*

Jackson, Sir Geoffrey, 170*n20*
JP. *See* Peronist Youth
JTP. *See* Peronist Working Youth
JUP. *See* Peronist University Youth
July Days, 71, 90–91, 148, 203*n57*

Kloosterman, Dirk, 34
Krieger Vasena, Adalbert, 17
Kunkel, Carlos, 176*n62*

Lambruschini, Rear Admiral Armando, 61, 87, 180*n7*
Lambruschini, Paula, 61
Lanusse, General Alejandro A.: 20, 37, 47, 58, 175*n49*; inauguration, 21, 28; confrontation with Perón, 30–31, 33, 175*n50*
Laplane, General Alberto Numa,
Lastiri, Raúl, 36
Lenin, Vladimir Ilyich, 8, 170*n24*
Levingston, General Roberto M., 20, 21
Lewinger, Arturo, 134
Liberation Antiterrorist Groups (GAL), 95, 193*n28*
Liberation Armed Forces (FAL): 22, 26, 39, 53, 55, 138, 142. *See also* armed struggle in Argentina
Liberation Popular Commandos (CPL), 26, 39
Liberators of America Commando, 82
Lima, Vicente Solano, 36
Lockwood, Charles, 57
Lonardi, General Eduardo, 12, 13, 14, 71
López, Atilio, 38
López Rega, José: 38, 71, 82, 83, 188*n14*, 188*n16*, 188*n18*. *See also* Argentine Anti-Communist Alliance; hedge theory

Malvinas-Falklands war, 41, 91
Martínez Baca, Alberto, 178*n86*
Massera, Admiral Emilio Eduardo, 47, 86, 87, 164, 180*n7*
Mattini, Luis, 140, 201*n25*
Mendizábal, Horacio, 25, 174*n36*
Menem, Carlos, 16, 91, 180*n7*, 191*n9*, 204*n82*
Menna, Domingo, 42, 198*n44*

militarism: definition of, 5–6, 163; determinants of, 6–7, 9, 46, 101–102, 120–126, 132–133, 159, 160–163; within guerrilla groups, 6, 7, 8, 12, 126–127, 131, 146, 152, 153, 156, 157, 163; indicators of, 7, 8, 50, 56, 108, 123, 161; contribution to development made by right-wing violence, 75–76, 158–159, 164; contribution to development made by collective violent protest, 90–91, 158

Montoneros: 42, 47, 52, 80, 136, 140; founding of, 22, 23, 24; operations, 25, 38, 41, 57, 58, 61, 62, 154–155, 176n62; and Trelew massacre, 28, 29, 175n49; and Ezeiza massacre, 35, 177n69; fusion with FAR, 39, 53; relations with Peronism, 40, 54, 138, 176n63, 177n77; relations with mass fronts, 132, 150–151; return underground, 41, 150; organizational splits, 202n45, 204n82; internal organization, 104, 121, 148–151, 152–154, 203n58, 204n72. See also alternativism; Aramburu, General Pedro Eugenio; armed struggle in Argentina; hedge theory; July Days; movementism; Revolutionary Tendency; socialismo nacional

Moreno Ocampo, Luis, 191n8

Mor Roig, Arturo, 157, 175n49

movementism, 40, 143–145, 150

Movement of Peronist Slum Dwellers (MVP), 39, 150, 151

Mugica, Father Carlos, 135–136, 151

Muñiz Barreto, Diego, 176n62, 193n29

National Commission on the Disappearance of Persons, 48, 74, 91, 179n7, 188n24, 191n8

Navy Mechanics School (ESMA), 2, 79, 86, 190n36

Nell, José Luis, 187n9

Night of the Long Batons, 18–20, 28, 29, 65, 117

Obregón Cano, Ricardo, 38, 190n6

Olmedo, Carlos Enrique, 134, 140

Onganía, General Juan Carlos: 34, 42, 51, 65, 74, 77, 152; seizes power, 11, 16; as president, 17, 18, 164, 191n9; deposed, 20, 25

Onganiato: 11, 12, 16, 33, 40, 63, 75, 83; popular dissatisfaction with, 17, 27, 65, 73, 89. See also Argentine Revolution; Onganía, General Juan Carlos

Osatinsky, Marcos, 134

Osinde, Colonel Jorge, 35, 36

Palestinian Liberation Organization (PLO), 158, 181n12, 182n22

Pardo, Héctor, 190n6

People's Revolutionary Army (ERP): 42, 49, 79, 138, 140; founding of, 22, 26–27; operations,

38, 41, 56–57, 58, 60–61, 178n94, 188n18; and Trelew massacre, 28, 29, 175n48; attitude toward Peronist presidencies, 34, 131, 142; rural front, 39–40, 51, 53, 92, 180n6, 195n14, 196n15, 205n5; organizational splits, 39, 40, 53, 187n9; internal organization, 92, 140–142, 146–148, 202n49–50; relations with mass fronts, 148; decline after 1976, 54, 203n64. See also armed struggle in Argentina; Workers' Revolutionary Party

Perdía, Roberto, 190n6

Pérez, Juan Carlos, 61

Perón, Juan: 3, 7, 8, 15, 16, 64, 69, 76, 82; 1946–55 presidencies, 12–13, 45; ouster in 1955, 11, 12, 13, 14, 167n1, 178n83; political activities in exile, 30, 33; and March 1973 elections, 3, 30, 31, 33; relations with armed organizations, 33, 38, 40, 56–57, 143, 176n59, 176n63; returns to Argentina, 35, 36; and September 1973 elections, 36–37; support for death squad activity, 94–95; death, 40, 41, 71, 75. See also hedge theory

Perón, María Estela (Isabel) Martínez de, 36, 40, 57, 58, 92, 157

Perón, María Eva (Evita) Duarte de, 13, 14, 25, 30, 40, 41, 58

Peronist Armed Forces (FAP): 22, 25, 33, 54, 136, 138; operations, 23, 34, 61, 145; organizational splits, 23, 39, 53, 173n31, 187n9, 201n37, 202n41. See also alternativism, armed struggle in Argentina, movementism

Peronist left: 14–15, 34, 36, 72, 187n11. See also Revolutionary Tendency

Peronist party, 65, 72, 129

Peronist Resistance, 14–15

Peronist right: 34, 35, 36, 46, 72, 75, 76, 80, 192n22; component groups, 79, 80, 187n11

Peronist University Youth (JUP), 80, 150

Peronist Working Youth (JTP), 39, 48, 80, 150

Peronist Youth (JP): 22, 25, 39, 40, 47–48, 80, 149–150, 187n10. See also Revolutionary Tendency; universities

Pirles, Roberto, 108

Pita, Colonel Juan Alberto, 59

Popular Indoamerican Revolutionary Front (FRIP), 26

Process of National Reorganization, 41, 63, 180n6. See also dirty war

Puig, Juan Carlos, 34

Puiggrós, Rodolfo, 34

Pujadas, Mariano, 29

Pujals, Luis, 79, 134, 198n44

Quieto, Roberto, 29, 95, 134, 140, 201n25

Quijada, Rear Admiral Hermes, 29, 30

Quiroga, Jorge, 175n48–49

Rabossi, Eduardo, 191*n8*
radical Catholicism, 65
Radical Civic Union (UCR), 12, 13, 15, 31, 45, 65, 129
Ragone, Miguel, 178*n86*
Ramus, Carlos Gustavo, 136, 187*n9*, 198*n44*
Rapaport, Luis, 108
Red Brigades, 4, 90, 115, 119, 161–163, 164, 197*n34*
Revolutionary Armed Forces (FAR): 22, 26, 35, 64, 138, 140; and Trelew massacre, 28, 29; fusion with Montoneros, 39, 53. *See also* alternativism; armed struggle in Argentina; movementism
Revolutionary Tendency: 25, 34, 35, 36, 38, 40, 62, 80. *See also* Peronist left; Peronist Youth
Righi, Esteban, 34, 176*n67*, 185*n31*, 188*n22*
Roqué, Julio, 52, 180*n7*
Rosas, General Juan Manuel de, 45
Royal Ulster Constabulary (RUC), 95, 193*n28*
Rucci, José Ignacio, 38, 54

Sabino Navarro, José, 140
Sallustro, Oberdan, 58
Santucho, Mario Roberto, 26, 29, 42, 134, 140, 142, 174*n41*, 198*n44*
Schlieffen plan, 157
Second War of Independence, 51, 92, 137, 151–152
socialismo nacional, 33, 69, 145–146, 202*n47–48*
Social Pact, 37, 69
Solari Yrigoyen, Hipólito, 38, 83
Sylvester, Stanley, 27, 181*n17*

Tacuara, 76, 79, 187*n9*
terrorism: definition of 3, 4, 168*n11*; and guerrilla warfare, 3, 4, 169*n16*; and armed struggle in Argentina, 5, 91–92
Toranzo, Higinio, 197*n24*

Torres, Camilo, 135
torture: 26, 36, 42, 93, 160, 189*n32*, 192*n19*. *See also* dirty war
Trelew massacre, 20, 28–30, 117, 174*n47*, 175*n48–49*, 183*n3*
Triple A. *See* Argentine Anti-Communist Alliance
Tupamaros, 26, 118, 170*n20*, 181*n15*, 187*n9*

Union of Secondary School Students (UES), 39, 150
universities, 13, 15, 18, 64, 65–67, 71
Urondo, Francisco, 52, 180*n7*, 193*n29*
Urteaga, Benito, 42

Vaca Narvaja, Daniel, 203*n64*
Vaca Narvaja, Fernando, 29, 190*n6*, 203*n64*
Vaca Narvaja, Miguel, 197*n24*
Valenzuela, Tulio, 87
Valle, General Juan José, 14, 25
Vélez, Ignacio, 198*n44*
Verdinelli, Néstor, 22, 173*n31*
Vergara, Esteban, 174*n47*, 175*n48*
Viborazo, 20, 21, 27, 28, 67, 68
Vidaña, Roberto, 176*n62*
Videla, General Jorge R., 64, 74, 152, 180*n7*
Villar, Alberto, 82, 188*n13*
Viola, General Roberto E., 180*n7*
Vittar, Rodolfo, 176*n62*

Walsh, Rodolfo: 1–2, 104, 167*n1*, 170*n19*; Walsh Papers, 1–2, 157
Walsh, Victoria, 2, 170*n19*
Workers' Revolutionary Party (PRT): 26, 27, 42, 131–132, 140, 141, 142, 152. *See also* People's Revolutionary Army
Workers' Word, 26

Zabala Rodríguez, Miguel, 22, 173*n32*

DATE DUE

AUG − 4 1995	
OCT 1 0 1995	
DEC _ 9 1996	
OCT 2 8 1997	
OCT 2 9 1997	